Gender and Politics

Series Editors: Johanna Kantola, Senior Lecturer in Gender Studies, University of Helsinki, Finland; and **Sarah Childs**, Professor of Politics and Gender, University of Bristol, UK

This series publishes leading monographs and edited collections from scholars working in the disciplinary areas of politics, international relations, and public policy with specific reference to questions of gender. It showcases cutting-edge research in Gender and Politics, publishing topical and innovative approaches to gender politics from new authors and well-known academics as well as practitioners working on related issues.

The series covers gendered engagement with mainstream political science issues, such as political systems and policymaking, representation and participation, citizenship and identity, equality, and women's movements; gender and international relations, including feminist approaches to international institutions, political economy, and global politics; and interdisciplinary and emergent areas of study, such as masculinities studies, gender and multiculturalism, and intersectionality.

Series Advisory Board:
Louise Chappell, University of New South Wales, Australia
Joni Lovenduksi, Birkbeck College, University of London, UK
Amy Mazur, Washington State University, USA
Judith Squires, University of Bristol, UK
Jacqui True, Monash University, Australia
Mieke Verloo, Radboud University Nijmegen, the Netherlands
Laurel Weldon, Purdue University, USA

Titles include:

Gabriele Abels and Joyce Marie Mushaben (*editors*)
GENDERING THE EUROPEAN UNION
New Approaches to Old Democratic Deficits

Phillip Ayoub and David Paternotte
LGBT ACTIVISM AND THE MAKING OF EUROPE
A Rainbow Europe?

Elin Bjarnegård
GENDER, INFORMAL INSTITUTIONS AND POLITICAL RECRUITMENT
Explaining Male Dominance in Parliamentary Representation

Elgin Brunner
FOREIGN SECURITY POLICY, GENDER, AND US MILITARY IDENTITY

María Bustelo, Lucy Ferguson, and Maxime Forest (*editors*)
THE POLITICS OF FEMINIST KNOWLEDGE TRANSFER
Gender Training and Gender Expertise

Sarah Childs and Paul Webb
SEX, GENDER AND THE CONSERVATIVE PARTY
From Iron Lady to Kitten Heels

Jonathan Dean
RETHINKING CONTEMPORARY FEMINIST POLITICS

Meryl Kenny
GENDER AND POLITICAL RECRUITMENT
Theorising Institutional Change

Andrea Krizsan, Hege Skjeie, and Judith Squires (*editors*)
INSTITUTIONALIZING INTERSECTIONALITY
The Changing Nature of European Equality Regimes

Mona Lena Krook and Fiona Mackay (*editors*)
GENDER, POLITICS AND INSTITUTIONS
Towards a Feminist Institutionalism

Emanuela Lombardo and Maxime Forest (*editors*)
THE EUROPEANIZATION OF GENDER EQUALITY POLICIES
A Discursive-Sociological Approach

Birte Siim and Monika Mokre (*editors*)
NEGOTIATING GENDER AND DIVERSITY IN AN EMERGENT EUROPEAN PUBLIC
SPHERE

Anna van der Vleuten, Anouka van Eerdewijk, and Conny Roggeband (*editors*)
GENDER EQUALITY NORMS IN REGIONAL GOVERNANCE
Transnational Dynamics in Europe, South America and Southern Africa

Polly Wilding
NEGOTIATING BOUNDARIES
Gender, Violence and Transformation in Brazil

Gender and Politics Series
Series Standing Order ISBNs 978–0–230–23917–3 (hardback) and
978–0–230–23918–0 (paperback)
(*outside North America only*)

You can receive future titles in this series as they are published by placing a standing order. Please contact your bookseller or, in case of difficulty, write to us at the address below with your name and address, the title of the series and the ISBN quoted above.

Customer Services Department, Macmillan Distribution Ltd, Houndmills, Basingstoke, Hampshire RG21 6XS, England

The Politics of Feminist Knowledge Transfer

Gender Training and Gender Expertise

Edited by

María Bustelo
Associate Professor, Departamento de Ciencia Política de la Administración II, Universidad Complutense de Madrid, Spain

Lucy Ferguson
Associate Researcher, Unidad de Género, Instituto Complutense de Estudios Internacionales, Universidad Complutense de Madrid, Spain

Maxime Forest
Senior Researcher and Lecturer, Sciences Po Paris, OFCE, CEVIPOF, France

First published 2016 by
PALGRAVE MACMILLAN

Palgrave Macmillan in the UK is an imprint of Macmillan Publishers Limited, registered in England, company number 785998, of Houndmills, Basingstoke, Hampshire RG21 6XS.

Palgrave Macmillan in the US is a division of St Martin's Press LLC, 175 Fifth Avenue, New York, NY 10010.

Palgrave Macmillan is the global academic imprint of the above companies and has companies and representatives throughout the world.

Palgrave® and Macmillan® are registered trademarks in the United States, the United Kingdom, Europe and other countries.

ISBN 978-1-349-57749-1   ISBN 978-1-137-48685-1 (eBook)
DOI 10.1057/978-1-137-48685-1

This book is printed on paper suitable for recycling and made from fully managed and sustained forest sources. Logging, pulping and manufacturing processes are expected to conform to the environmental regulations of the country of origin.

A catalogue record for this book is available from the British Library.

Library of Congress Cataloging-in-Publication Data
Names: Bustelo, María, editor. | Ferguson, Lucy, 1978– editor of compilation. | Forest, Maxime, 1976– editor of compilation.
Title: The politics of feminist knowledge transfer: gender training and gender expertise / edited by María Bustelo, Lucy Ferguson, Maxime Forest.
Description: New York, NY: Palgrave Macmillan, 2016. | Series: Gender and politics | Includes bibliographical references and index.
Identifiers: LCCN 2015026440 | ISBN 9781137486844 (hardback)
Subjects: LCSH: Feminist theory. | Knowledge, Theory of. | Sex role. | Women's rights. | Women in development. | BISAC: POLITICAL SCIENCE / History & Theory. | SOCIAL SCIENCE / Feminism & Feminist Theory. | SOCIAL SCIENCE / Gender Studies.
Classification: LCC HQ1190 .P655 2016 | DDC 305.4201—dc23
LC record available at http://lccn.loc.gov/2015026440

We would like to dedicate this book to our fellow community of practitioners and researchers, united in our ongoing search for feminist transformation.

Contents

Figures and Tables

Figures

Tables

Foreword

Gender Inequality and Institutional Knowledge: The Politics of Knowledge Transfer

The chapters in this book offer a rich variety of critical perspectives on the "knowledge work" being undertaken today to increase awareness of gender inequality; help understand how it operates as a system; and intervene in specific ways to transform organizations where gender is embedded and reproduced. Encouraged by mandates from the UN and EU to "mainstream gender" into policy processes, gender equality advocates around the world have taken up the challenge to help train policymakers. Training policymakers is intended to help them recognize how gender operates systematically in their areas of competence and to be able to respond with new policy initiatives designed to shift their organizations' routines towards producing equality rather than reproducing inequalities.

Mainstreaming gender, however, is never just about educating willing learners. Gender inequality is actively supported by the ongoing activities, conscious and unconscious, of a wide range of actors, some of whom benefit from current configurations of gender relations. Thus, gender mainstreaming, gender training, and feminist knowledge transfer inevitably engage in a "gendered politics" of knowledge. By politics, we mean here not only that there are different ideas about what knowledge is, or which knowledge is considered more real or valuable than others. We also mean that power is dynamically at work in the processes of knowledge construction and knowledge diffusion. Gender-based power and gender-based knowledge are embedded in ideological, material, and positional differences, all of which are deeply rooted in historical legacies that are context dependent.

The processes of feminist knowledge transfer that facilitate awareness and understanding of the dynamics and consequences of gender inequality thus occur in settings where participants have real differences in their interests. Alongside the participants who are eager and willing to learn, there always are participants who are sceptical and reluctant, and participants who actively oppose any challenge to their understanding of the gender unequal reality as being "normal", "just", or "inevitable". Working to transfer feminist knowledge for the purpose of increasing equality therefore also means challenging the tenets of knowledge whose purpose is to secure and legitimate gender inequality. This cannot be done without also working to change the relations of power that create the facts on the ground that "everybody knows".

If we want to improve gender mainstreaming and gender training, it has emerged as necessary to have a solid perspective on how to deal with the resistances and rejections inherent in the inequality-supporting politics of knowledge. Recognizing that this is not just the training of somehow unknowing or unskilled learners, but rather engaging with others whose "truth commitments" are structured around different premises, can lead to more effective change strategies. This is true if different interests are organized around feminist and anti-feminist claims about inequality. However, it can also reflect a struggle between those whose claim to truth is based on their experiences and those whose claim to truth is grounded in a set of theoretical claims about how the world works, only some of which can be empirically tested in a given situation.

In this Foreword, we draw from scholarly insights about gender mainstreaming and the discursive dynamics of gender equality, combining this with our experiences as academics engaging in teaching and learning about gender, to present some ideas about the politics of knowledge transfer. We find the book helpful in moving the discussion of knowledge transfer away from views of learners as passive, disempowered, or ignorant, and instead in questioning the hierarchy of knowledge sometimes imbedded in the term "training". We applaud the book's explicit recognition that what is going on under the name of "training" actually involves a more contested politics, particularly since this engagement is so poorly captured in the typical evaluations of training itself as being "successful" or "unsuccessful" in a particular organizational context.

As members of the US-EU knowledge-creating project TARGET (Transatlantic Applied Research in Gender Equity Training), we participated in many workshops in which trainers and researchers exchanged perspectives based on their experiences with the goals of increasing knowledge about gender in the policymaking world. The grounding of the trainers' knowledge in work with commissioners of gender equality interventions, as well as with the recipients of such gender training programmes, provided us with a level of critical insight into the knowledge transfer process that we, as academically based researchers, would not otherwise have had. The OPERA subproject of the QUING initiative further emphasized the needs that trainers have for a broader and deeper view of the field as a whole. It also encouraged us as researchers to see what we could contribute to the mutual learning process surrounding feminist knowledge transfer.

Because QUING (Quality in Gender+ Equality Policies, see www.quing.eu) in particular was oriented to thinking more intersectionally about multiple inequalities, the questions of knowledge transfer that it raised also went beyond a uni-dimensional process of transferring gender knowledge from the "expert" to the "trainee". Although gender maintains a central position in "gender+" analysis, the intersectional approach that it advocates is itself an extension of feminist knowledge that arose out of the practical experiences of trying to create "gender equality" in conditions of racial-ized inequalities. Kimberlé Crenshaw's (1989, 1991) introduction of the term "intersectionality" arose from her experience as an African American woman lawyer who was working on applications of US laws concerning employment discrimination and violence against women to women of colour. The era-sure of their situation from the eyes of the law was a practice-based form of knowledge construction that today informs feminist theory across a wide variety of fields.

Both TARGET and QUING provided concrete situations for mutual listen-ing to occur. Practitioners working regularly in organizations mandated to include a "consideration of gender" in their ordinary processes of decision-making faced very different challenges than those of us whose jobs were defined as reflecting on, and theorizing about, the work of organizational change. Rather than coming into these workshops thinking that either prac-titioners or social scientists were the possessors of "truth" that needed to be taught to the other, we encountered each other with a sense of curiosity about what the other knew and how they came to know this. By establish-ing sites for mutual learning, TARGET and QUING challenged the common assumption that knowledge transfer is always from academic to practitioner, from theory to application, from the general to the specific. The specificity of each practitioner's skills and experience created standpoints from which particular knowledge could be constructed and from which empirical gen-eralizations could be made. Rather than "theory" being constructed and applied to these practices, the practitioners offered their own theories to academic researchers to investigate further.

What made this mutual learning possible? We suggest that there are several important preconditions for engaging in a shared process of knowl-edge construction that were met in these projects and could be more often attempted. First, the participants came together with a common commitment to making feminist change happen, rather than positioning themselves as either teachers or learners. On the one hand, the idea of a "workshop" potentially challenges the hierarchies built into academia and how it treats students and research subjects as subordinate to the author-ity of researchers. On the other hand, it challenges the hierarchy built into the practices of gender training, which give authority to "gender experts" to frame the experiences of the members of the organization being trained. As several of the chapters of this book explain, the competing claims to episte-mological authority by feminist academics and practice-based gender experts can easily become a battleground for the power to define knowledge and to rank methodologies. This risks allowing their common interests in equality politics to fade from view.

The absence of financial incentives for controlling the definitions of expertise in these projects was another important precondition for work-ing together in a less hierarchical way. Because there was no contract to be won or research findings to be written up, at least in the short term, all participants could be persuaded that their own interest lay in the common endeavour of understanding how gender knowledge was being produced and (re)distributed rather than deciding who knows "best". The commodification of knowledge, by contrast – whether marketed by means of consultancies, expert reports, training contracts, research grants, or peer-reviewed books and articles – is a condition encouraging knowledge producers to claim ownership ("intellectual property rights") and fight for returns on their investments.

In capitalist systems, it may often be impossible to assume a financially disinterested stance towards knowledge as a good in its own right. Nevertheless, there still may be compelling alternative forms of reward in shared recognition of contributions to political and interpersonal goals. Taking financially costly stands on principle, or for the sake of peer approval, for example, is a common feature of shared-value networks that discriminate, like the "old boys" who affirm their group membership by acts of exclusion that may cost their organizations talent or social respect. It may also be common among those that contest discrimination, as transnational feminist advocacy groups and feminist trainers do. Nonetheless, the typical gap in interpersonal connections between "academic" and "activist" researchers may contribute towards mutual suspicion rather than perceptions of shared purpose. For example, each group of participants may impute merely instrumental motives for contact and cooperation to the other group. Certainly, during the TARGET project, we always had to deal with anxiety on both sides about who was "using" whom and who was "being used".

A third issue that arose in attempting to "meet in the middle" of the academic-activist gap was the problem of languages and translation. Although these workshops were always multi-national, it is not language in a national sense that posed a significant barrier. For better or worse, the dominance of English was normal. Instead, the academic-activist language gap about gender equality measures and organizational politics manifested as differences in what could easily be spoken about and what produced misunderstandings. The "commissioners" of research, for example, loomed large on the horizon of practitioners, whose work conditions and even livelihoods depended on them. By contrast, these commissioners were less obviously relevant to academic researchers, who looked to the implementation of a law or policy about mainstreaming as a more abstract and disembodied process. To speak of the "design" of an intervention, therefore, meant to practitioners a process entailing the power of commissioners to define goals, allocate resources, and demand results in a specified (and often unrealistic) timeframe. To academics, it meant the way that the practitioners responded to the charge of doing mainstreaming work – that is, the skills they developed, the tools they used, and the pedagogic rationales they offered for their approach.

Another language trap in addition to "design" was the very nature of "gender inequality" as the target of transformational processes. As Verloo et al. (2007, 2011) have found in their Critical Frame Analyses of gender policy documents in the EU 27, "gender" is often thinned out into meaning only women. That is, policy speaks about what women do, and what happens to women in an organization, rather than addressing the ways that gender is about a relationship in which both men and women have positions and act on that basis. Is gender equality in an organization achievable by changing discriminatory attitudes that are interfering with what the organization was designed to do, or was producing gender inequality part of its basic function? Thinking about gender relationally, rather than as a synonym for women in organizations designed around men, raises different questions about what kinds of organizational features are "inequality-producing". For example, gender relations would need to be seen as part of how organizations relate to each other, not just how managers relate to the female- and male-bodied individuals they employ or serve.

The broader the questions, the more difficult the answers become. If "gender equality" could be produced within one ministry or one corporation without thereby upsetting the complex ordering of gender across other organizations and institutions, what does that imply about the social importance of that one ministry or corporation? What would "gender equality" mean if it were confined to one institutional setting, since the very complexity of gender relations makes every element intersect in multiple institutions? Implementing equal pay in a single organization still triggers changes in workplaces, families, state pension systems, and insurance markets, for example.

Another linguistic struggle arises with regard to understanding "diversity". Especially in the United States today, the word "diverse" is applied to describe populations that are actually mostly or entirely "persons of colour". Thus recruiting "diverse" students does not actually mean what it seems to say, but focuses attention on ethnic minorities who will bring their "diversity" into an organization by their very bodies, often without challenging how the organization defines itself already in terms of its "whiteness". In academic feminist discourse, "intersectionality" often serves a similar function of bringing in "the other", while obscuring the norms already embedded in social relations organized around heterosexism, national-religious loyalties, age, and able-bodiedness.

When intersectionality is thinned into merely examining women with non-normative positions who "bring in diversity", a supposedly intersectional analysis is not really going to be about "gender+" relations, but merely about "women-who-are-also" disadvantaged in multiple ways. Thin versions of diversity and intersectionality are more readily fed into existing systems. They underline the very "normality" of the unmarked that they were imagined as undermining and allow the marking of the "other" women or men to proceed unchecked. Treating diversity and intersectionality as if they were categories, rather than processes (Ferree, 2009), is often criticized by practitioners as well as academics. While we have often seen a thinning (or "smothering"), of the critique that the concepts of diversity and intersectionality offer, we are also encouraged to see an energetic debate about what these words mean, and what they actually do, in specific contexts. Our TARGET workshops convinced us that both academic and activist communities are internally heterogeneous in the ways they work to make their gender politics "diverse" and "intersectional".

This book not only captures some of the insights collectively constructed in the OPERA and TARGET workshops but invites reflection on the challenges for all feminists interested in advancing social justice in the world. If our purpose as feminists is not just to understand the world, but also to transform it, we require self-critical examination of our practices both within and outside of academia. By identifying valuable steps or dangerous missteps on the road to justice, self-evaluations of the processes by which we adopt specific goals, strategies, and tactics in various settings and with what resistances can be very fruitful types of analysis.

Moreover, consideration of the effects which these choices have on us is part of the reflexivity demanded by feminist models of truth-seeking. Taking ourselves seriously as situated change agents is not the same as expressing guilt about our social locations of privilege and disadvantage. In fact, it is unrealistic to demand that we be most aware of that which we are most likely to be overlooking, that is our own situated perspectives. Awareness of the partial and temporary nature of what we know is a realistic expectation that should spur efforts to listen respectfully, and even appreciatively, to those whose position is differently constituted. But at the same time, awareness of all knowledge as situationally conditioned and politically contested should also give us a more realistic view of the struggles that we encounter in the classroom, the research project, the training commission, or any other setting where differences are present and should be allowed to have a voice.

The authors in this valuable book come to their common project of understanding the politics of feminist knowledge transfer from positions that are identifiably different. Their very specificity of perspective is part of what informs their analysis and makes it so generally useful. While less than half of the contributors were part of the TARGET or OPERA projects directly, they have all been moving back and forth between trying to bring a gender+ analysis into use in policymaking and trying to analyse reflexively what such application efforts demand and produce. Perhaps not surprisingly, there are common themes of hope and disappointment mingled in their reflections on practice. But there are also differences in how much optimism they seem to have for the longer term project of provoking change in gender relations through feminist knowledge transfer and how critical they have become of aspects of this strategy.

As already noted, one such important position shaping perceptions of possible, effective, and desirable courses of action is the academic/activist divide. A feminist politics of intersectionality demands some attention to how academics and activists relate to each other, not merely through the lens of difference but in a relationship of inequality. Professional status and employment security are significant resources in the struggle over whose knowledge is to be valued. Both status and security are unevenly distributed between academic and practitioner positions, without being uniformly high on one side and low on the other. Heterogeneity within each type of work, as well as between them, became apparent in the TARGET workshops. Along with this, a much more self-critical understanding of what makes an "ideal" trainer or researcher came to the fore.

On the one hand, each trainer or researcher is specific as to their particular discipline or type of intervention work and commands a variety of skills and insights. On the other hand, the inequality of position between academic and activist sets up certain types of locations of privilege for one or the other. To the extent that academic researchers enjoy the privileges of status and security, and not all do, they can afford a "longer view". Thus, they set their sights on more fundamental transformations ("radical changes") than practitioners in most situations, who tend towards categorizing more achievable "reforms". Without the luxury of being radical that longer term imagination offers, and needing to get up every morning and return to fight the good fight, practitioners may sell short, specific strategies that look "unrealistic" in the shorter time frame in which they operate. But to the extent that activists are engaged in actually having to use the limited power they have in a practical setting, they can see their allies more realistically and be more accurate diagnosticians of the resistances they face. Academics can idealize common interests abstractly, while practitioners will take their help where they find it. In sum, we come from our workshop experience sceptical about academics who think that practitioners don't "do theory" or "have vision". Instead, we have come to recognize that what is being imagined as relevant reflects quite different, but equally important, socially constructed needs for knowledge of particular kinds.

In fact, the reality that gender researchers and gender trainers face is one in which multiple discourses about gender are already circulating with different kinds of authority attached to their various truth claims. In addition to the important positionality to be recognized between academics and activists, we urge attention to differences that depend on positions in the wider world system of inequalities. That is, it is vital to recognize the gaps among knowledges produced in the Global South and North; in languages shared by large communities of native speakers, such as English, Spanish, or Chinese, and those expressed in the languages that few understand, such as Finnish, Turkish, or Korean; in the media of intellectuals, such as academic books and journals, as opposed to the media of mass communication, such as radio, TV, or films, or the media of the politically engaged, such as newspapers, blogs, and formal organizational training. This book only begins a conversation about how gender knowledge gets transferred within the context of bureaucratic organizations that choose to engage deliberately in this process. Nevertheless, the authors also do a wonderful job of making clear that this is never the only kind of gender knowledge transfer going on.

Additionally, the authors point to the great question of what kind of authority "gender training" is actually appealing to when it is introduced into an organization. Surely in the training process itself, it is sometimes "science", sometimes "law", and sometimes "managerial power" that provide authority backing the trainers' claims to impart knowledge and challenge existing beliefs among participants. But how do the counter-claims of the resistant participants receive their authority? Is it in the existing practices of the organization ("but we've always done it this way"), or in experience with a variety of gender-inequality-producing institutions ("but women are just not as competent/motivated/etc."), or in the managerial-technocratic logic of the bureaucracy itself ("but that has nothing to do with our main goal"). Engaging effectively with such varieties of knowledge claims demands a practical theory of gender transformation.

Practical theory is what this book offers in abundance, presenting both general visions and individual cases that illuminate the situations where gender equality advocates are actually struggling to turn out some version of a new, more gender-just reality. Because these struggles are concrete and site-specific, even the general claims in the first section are tied to the kinds of support and resistance that become visible in actual struggles to frame problems and change interconnected systems. All of the authors in this section are not merely critics of what others have done, but are engaged in imagining the undertaking of the best possible feminist transformation work. They offer concrete suggestions about ethical principles in the abstract sense, but they also provide examples of how places to meet among themselves, as well as strategies to hear from the grassroots level, can function to resist the power exercised by donors over the work being done. Their pragmatic realism suggests that truth is known at different scales, as well as from different social locations.

As a guide for thinking about how feminist knowledge can circulate, the model this book offers is less one of orderly "transfer", as from a bank of accumulated knowledge, and more like a global storm than even the "waves in motion" metaphor suggests. In this storm, there are many forms of action – wind, waves, tectonic shifts – that are stirring things up and creating both positive and negative feedback into each other's effects, so that it is hard to tell what the shape of the world will ultimately be. The storm is not local but it is felt locally, and it is not directed, even if at different times different actors think that they have everything under control. But through the power of the storm, even that which has been seen as immovable can be shifted and new features of the landscape emerge. Gender equality is one such feature that feminist knowledge practices are making visible, even if as a still distant place on the horizon.

Myra Marx Ferree and Mieke Verloo

References

Crenshaw, Kimberlé (1989) "Demarginalizing the Intersection of Race and Sex: A Black Feminist Critique of Antidiscrimination Doctrine, Feminist Theory and Antiracist Politics", *The University of Chicago Legal Forum*, 140, 139–167.
——— (1991) "Mapping the Margins: Intersectionality, Identity Politics, and Violence against Women of Color", *Stanford Law Review*, 43(6), 1241–1299.
Ferree, Myra Marx (2009) "Inequality, Intersectionality and the Politics of Discourse: Framing Feminist Alliances", in Emanuela Lombardo, Petra Meier, and Mieke Verloo (eds.) *The Discursive Politics of Gender Equality: Stretching, Bending and Policy-Making*. Abingdon and New York: Routledge.
Verloo, Mieke (ed.) (2007) *Multiple Meanings of Gender Equality: A Critical Frame Analysis of Gender Policies in Europe*. Budapest: Central European University Press.
Verloo, Mieke et al. (2011) *QUING Quality in Gender+ Equality Policies: Final Report*. Vienna: Institute for Human Sciences (IWM). http:// www.quing.eu/files/ QUING_Final_Report_Jan%2012.pdf (accessed 26 May 2015).

Acknowledgements

This book has been partly funded by the QUING project (Quality in Gender+ Equality Policies, 2006–2011) financed by the European Commission, DG Research, through the Sixth Framework Research Programme, grant agreement 028545–2.

We would like to acknowledge and express our appreciation for the inspiration provided, and the collective work done by all the QUING and TARGET researchers as well as the participants of the TARGET meetings, the OPERA training pilots, online forums, and the Madrid Seminar. We would also like to thank the esteemed contributors to this book, as well Myra Marx Ferree and Mieke Verloo for the Foreword, and Ruya Leghari for copyediting and editorial assistance.

Preface

The idea for this book started to take form over five years ago while working on the QUING project. QUING ("**QU**ality **IN** Gender equality policies") was a European research project funded under the EU's Sixth Framework Programme, involving 12 European project partners. Led by Mieke Verloo, it placed under scrutiny gender equality policies across the EU and Turkey and encompassed five different streams. One of these, OPERA,[1] consisted of the integration of knowledge on gender, intersectionality, and European gender equality policies into operational standards for gender+ training, including the training of trainers. Thus, one of the QUING/OPERA objectives was to formulate policy recommendations and standards for gender training as a way to comply with gender mainstreaming. Hence, "Gender+ training"[2] was consequently understood as part of a gender mainstreaming strategy, and duly taken to mean training planned, organized, and/or commissioned by public institutions, and targeted at public staff and professionals.

However, early on in the project, we realized that the subjects of gender training, in particular, and of knowledge transfer through gender expertise and training, in general, were substantially under-researched. Secondly, the complexity of the subject matter and practices we encountered persuaded us to take a much broader view, coming to include other actors, such as NGOs, universities, and international development practitioners. To this end, we benefited from the TARGET project ("Transatlantic Applied Research on Gender Equity Training"), which allowed us to work jointly with North American partners, including Myra Marx Ferree (University of Wisconsin-Madison) and Kathrin Zippel (Northeastern University, Boston).

As part of this cooperation, four inspiring seminars were organized in 2008 and 2009. In May 2008 in Berlin, at the invitation of Susanne Bauer (Humboldt University), we tackled issues pertaining to the content of gender+ training, including intersectionality, the theoretical understanding of learning organization, the political dimensions of gender training, equality legislation, quality assessment, and knowledge from feminist movements. In November of that year, Mieke Verloo's team at Radboud University Nijmegen, the Netherlands, organized the second TARGET expert meeting. The gathering focused on gender training methodologies, bringing together experts and commissioners, to jointly identify which type of training would be most useful for the latter's needs. In March 2009, a seminar was held at Northeastern University, Boston, MA, on the global dimensions of gender+ training. Finally, in Madrid in June 2009, led by Emanuela Lombardo and María Bustelo of Complutense University, we engaged with gender training curricula, practices, and standards.

Through the OPERA project, we quickly came to appreciate the richness and diversity of gender training experiences in Europe, even though these were neither systematic nor regularly organized. Focusing on the discernable gaps, problems, weaknesses, and strengths of gender training, and identifying characteristics which would feature in an "ideal" gender+ training initiative, we produced guidelines that could be useful across the board. For example, having identified several existing manuals for trainers, mostly in the international development sector, we produced a set of "guidelines" for gender training commissioners. These included explanations of the concept, content, and methodology of gender+ training, as well as practical information about the design of gender+ training initiatives, such as recommendations concerning group composition, quality control. So too did these entail recommendations on how to address resistances, alongside tools for the evaluation and monitoring of gender+ training.

In addition to the aforementioned meetings, jointly held with the TARGET project, several other valuable research activities were carried out under the QUING/OPERA initiative and have served to inspire this book. Especially worth mentioning are a survey on existing gender training practices in Europe; a database on gender trainers, which was transferred to the European Institute for Gender Equality (EIGE) upon completion of the QUING project in 2011; and numerous activities for training trainers. Moreover, gender+ training pilots of selected "best practices" were undertaken, which we felt should be embedded within broader gender equality strategies. This was done in order to contribute to the theoretical development of gender and feminist knowledge transfer, particularly in light of our conviction that inductive "learning from practice" was sorely needed.

Finally, we learnt that effective "training the trainers" activities should emphasize the need for trainers to be self-reflective about their own practices and that networking with the community of active gender trainers helps to foster such self-reflexivity. With the model of Communities of Practice in mind, three online forums were organized. These concerned how to integrate intersectionality and gender/feminist theory; how to use truly participatory and experiential methodology; and how to deal with resistances to gender+ training. Thereafter, a final face-to-face conference was also held.

This final conference was a key international one held at Madrid's Complutense University, on the 3rd and 4th of February, 2011, with the overarching theme "Advancing Gender+ Training in Theory and Practice". The event brought together academics, practitioners, policymakers, and commissioners to explore key issues in gender+ training. Topics discussed included ensuring quality in gender+ training – encompassing the definition of curriculum standards, the monitoring and evaluation of training activities, and the definition of quality criteria – and developing practice through reflexivity, involving the communication of feminist and gender studies theory in training, participatory-experiential methodologies, and mainstreaming intersectionality. Debates also revolved around strengthening gender+ training through a Community of Practice and addressing how best to address resistances and negotiate with commissioners, as well as the professionalization of gender+ training activities.

At the conference, the *Madrid Declaration on Advancing Gender+ Training in Theory and Practice* (see the Appendix to this book) was developed. This Declaration aims at producing a mission statement wherein gender+ training is based on feminist and gender theories translated into practice, and combines competence and capacity building with knowledge transfer. It also seeks to confront attitudes which could hinder the application of said knowledge and competences.

Thus, the challenge had begun. The principles outlined in the Madrid Declaration have served as a step forward in the professionalization of gender+ training in several countries, contributing to the global discussion on feminist knowledge transfer and supporting the development of a general framework for conducting gender+ training as part of broader gender mainstreaming strategies. At the individual level, this has enriched the editors of this book in terms of their own reflections and practice as researchers, policy advisors and evaluators, and gender trainers. These have been developed in contexts as different as those of the European Evaluation Society, chaired by María Bustelo in 2012–2013, the online community of practice launched by the UN Women Training Centre on gender+ training and moderated by Lucy Ferguson, or the development of gender training strategies in research and academia as part of the EU-funded EGERA project (FP7, 2014–2017) for Maxime Forest.

But, it is clear that in-depth discussion of many of the issues raised during the QUING/OPERA project is still very much needed. So too is a theoretical contribution regarding processes of feminist knowledge transfer through gender+ training and gender expertise. We hope this book will go some way towards filling this gap.

María Bustelo, Lucy Ferguson, and Maxime Forest
May 2015

Notes

1. In addition to the OPERA project, the other five sub-programmes of the QUING initiative were: (1) LARG, which consisted of a comparative analysis of the differences, similarities, and inconsistencies in the field of gender+ equality between the EU and its Member States, as well as developing a methodology that combined Frame and Voice; (2) WHY, which aimed at explaining those similarities, differences, and inconsistencies in gender+ equality policies across Europe, paying specific attention to differences in civil society interfaces; (3) STRIQ, a study of how intersectionality is dealt within gender+ equality policies across the EU and

its Member States, including the study of intersectional bias; and (4) FRAGEN, the construction of a database of gender+ equality frames that originate in feminist movements across Europe, leading to an open database.

2. "Gender+" is taken to denote the intersections between gender and other inequality grounds.

Contributors

Viviane Albenga is a French sociologist who specializes in the sociology of gender in the spheres of cultural practices and educational policies. Her PhD, attained in 2009 at the Ecole des Hautes Etudes en Sciences Sociales (Paris), advocates a gender approach for reading practices, and she won the Prize for Gender Studies PhD of the city of Paris in 2010. She has published several papers in peer-reviewed journals, as well as a number of books regarding gender and reading; gender and musical practices; and policies addressing the issue of gender-based violence in schools. She has recently co-edited a special issue for the French journal *Politix* (2015/1, Number 109) on ordinary appropriations of feminist ideas. She is also a member of the French team of EGERA (Effective Gender Equality in Research and the Academia) at Paris' Sciences Po-OFCE and takes part in the PRESAGE project, the gender studies programme concerning teaching and research at Sciences Po.

María Bustelo is Associate Professor of Political Science and Public Administration at Madrid's Complutense University (UCM), teaching on evaluation, public policies, and gender and politics. She is Director of UCM's Master's degree on the Evaluation of Programmes and Public Policies, and a member of UN Women's Global Evaluation Committee (2014–2016) and the UN Women Training Centre's Expert Group on Gender Training. She has been President of the European Evaluation Society (2012–2013), a member of the Board of Directors Committee of the Spanish National Agency for the Evaluation of Public Policies (2007–2011), and leader of several national and European research projects at UCM on the quality of gender equality policies, such as MAGEEQ (FP5) and QUING (FP6). She and her team act as project evaluator for GENOVATE ("Transforming Organisational Culture for Gender Equality in Research and Innovation") (2013–2016) under FP7. She has published widely on evaluation theory and methodology, and gender equality policies, including intersectionality, gender mainstreaming evaluation, and policy frame analysis. Her latest publications include "Three Decades of State Feminism and Gender Equality Policies in Multi-Governed Spain" in *Sex Roles* and a contribution to *Revista de Investigaciones Feministas'* special issue on public policies in 2015.

Anne-Charlott Callerstig is a researcher at Örebro University, Sweden, in political science (public policy and administration) and gender studies. She has extensive experience in both research and practical work surrounding equality issues in public sector organizations, including the Swedish Equality Ombudsman. She is currently involved in a research project studying the implementation of national gender equality objectives and gender mainstreaming in local municipalities. She is also an expert in national investigation on Sweden's gender equality policy and organization, launched by the government in 2014. Her research interests include equality policies and organizations; policy implementation and evaluation; public administration; labour market politics; European equality politics; and interactive research approaches. Her doctoral thesis, "Making equality work: Ambiguities, conflicts and change agents in the implementation of equality policies in public sector organisations", was published in 2014 at Linköping University, Sweden.

Tine Davids is a lecturer and researcher at the Department of Anthropology and Development Studies, as well as the Centre for International Development Issues (CIDIN), at Radboud University Nijmegen, the Netherlands. She is involved in teaching and research on gender, politics, globalization, and (return) migration. She has published internationally on these themes, including in such prestigious journals as the *European Journal of Women's Studies*, *New Diversities*, and *Third World Quarterly*. She was also co-editor of a special issue of the *Women Studies International Forum*, "Embodied Engagements: Feminist ethnography at the crossing of knowledge production and representation" (2014), as well as the books *Women, Gender and Remittances* (2015) and *The Gender Question in Globalization* (2005/2007). She further participated in the "On Track with Gender" initiative, in which CIDIN, the Dutch Ministry of Foreign Affairs, Hivos, Oxfam Novib, ICCO, Cordaid, and the Royal Tropical Institute (KIT) engaged in a process of reflection on the policy, practice, and theory of gender mainstreaming. One of the results in this process, amongst others, was a special issue for the *Journal of International Development* (2014), which she co-edited with Anouka van Eerdewijk.

Lucy Ferguson explicitly combines the roles of academic, consultant, and practitioner. As a researcher, she is associated with the Unidad de Género, Instituto de Estudios Internacionales, of Madrid's Complutense University. Her research on working as a gender expert has been published in the *International Feminist Journal of Politics*. She was also a member of the QUING/OPERA research team. As a consultant, she works for the UN Women Training Centre, moderating the Community of Practice and producing content on Training for Gender Equality, for example a recent review of gender training since the Beijing Conference. She has coordinated Virtual Dialogues on topics such as transformation, resistances, and online learning. As a practitioner, she has worked as a gender expert and trainer in her specialist field of tourism, on which she has published widely in academic journals. From 2010 to 2012, she was a gender advisor to the United Nations World Tourism Organization, developing projects and providing policy advice. She

is a founding director of Equality in Tourism, an organization which promotes gender equality in the sector and has provided gender training to
several tourism companies. In combining these three roles, her work offers
a reflection on the politics of feminist knowledge transfer that is strongly
grounded in both theoretical and practical feminist knowledges.

Maxime Forest is a senior researcher and lecturer at Sciences Po Paris
(OFCE, CEVIPOF), and scientific supervisor of the EU-funded EGERA project
(Effective Gender Equality in Research and the Academia, FP7, 2014–2017).
From 2008 to 2011, he was a post-doctoral fellow at Madrid's University
Complutense, under the QUING project (EU FP6). He has taught at political
studies institutes in Strasbourg (2007–2008) and Toulouse (2009–2010) and
been a lecturer at Paris Sorbonne University (2010–2015). His research inter-
ests include the Europeanization of gender and other equality policies; the
gendered dimensions of political and social change in Eastern and Southern
Europe; women in parliamentary politics and executive power; and the pol-
itics of intersectionality. He has published in *Comparative European Politics*,
Perspectives on European Politics and Societies, *Revue Internationale de Politique
Comparée*, and *Politique Européenne*. He also co-edited *The Europeanization
of Gender Equality Policies: A Discursive-Sociological Approach* (2012) with
Emanuela Lombardo. Appointed an executive member of the French High
Gender Equality Council in 2013, he chairs its International and EU Affairs
Committee. He regularly provides expertise to the European Institute for
Gender Equality, the French Ministry for Women's Rights, and the Council
of Europe.

Rahel Kunz is a lecturer at the Institute of Political and International Studies,
University of Lausanne. Her main research interests are feminist international relations; and feminist, poststructuralist, and postcolonial theories.
She has published in the *Journal of International Political Sociology*, *Journal of European Integration*, *Migration Studies*, *Review of International Political
Economy*, and *Third World Quarterly*. She is also the author of *The Political Economy of Global Remittances: Gender, Governmentality and Neoliberalism*
(2011) and co-editor of *Multilayered Migration Governance: The Promise of Partnership* (2011). She is currently involved in a collaborative research project
on gender experts and gender expertise.

Emanuela Lombardo holds a PhD in Politics from the University of Reading, UK. She is a lecturer at the Department of Political Science and
Administration II of Madrid's Complutense University, Spain. Her research
concerns gender equality policies and their intersections with other inequalities, particularly in the European Union and Spain; gender mainstreaming;
gender training; Europeanization; and political representation from a gender perspective. On these issues, she has published articles in peer-reviewed

journals, such as *Comparative European Politics, Political Science, Social Politics, European Integration online Papers, Journal of Women Politics and Policy, Women's Studies International Forum, International Feminist Journal of Politics, European Journal of Women's Studies, Feminist Review, Nordic Journal of Women's Studies*, and *Citizenship Studies*, as well as chapters in edited volumes. Her latest book, co-authored with Petra Meier, is *The Symbolic Representation of Gender*. She has worked as a researcher in different European and Spanish projects, such as the European Commission's FP4, FP5, FP6, and POM programmes, two of which – QUING and TARGET – concern gender training as part of a broader gender mainstreaming strategy.

Lut Mergaert holds a PhD in Management Sciences from Radboud University Nijmegen, the Netherlands. For her dissertation, she studied gender mainstreaming implementation by the European Commission in the policy area of research. She is Research Director and member of the management team at Yellow Window, a consultancy company based in Belgium. She has been principal investigator and coordinator of three pan-European research projects on gender issues for the European Institute for Gender Equality (EIGE). One of these analysed the institutional capacity for gender mainstreaming in the European Commission, and the EU's 28 Member States, with a specific focus on research policies (2013). She was the research leader for the study *Monitoring progress towards gender equality in the EU Sixth Framework Programme for Research and Development*, covering the "Science and Society", and Social Sciences and Humanities fields (2004–2007). Also for the European Commission, she coordinated a project under which a gender toolkit was developed and 73 training sessions were organized throughout Europe to raise the research community's capacity for integrating gender aspects into research (2009–2012).

Daniela Moreno Alarcón specializes in tourism analysis with a gender focus in the field of responsible tourism. She is a Tourism Planning and Management Graduate (SEK International University, Chile), with a Master's in Tourism Planning and Management (University of Alicante, Spain), and a specialization in Gender Relations (IUDC – UCM). A PhD candidate of the programme "The Feminist Perspective as a Critical Theory", at the Faculty of Political Science and Sociology of Madrid's Complutense University, her doctoral thesis is entitled "Tourism and Gender: An essential approach in the context of responsible and sustainable development". Over the last eight years, she has promoted gender equality through incidence programmes; social inclusion; awareness raising; education for development; international cooperation; and corporate social responsibility regarding consultancy, research, education, project cycles, and emotional intelligence. She co-authored FIAPP's *Tourism and Gender Guide* with Lucy Ferguson, and has supported the United Nations World Tourism Organization and the Spanish

Forum of Responsible Tourism in integrating gender issues. She is also a co-director of Equality in Tourism, an organization which promotes women's equal share of the benefits of tourism.

Elisabeth Prügl is Professor of International Relations at the Graduate Institute of International and Development Studies in Geneva, where she directs the Programme on Gender and Global Change. From 2010 to 2014, she served as Deputy Director of the Institute. She previously taught at Florida International University in Miami. Her research focuses on gender politics in international governance, in particular in the areas of agriculture, development, and conflict. She currently directs research projects on gender experts and gender expertise, gender and armed conflict, and gender and land commercialization. Recent publications include "Neoliberalising Feminism", *New Political Economy* (online) (September 2014), "Equality Means Business", *International Political Economy*, Vol. 22, 6, with Jacqui True, and *Feminist Strategies in International Governance*, with Gülay Caglar and Susanne Zwingel (2013). She is spending the 2014–2015 academic year as a fellow at the Women and Public Policy Program of the Harvard Kennedy School.

Anouka van Eerdewijk is a senior advisor at the Royal Tropical Institute (KIT, Amsterdam) and an affiliated researcher at the Institute for Gender Studies, Radboud University Nijmegen. Her work concerns gender mainstreaming and transformational change; norm diffusion processes and transnational dynamics; gender, sexuality, and rights; and gender in agricultural research. Her PhD thesis, "The ABC of Unsafe Sex: Gendered Sexualities in Dakar (Senegal)", brought together development studies, anthropology, and gender and sexuality studies. Her engagement with feminist knowledge transfer stems from both academic research and writing, and her work as an advisor at the interface between theory and practice. She coordinated the On Track with Gender trajectory on gender mainstreaming with Dutch development NGOs and the Ministry of Foreign Affairs. More recently, she worked with international research institutes and development agencies on capacity building, applied research, organizational learning, and policy advice to support the institutionalization of gender equality. She also co-edited a special issue of the *Journal of International Development* on gender mainstreaming with Tine Davids; published in *Globalizations* and *Gender and Development*; and co-published an edited volume *Gender Equality Norms in Regional Governance*.

Introduction

María Bustelo, Lucy Ferguson, and Maxime Forest

This book explores the politics of feminist knowledge transfer, offering a critical reflection on the practice of gender expertise and gender training. It brings together analytical and theoretical work on feminist knowledge transfer with revealing experiences grounded in the practice of gender training and gender expertise. These processes are explored in a reflective and analytical way, bringing what has up to now been primarily a practice-based debate into the academic arena. Overall, the book aims to critically reflect on the politics of feminist knowledge transfer and the relationship between gender expertise, gender training, and broader processes of feminist transformation.

This book is located at the intersection of two emerging literatures – gender expertise and gender training. Research on gender expertise has a longer tradition, and a number of key works have addressed the ethical and political dilemmas of feminist engagement, both with international institutions and within the development context (Cornwall et al., 2007; Prügl and Lustgarten, 2006). More recently, the edited collection by Caglar et al. (2013a) offers a detailed intervention into these debates, focusing on "feminist strategies" in international institutions. The authors question whether the primary effect of feminist practices in international organizations has been to govern, albeit through "subtle and indirect means", and how sometimes feminist strategizing "is turned from a model of resistance to an instrument of power" (Caglar et al., 2013b, pp. 5–6). The substantive chapters of their work offer detailed case studies of feminist engagement with international institutions, and the range of challenges and dilemmas this has produced.

While we follow Caglar et al. in their concerns about gender expertise, in this book we aim to engage more explicitly with the reflections of authors who identify primarily as gender experts and/or trainers. Moreover, we also develop a substantive focus on gender training. In contrast to the existing literature on gender expertise, there is currently little academic research that focuses specifically on gender training. Two recent research projects – OPERA-QUING[1] (in the European Union) and TARGET (EU–North

America)[2] – have explored the practical and political aspects of contemporary gender training, but to date have produced few concrete academic outputs on this specific area. Knowledge generation in gender training has tended to involve a more informal, non-academic process, evolving through events such as the OPERA Conference in Madrid in 2011, and networks, including the EIGE Gender Trainers Database[3] and the UN Women Training Centre Community of Practice.[4] While these fora are relevant for sharing good practices and engaging gender experts and trainers in a collective process of professionalization, a considerable void exists for more analytical reflection. In particular, there are very few avenues at present for discussing practice in the light of different bodies of literature, including those on feminist knowledge transfer and sociological-institutionalist approaches to the implementation of gender mainstreaming. This book brings together authors from diverse backgrounds, including academics, practitioners, and those whose experiences span both realms. As such, it offers a substantive contribution to the existing literature by combining a focus on both gender expertise and gender training, while providing a mix of practice-oriented and more theory-focused chapters.

This introductory chapter begins by constructing the analytical framework of the book and defining key concepts: feminist knowledge transfer, gender expertise, and gender training. We also set out the goal of feminist knowledge transfer, as well as the process, vehicle, channels, and instruments through which we understand it to take place. Throughout the book, we explore and refine these key concepts, engaging explicitly with the politics of feminist knowledge transfer and transformation. Next, the chapter maps the contours of contemporary gender training and gender expertise at the national, EU, and international/global levels. This sets out preliminary mapping efforts conducted through EU-funded research and by Communities of Practice at the international level. We explore how emerging markets for gender expertise and gender training are being structured, looking at issues such as quality criteria or standards and professionalization. Building on this mapping exercise, the chapter develops some key analytical questions for framing the discussions developed in the successive chapters around governmentalities, postcolonial analysis, intersectionality, and resistances and tensions in feminist and gender knowledge transfer. The final section outlines the overall structure and rationale of the book.

Analytical framework and key concepts

There are currently no agreed definitions of the various concepts and processes associated with feminist knowledge transfer. For example, Caglar et al. (2013b) use the term "feminist strategizing" to encompass the dynamics involved in such a process. They are concerned with how "feminist actors" in international institutions are "profoundly unstable and always mobile"

(Caglar et al. 2013b, p. 4). In their framework, such actors adopt feminist strategies. For them, gender expertise is one such "strategic tool", which helps identify "the reasons for continued gender inequality and subordination, and to advance feminist goals" (2013, p. 58). We follow Claudia von Braunmühl (2013, p. 176) who, in her discussion of feminist strategies in security governance, calls for a "strategic unbundling" of gender mainstreaming and feminist strategies. That is, in order to be clearer about the change we want and how to promote such change, further conceptual work is needed to define more clearly the processes and tools required. It is precisely one of the aims of this book, to make a further contribution to that discussion.

Here, we aim to construct an analytical framework for exploring the process of feminist knowledge transfer, which we consider to be inherently political, dynamic, and contested. First, we set out what we understand by "feminist" knowledge transfer, following key literature on gender mainstreaming and feminist evaluation (Brisolara, Seigart, and SenGupta, 2014; Hay, 2012; Podems, 2010; Seigart and Brisolara, 2002). We suggest that such a process may exhibit some or all of the following characteristics:

1. An understanding that gender inequality is "structural" and "systemic", and a capacity to use gender lenses or feminist glasses in knowledge transfer scenarios.
2. Transfer of knowledge which aims at being "transformative"; that is, knowledge use should aim not only at better understanding, but also at changing the world, fighting against social injustices, and redressing unequal power relations.
3. Feminist knowledge understood as situated knowledge, filtered through the standpoints of different knowers, in which some ways of knowing are privileged over others. This implies the acknowledgement of the plurality of feminist "knowledges".
4. An explicit acknowledgement of the inherently "political" nature of the contexts in which such knowledge is transferred, as well as of feminist knowledge transfer as a site for contestation.
5. A key focus on "reflexivity" in order to acknowledge biases and limitations and allow for the recognition of multiple perspectives.

Moreover, for the purposes of this book, we suggest that the overall goal of feminist knowledge transfer is a transformation in gendered power relations for more equal societies, workplaces, policies, and communities. The nature of such a transformation is addressed as a key theme throughout the chapters of this book. The process through which this takes place is knowledge transfer with the objective of feminist transformation. We pay particular attention here to the term "transfer" and are aware of its one-dimensional connotations and the danger of creating and sanctioning hierarchies of feminist knowledges, or knowledges on gender. Different contributors to this book approach the idea of feminist knowledge transfers in various ways, challenging the very notion of transfer and the hierarchies it may entail, and enriching this debate which we return to in more detail in the concluding chapter. However, we rely on a conceptualization of knowledge transfer which involves a dynamic participatory approach and necessitates the exchange of knowledge and ideas about gender as a fundamental part of the process. Moreover, as set out above, by using the term "feminist knowledge transfer", we firmly affirm the political nature of feminist knowledge and consider that transferring such knowledge is an inherently political and contested process.

In more concrete terms, we consider the primary vehicle for the process of feminist knowledge transfer to be feminist engagement – both externally and internally – by researchers, consultants, trainers, policy actors/agents, and activists with a range of institutions, organizations, and bodies – public, private, and semi-private. This engagement may be paid, unpaid, voluntary, or chronically under-paid and may be on a short-term, permanent, or contractual basis. Moreover, individuals may engage in different ways at different times and with different institutions. In terms of channels for engagement, this may be through broad public policy processes such as gender mainstreaming, as is the case of much feminist engagement in the EU context. Other channels for engagement include international development contexts, policy and advocacy work, and – increasingly – collaboration with the private sector, as addressed in Chapter 3. We are interested in the ways in which the channels for feminist engagement are being restructured in the current political and economic climate, and how this, in turn, affects the possibilities for transformation through feminist knowledge transfer.

In this book, we are primarily concerned with what we consider to be a range of instruments for feminist knowledge transfer through feminist engagement. Within each instrument, there is a subset of tools or methods that can be employed. These include, among others, "gender expertise", which employs methods such as policy work, general advisory work, activism, engagement with non-governmental organizations (NGOs), and engagement with the media. A further instrument – and one on which many of the authors in this book focus – is "training". Methods in training for gender equality are diverse and will be outlined further in the section on standards and professionalization. However, in general, we consider feminist training methods to be participatory, interactive, and with the ultimate goal of transformation. As Ziffer (2010, p. 5630) notes, the term "gender training" has included "primarily briefing, sometimes advocacy, occasionally learning (on knowledge, skills, or attitudes and values), but there is little rigour to the concept of gender training". In terms of institutional definitions, the UN Women Training Centre offers the term "training for gender equality" as opposed to gender training, with the aim of broadening the scope of what such training can achieve. Training for gender equality is defined as

> a transformative process that aims to provide knowledge, techniques and tools to develop skills and changes in attitudes and behaviours. It is a continuous and long-term process that requires political will and commitment of all parties in order to create an inclusive, aware and competent society to promote gender equality.
>
> (UN Women Training Centre, 2015)[5]

Throughout the development of this book, we have collectively aimed to develop and refine the concepts of feminist knowledge transfer, gender expertise, and gender training, bearing in mind two broad goals – both analytical and normative. Analytically, the book aims to provide a critical reflection on the practice of feminist knowledge transfer. The broader political or normative goal of the book is to use this process of critical reflection to enhance the potential of feminist knowledge transfer, in order to promote transformation in gendered power relations.

It is useful to frame the overall reflections of this introductory chapter in the broader context of the implementation of gender mainstreaming strategies and policies. Since the first emergence of the term in the early 1990s, gender mainstreaming has been defined in a range of ways. The most influential were developed in the mid-1990s to support the implementation of gender mainstreaming by major international actors such as the EU, the UN, the World Bank, and the Council of Europe. In 1996, the EU referred to the process as

> mobilising all general policies and measures specifically for the purpose of achieving equality by actively and openly taking into account at the planning stage their possible effects on the respective situations of men and women (gender perspective).
>
> (European Commission, 1996)

It received a more extensive definition from the Council of Europe, which described it as

> the (re)organisation, improvement, development and evaluation of policy processes, so that a gender equality perspective is incorporated in all policies, at all levels and at all stages, by the actors normally involved in policymaking.
>
> (Council of Europe, 1998)

In 1997, the United Nations Economic and Social Council (ECOSOC) defined gender mainstreaming as the process of assessing the implications for women and men of any planned action, including legislation, policies or programmes, in all areas and at all levels. It is a strategy for making women's as well as men's concerns and experiences an integral dimension of the design, implementation, monitoring and evaluation of policies and programmes in all political, economic and societal spheres so that women and men benefit equally and inequality is not perpetrated. The ultimate goal is to achieve gender equality.

(United Nations, 1997)

Implemented in different scenarios and policy settings – from internal EU policy transfers and international organizations to the arena of international development in the Global South – gender mainstreaming has generated a considerable need for knowledge and capacity building. This has helped pave the way for both gender expertise and gender training to expand as global phenomena. In this book, we thus acknowledge these phenomena as a consequence of the development and implementation of gender mainstreaming, reflecting both the rationale and intrinsic ambiguities embedded in these processes. This points to one of the key objectives of this book, namely, to address these ambiguities or tensions at different levels and from different perspectives throughout the chapters.

Gender training and gender expertise as global phenomena

Here we begin by sketching the more well-documented field of gender expertise, before moving to a more detailed discussion of gender training, an area which has been relatively understudied in feminist literature. Demand for gender expertise has gained ground since the 1995 Beijing Platform for Action, particularly in the wake of its subsequent review processes. It has been drawn upon extensively by international organizations, public bodies, and, more recently, the private sector (AWID, 2014), to provide policy advice, research, training, and capacity development. However, gaps in knowledge persist in this field. There is no agreed definition of the term "gender expert", no common criteria of what their work entails, and no systematic mapping of the profession. Nevertheless, gender experts have been central to the development of tools, methods, and frameworks employed in international organizations and development institutions. Networks of gender experts have been formed to support the work of the United Nations Development Fund for Women (UNIFEM) and its successor agency, UN Women. Experts and trainers have also been at the forefront of the EU's ongoing institutionalization of gender mainstreaming. Increasingly, it is not just public bodies but private enterprises which are displaying an interest in gender expertise. This reflects wider changes in global political economy, wherein private actors are adopting concerns or practices previously limited to states (Prügl and True, 2014). The implications of such a shift are addressed in the contribution to this book by Ferguson and Moreno.

In terms of gender training more specifically, this has recently become one of the most widely used tools for supporting the implementation of gender mainstreaming strategies in public and private organizations worldwide (EIGE, 2013). Indeed, by the late 2000s, it appeared to have the potential for effective structural change, by transferring knowledge, raising awareness, and strengthening capacities in terms of gender equality for a number of actors, including policymakers, civil servants, trade unionists, and researchers. These promising developments took place in the windows of opportunity opened at the international, EU, and domestic levels in the realms of the implementation of gender mainstreaming strategies, and the expanding regulation and institutionalization of gender equality (Kantola, 2010; Lombardo and Forest, 2012). This opportunity, however, has not yet fully materialized. Gender training has remained a highly contextual, weakly institutionalized activity, which is developing at a different pace across geographical areas and policy sectors and involving a multifaceted range of actors.

The first reason for these as yet unfulfilled promises relates to the quality of gender training. The potential of gender training for changing power relationships, challenging gender stereotypes, and revisiting organizational cultures very much depends on the existence of minimum quality standards in terms of methodology and theoretical background. However, these have not been agreed upon thus far. Another reason is the fact that gender training is also a profession in the making. Yet, since legislative, institutional, and policy frameworks for gender training vary strongly between domestic and international contexts, and across fields of intervention, so too does the professionalization of gender expertise. Last but not least, the global economic and financial crisis that began in 2008 affected the prospects opened for changing organizations through the means of gender training. It did so not only by limiting available resources but also by either moving gender equality lower down on the public agenda or by making polities less inclined to embrace the objective of gender equality (Annesley and Sheele, 2011; Briskin, 2014).

These tensions and questions regarding the limitations of gender training are highlighted in several of the contributions to this book. However, overall the book is more concerned with the relevance of different scenarios for gender and feminist knowledge transfer. By scenarios, we mean not only differentiated institutional, organizational, and cultural contexts but also, more substantively, different arenas for political contestation and knowledge circulation. Indeed, as several contributors to this book point out, while transferring feminist knowledge on gender can trigger contestation and resistance anywhere, those may be manifested in different ways in different contexts, such as where such knowledge is meant to be transferred from the "Global North" to the "Global South".

Building communities of practitioners in gender training

Incipient efforts have been made to map out the developments of Communities of Practitioners at the international level, such as those undertaken as part of the QUING and TARGET projects. Rather than extensive – through an accurate mapping of gender training institutions, provisions, and actors – their contribution has been intensive, pointing out the diversity of legal and policy settings for gender training. Along with the role to be played by the knowledge grounded in gender and feminist theory, the mobilization of experiential and participatory methods, and the key issues of institutional and individual resistances, this contribution has also acknowledged the considerable variety of actors and approaches involved in gender training activities. This primary feature of gender training worldwide was more thoroughly addressed through the building of communities of practitioners. Bringing together nearly 140 gender trainers, commissioners, and experts, the first international conference on gender training as a global issue was held as part of the OPERA-QUING project in February 2011. This clearly illustrated the different skills and institutional resources mobilized by gender training in a variety of fields, including gender and development, justice, post-conflict management, and policy design and implementation.

This pattern was clearly evidenced in the study *Mapping Gender Training in the European Union and Croatia* (EIGE, 2013). The publication indicates that gender trainers affiliated with a private company, an NGO, or a university account for some two-thirds of the database established by the European Institute for Gender Equality. Most having attained higher education, the types of degree held by gender trainers cover a variety of fields, from psychology to political science, to clinical sexology. Additionally, it is revealed that trainers have followed different paths to achieve their current level of expertise and qualification. The availability of gender-related curricula, in particular, depends on the institutionalization of gender studies at the national level, which are uneven across EU member states.[6] This diversity is also related to the different areas of intervention in which gender training has blossomed. Development policies and international cooperation have provided feminist and gender knowledge transfer through action learning as their most extensive field of experimentation. Mainstreaming gender equality throughout funding schemes, policy monitoring, and evaluation, as well as through specific projects in a wide range of cultural, religious, economic, and social environments, has truly constituted a real-scale empirical test. While providing gender training with a broad set of experiences, it also triggered first attempts at institutionalization, as evidenced by the resources jointly developed by the UN Women Training Centre for practitioners and researchers.

This diversity of experiences, standpoints, and tools is extensively addressed in this book, reflecting the pioneering role of gender and development in the diffusion of gender training. This role is notably analysed in the light of the postcolonial politics of feminist knowledge transfer, highlighting that knowledge about gender training and capacity building is generated at every level, is often context-specific, and is fuelled by empirical reality (see the chapters by Prügl [Chapter 1], Davids and van Eerdewijk [Chapter 4], and Kunz [Chapter 5] in this book). Nevertheless, both in this section and in the second part of this book, we adopt a broader perspective on gender training as a global phenomenon than the sole lens of those fields where it primarily developed. Our argument is that major challenges and issues concerning gender training are not specific to those fields. Rather, these embrace the variegated landscape of building capacity for gender mainstreaming worldwide.

Internal vs. external and top-down vs. bottom-up organization of gender training expertise

By and large, public and private demand for gender expertise and gender training is being answered by a wide range of specific external expertise, offered by trainers with individually distinct backgrounds. As gender training increasingly features as a key component of gender mainstreaming strategies, the need for better controlled qualifications, theoretical backgrounds, and methodological approaches has resulted in different attempts to organize gender training expertise, either vertically or horizontally. These can be broadly distinguished as follows:

1) At the domestic level, some public institutions and gender equality machineries have developed in-house expertise. Training is provided either internally (to the organization itself, as in the case of a ministry or a regional administration or to the broader organization under which they are placed) or on an inter-ministerial/interdepartmental basis.
2) In a few national contexts, top-down efforts have been initiated to better structure the emerging "gender training market", through the definition of minimum standards, the building of qualification procedures, or the creation of labels distinguishing qualified trainers and training organizations.
3) Qualified gender trainers themselves appear to be increasingly eager to constitute communities of practitioners as a means of achieving bottom-up professionalization through commonly agreed standards and peer recognition of qualifications and experience.

These strategies, to be briefly described below, have also been complemented by UN and EU level efforts to establish Communities of Practice across borders and fields of intervention. These further seek to make common resources available to gender trainers, including train-the-trainers activities.

In terms of the first (1) building in-house gender training capacities requires the mobilization of considerable resources. In the EU, it is reported that gender capacity-building activities are not implemented on a wide scale, with the number of such activities decreasing as a result of the economic crisis (EIGE, 2011). Nevertheless, it is worth underlying that the EU level has been key in terms of triggering the institutionalization of public gender training capacities. Rather than from the mere recognition of gender mainstreaming as a policy paradigm, these capacities have resulted from its concrete implementation through the management of EU structural funds, such as the European Social Fund and the European Regional Development Fund. This has entailed capacity building on gender issues for different categories of public actors. In turn, one of the reasons why the development of in-house gender training capacities has been uneven across policy areas, and across member states, has been its varying relevance to structural funds. As a result, most examples of in-house gender training capacities are directly related to the implementation of EU-funded projects, and the fact that "almost all Member States have received EU funding for gender training initiatives", as put forward in EIGE's study (2011).[7] Building public gender training capacities also entails train-the-trainers activities, mostly supported by EU funding, as in Estonia, Finland, Lithuania, Luxembourg, or Germany. In the latter, both public and private sector organizations have taken part in a European Scientific Foundation (ESF) project (2008–2011) aimed at building qualified in-house gender equality expertise.[8] It should be added that in Spain, managing EU structural funds led to building up gender training capacity in different "Objective 1" regions, such as Galicia and Andalusia (Alonso and Forest, 2012).[9]

Similar developments can occasionally be triggered by windows of opportunity, mainly at the domestic level. This has been the case for Sweden, where mainstreaming gender led to the strengthening of gender training capacities at the local and regional levels (EIGE, 2011).[10] More recently, following a renewed commitment to gender mainstreaming, French institutions have proved eager to develop in-house gender training expertise. This is notably the case for central gender equality machineries working on an inter-ministry basis, specifically the Women's Rights and Gender Equality Ministry, and the Women's Rights service, as well as for gender units within respective ministries. While gender training has not developed to the same extent under individual UN agencies (EIGE, 2011), UN Women has developed specific in-house expertise in this field, to be provided to other, larger UN bodies. This expertise, first of all, involves collecting data on gender knowledge transfer and capacity-building activities, with view to capturing major trends, and building empirically grounded knowledge on these issues. Secondly, it entails the development of innovative resources and tools, in the form of databases, case studies, and toolkits.

Given the highly differentiated institutional and policy contexts in which gender training activities are being implemented, and the diversity of actors intervening in this field, as yet (2), top-down efforts to structure gender training activities have been almost non-existent. In France, the Women's Rights Ministry established a working group in 2013 on minimum quality criteria in gender training. It aimed at producing a national framework, as well as a public label for gender trainers, while bringing together public and private expertise, academic and practical knowledge, and sharing views between practitioners and commissioners.

While the achievement of its goals has not yet materialized, this collective effort nonetheless triggered developments in the sphere of private enterprise and social dialogue, where it encouraged the discussion and adoption of quality standards for gender training. Public attempts to structure this emerging market very much depend on the contribution of public authorities to stimulating demand. For instance, provisions on gender equality in the workplace in France, strengthened since the early 2010s, now make it necessary de facto to carry out gender training activities in both public and private organizations. Consequently, this has reinforced the need for minimum standards and qualification procedures. The fact remains, however, that in most cases where national gender equality machineries have attempted to set minimum quality standards for gender training activities, this has mostly consisted of facilitating experience sharing and providing resources, as reported in Denmark, Germany, Sweden, and the United Kingdom (Ferguson and Forest, 2011; EIGE, 2013).

To date, (3) establishing communities among practitioners, that is building common standards from below, appears to be the most developed means of fostering professionalization in the field of gender training. The notion of a Community of Practice (CoP), coined by pedagogue Etienne Wenger (1998, 2007), refers to "groups of people who share a concern or a passion for something they do and learn how to do it better as they interact regularly" (Wenger, 2007). Theirs is "an identity defined by a shared domain of interest", wherein they "develop a shared repertoire of resources: experiences, stories, tools, ways of addressing recurring problems – in short a shared practice" (Wenger, 1998). Put in more normative terms, a CoP is meant to foster the collective involvement of practitioners in a concrete area of interest and expertise, enabling joint activities and discussions, and the sharing of information. As a context for the safe exploration of new ideas and expanding the boundaries of knowledge from multiple experiences, CoPs are especially suited in the case of gender knowledge, which is in itself a life-long learning process drawing on self-reflexivity.

Scarce evidence of such communities is found at the national level. One exception is the case of Germany, where they may be illustrated by the "Gender Manifesto" (2006) initiative. This call for critical reflection on gender-oriented capacity building and consultancy, launched by gender training experts, supports the adoption of quality standards in gender training and consultancy. It does so most notably to eliminate gender stereotypes from the gender community itself, as well as to foster methodological reflection. At the international level, however, CoPs are blossoming in the field of gender training and gender expertise. Beyond those established in the realm of EU-funded projects, as discussed above, the UN Women Training Centre also has a well-established transnational community of practitioners, with over 1,500 members at the time of writing. While still in their infancy, these attempts already provide useful insights for further exploring the potential of CoPs of experts and trainers to engage in bottom-up professionalization.

Another type of tension which appears with regards to knowledge transfer in general, and gender training and gender expertise in particular, is the tension between academics and practitioners. In the case of gender training, it seems that practitioners are the ones to step forward, while academics pay little attention to gender training as such. The latter tend to consider that gender training does not really draw on theory. On the other hand, gender trainers normally pay little heed to academics, whom they feel do not cover their needs. Although trainers understand the theory of training, they are not necessarily interested in writing it down. A Virtual Dialogue on "Knowledge on Training for Gender Equality", held by the UN Women CoP in February 2014, revealed that many practitioners feel that a demand for "real-life experience" in training does not necessarily "fit with strict academic analytical criteria" (UN Women Community of Practice, 2014, p. 3). Others argue that academic knowledge may be rejected in certain training scenarios for not being "practical" or "concrete". This book proposes to pay attention also to this tension, as the separation of academia and the world of practice can only contribute to simplistic or technocratic responses and approaches to gender training and gender expertise. Standing, for instance, indicates that there is an "inevitable by-product of professionalizing gender and development, particularly in contexts where many of the practitioners do not come from a background in political activism" (2007, p. 109). She acknowledges that academically based courses taught mainly by academics, who often also have a background in feminist advocacy, provide an excellent basis for theoretically rigorous analysis. However, she notes that they fail "to carry this forwardinto the recalcitrant arenas of policy and implementation" and do not cover "how institutions work, how to develop contextually-based strategies and create workable alliances in constrained environments" (Standing, 2007, p. 109). In sum, practitioners frequently feel that academically based approaches might not be realistic or practical, whereas academics tend to think that many practitioners are in danger of becoming technocratic and banal.

The different, often multiple standpoints of the contributing authors to this book encourage us to pay attention to how bridges are built between these two perspectives. Indeed, this diversity reflects the fact that gender training and gender expertise have become global phenomena which mobilize different kind of profiles, with individuals often working under different capacities at once. It is one of the specific contributions of this book to bring together authors who are primarily academics (Albenga, Bustelo, Davids, Kunz, Lombardo, and Prügl) with those who are both academics and experts/trainers (such as Callerstig, Ferguson, Forest, Mergaert, and Moreno-Alarcón). Although this dichotomy does not fully account for the multiple positioning or self-definitions by contributors themselves, it nevertheless illustrates different perspectives, objectives, and practices which are rarely tackled collectively. Additionally, authors are working on/in different knowledge transfer scenarios, including at the EU or domestic levels; in public and private organizations; and in the arena of international development and international organizations, such as the UN. For these reasons, the contributors represent the broad spectrum of backgrounds and skills mobilized by feminist knowledge production and circulation. This diversity is very much present in the substantive chapters of this book, making it possible to address its overarching themes from a range of both theoretical and practical standpoints.

Overarching themes

Several key issues structure this reflective and analytical contribution to the literature on feminist knowledge transfer, which are developed throughout the substantive chapters of this book. This analysis combines both recent literature in feminist and gender governance in international settings (Caglar et al., 2013; Cornwall et al., 2007) and empirical studies of gender training developed by the QUING-OPERA project and EIGE, as outlined above. Four key issues are of particular concern for this book: gender training and expertise as instruments of governmentality, and the related issue of the co-optation of feminist goals by public and private organizations; the role of postcolonial analysis in challenging the very notion of gender and feminist knowledge transfer as unidirectional; the identification of different resistances and tensions in the practice of gender training and gender expertise; and the role of intersectionality in feminist knowledge transfer. These themes are tackled to different extents in the contributions to this book, reflecting the diverse positions of the authors and the different issues of priority for scholars and practitioners.

Gender expertise and gender training as instruments of governmentality

The fear for co-optation of feminist goals and agendas has always been present in feminist action. Traditionally, some feminists consider the state to be patriarchal and insist that it is important for women's movements and strategies to remain autonomous from the state. Others, however, conceive of the state as women-friendly, or at least as an actor potentially attentive to feminist demands. Thus, they underline state participation in promoting gender equality and for "change from within" (Prügl, 2013). Moreover, post-structuralist feminist theories of the state (Kantola, 2006) do not see the state as a unified entity and instead emphasize the differentiated and fragmented nature of states and institutions. Thus, state structures and organizations can have both empowering and disempowering effects on gender relations. By the same token, feminist action should be analytically aware and attentive. These potentially empowering and/or disempowering effects of feminist action and the discursive nature which leads to different interpretations and "uses" of gender equality policies by institutions are already well-documented for gender mainstreaming processes (see, for example, Jacquot, 2010; Lombardo and Verloo, 2009; True and Parisi, 2013). This has been made possible by analysing gender equality policies and gender mainstreaming through their actors, discourses, and instruments (Lombardo and Forest, 2012; Woll and Jacquot, 2010).

With the proliferation of capacity development activities as tools for gender mainstreaming in governments, international organizations, and private companies, the use of gender training and gender expertise as instruments of power deserves exploration on a much larger scale and in an increasingly diverse scope of scenarios. In this book, several authors have opted to focus on these aspects through the concept of "governmentality". This is a Foucauldian concept for expressing the way in which governments try to produce citizens best suited to fulfil governmental policies. In other words, it denotes the organized practices (mentalities, rationalities, and techniques) through which subjects are governed (Mayhew, 2004). Therefore, using Prügl's words, as gender trainers and gender experts generate the knowledge necessary for practice, they are

> the Trojan horses of feminism in governmental processes [...] But they also reinterpret feminism to match governmental processes and thus become Trojan horses of governmentality in feminism. In this sense, gender experts and gender training are instruments in the government of gender.
>
> (Prügl, 2013, p. 60)

As such, this book aims to identify the challenges, dangers, and opportunities of governmentalities in feminist knowledge transfer through the use of gender training and gender expertise in different settings. This discussion is especially notable in the chapters by Prügl, Davids and Eerdewijk, and Kunz (Chapters 1, 4, and 5). It is further analysed at length in the Conclusions.

Mobilizing postcolonial analysis

As seen both in theoretical works and in empirical research by the QUING-OPERA project, context matters significantly. The policy sector in which gender is to be integrated matters, as does the organizational context, the actors involved, and the geographic location. How do gender training and gender expertise play out differently in different contexts? Here, we want to emphasize issues which have been extensively problematized by postcolonial feminism. How can feminist actors address the power relations embedded within the process of feminist knowledge transfer between institutions and actors of the Global North and the Global South? Feminist knowledge transfer is also addressed as a process of professionalization in which different categories of actors with varied resources, skills, and objectives are engaged. From this perspective, the role of feminist movements in providing gender expertise, as well as the postcolonial politics of international development consultancy and research, receives specific attention from contributors. The chapters by Kunz (Chapter 5) and by Davids and Eerdewijk (Chapter 4) engage with the postcolonial politics of feminist knowledge transfer. The former argues that existing metaphors conceptualize the circulation of feminist knowledges by reproducing existing hierarchies and power relations, thereby excluding and marginalizing ways of being and doing that do not conform to the knowledge transfer scenario. Kunz puts forth concepts such as the "queered gender advisor", "waves of women on the move", and "ethical encountering" as tools for addressing some of the issues raised in such contexts. Davids and Eerdewijk consider the central role of training and expertise in the context of techniques of individualization and externalization, precipitated by the articulation of gender mainstreaming governmentalities with neoliberal governmentalities. They discuss the "smothering of feminist knowledge on gender" and offer suggestions on how to recast change and agency to alter this situation.

Tensions, resistances, and contestation in a process of change

Tensions and resistances are inherent to feminist action. Capacity development for gender equality is also addressed as a dual process of structural/institutional change and individual learning. Resistances develop at these two different levels. How do experiences in gender training and gender expertise integrate and manage the individual and the institutional levels? In this respect, critical attention is paid to the institutional and personal resistances generated by such processes.

Alongside resistances, there are also tensions which play a role in feminist knowledge transfer through gender training and gender expertise. The first such tension is "gender versus feminist", that is, are gender approaches to gender training and gender expertise the same as feminist approaches? As set out above, the practice and implementation of top-down and technocratic approaches to gender mainstreaming have produced critical reactions by the feminist community. However, strong resistances to the term "feminism" or "feminist" from commissioners and trainees should also be taken into account. This issue was raised several times in the OPERA expert meetings and online fora. One reason identified for individual resistances is that some consider the political goal of transforming gender relations, implicit in gender mainstreaming, as "feminist". That is, as excessively based on ideological and emotional rather than on rational, scientific, or legal arguments (see Lombardo and Mergaert in this book).

In the field of evaluation, for example, Podems (2010) distinguishes between "feminist evaluation" and "gender approaches" to evaluation. This distinction for the evaluation field can be an illustrative example for understanding the tension we want to highlight here. Podem's views, however, are influenced by the reality of what is frequently done under the label of gender approaches in development evaluation. In order to distinguish between the two types of approaches, she overemphasizes the most technocratic, simplistic, and non-feminist applications of gender and development practices. However, it seems somewhat contradictory to oppose gender to feminism, when gender has been an analytical category proposed by feminists. Gender refers to a system of power, the analysis of which seeks to understand the mechanisms and origins of difference and oppression. It was conceived as an analytical category which goes well beyond the dichotomy of men–women and includes other inequalities and sources of oppression. It further intends to unmask androcentric biases present at the very core of how the world is organized and perceived (Hawkesworth, 1994, pp. 97–98).

If this is the case, we can conclude that, rather than an analytical category which has produced practices and effects contrary to its origins (feminism), "gender" is a term which has been somehow kidnapped. From this perspective, the distinction of gender versus feminism could be better understood as an interesting means of resistance, a way of diluting feminist goals and seeing to make them invisible. This book pays attention to the explicit, but also often implicit, resistances provoked by terms such as "feminism" and to the frequent use by gender trainers and experts of a "calculated ambiguity". That is, they simultaneously try not to end in technocratic and de-politicizing practices, while recovering significant meanings to solve the false dichotomy about gender-feminism. Gender trainers and experts are well-versed in resistances and thus often seek to bypass one form of resistance by omitting the word feminist from their trainings and practices. In such instances, they rely on persuasion rather than confrontation. Nevertheless, only very rarely are gender experts working in the real world not feminist themselves, and "it is still possible to find ways to work with gender that are congruent with transformational agendas" (Cornwall et al., 2007, p. 11).

An intersectional focus by gender experts and gender trainers?

Feminism was the first school of thought to propose the examination of the intersections of gender with other inequalities, recognizing that women are not a homogeneous category and that gender can never be considered as a single, stand-alone inequality dimension. Indeed, feminist theories and scholars have put the intersectionality issue on the political agenda, recognizing that gender is always intersected by other axes of inequality, be it class, ethnicity, disability, age, or sexual orientation, and so on. In the study of intersectionality, Weldon distinguishes between "additive" effects of different inequalities, wherein each inequality produces different effects which might add to each other, and their "multiple" effects, which are many and reinforce one another. The third effect of inequalities is "intersectional". That is, the effects of a concrete combination of inequalities produce different effects than the sum of the effects considered by themselves (Weldon, 2006).

Correspondingly, in her analysis of how governments tackle different inequalities, Hancock outlines three approaches. The first is a "unitary" approach in which each inequality is treated separately. The "multiple" approach entails that categories of inequality are all considered equally important in a predetermined relation with each other. Finally, she outlines the "intersectional" approach, wherein categories are all equally important but their relation to one another remains an empirically open question (Hancock, 2007). Analysis undertaken in Europe demonstrates that the most common approach followed by the EU and many member states has been one closer to a multiple than an intersectional approach (Kantola and Nousiainen, 2009; Lombardo and Verloo, 2009).

This European "multiple" approach raises two problems. First, it promotes a clear competition among inequality grounds. Second, the main approach seems to be a plain "anti-discrimination" one, which tends to "forget" the developments gained through gender policies, which analysed the need to comprehensively tackle "structural inequality", as well as through the gender mainstreaming strategy (Verloo, 2006). That is, the framework the EU is upholding has to do more with the concept of (anti)discrimination than with more complex political action concerning equality promotion or mainstreaming (Kantola and Nousiainen, 2009). While this anti-discrimination approach has the advantage of using "hard law" for combating discrimination, it tends to be reactive. That is, it fights against discrimination already committed, rather than being pro-active and fighting to prevent inequality. Consequently, it is normally conceived of as a mechanism targeting concrete individuals instead of society as a whole. This European approach, which is also similar to the approaches of many international organizations, has influenced much of the gender training and gender expertise propagated by European governments and international organizations, thus substantially limiting the development of a truly intersectional approach.

As such, the analytical development of the concept of intersectionality – understood as the interactions and mutually constitutive relationships of gender and other inequalities – tends to remain in theoretical terms rather than being translated concretely into practice. As McCall recognizes, "despite the emergence of intersectionality as a major paradigm of research in women's studies and elsewhere, there has been little discussion of how to study intersectionality, that is, of its methodology" (2005, p. 1771). Such discussions would include how the recognition of intersectionality is actually transferred in practice through gender training and gender expertise. In general, there is recognition of the complexities of bringing the intersectionality perspective to bear on empirical research on gender, as well as of the methodological challenges it implies (McCall, 2005; Shields, 2008). We would like to go a step further in this book, inquiring as to the methodological implications of embracing an intersectional perspective and translating it into practice in gender training and gender expertise. This book engages with the issue of integrating an intersectional focus in feminist knowledge transfer. Therefore, one of the objectives of this book is to explore to what extent a real intersectional perspective, rather than one merely identifying multiple inequalities, is part of feminist knowledge transfer and is integrated in the tools and methods of gender training and gender expertise. However, while intersectionality is incorporated into several chapters, there has been little explicit engagement with this issue as a key question for feminist knowledge transfer. We discuss the implications of this at length in the Conclusions.

Structure and rationale

In order to develop these themes more substantively, the book is divided into two parts – Key Issues in Feminist Knowledge Transfer and Critical Case Studies of Feminist Knowledge Transfer. Part I opens with Elisabeth Prügl's exploration of gender experts in governmental contexts. She develops a set of principles for the conduct of gender experts which, she argues, constitute a set of ground rules they can follow in order to minimize the potentially disempowering effects of their wielding of governmental power. This is followed by Emanuela Lombardo and Lut Mergaert's (Chapter 2) detailed empirical study of resistances in gender training processes. They posit that an exploration of the forms these resistances take can contribute to improving gender mainstreaming processes. In Chapter 3, the relationship between funding for gender equality and the private sector is articulated by Lucy Ferguson and Daniela Moreno *Alarcón*. Using original empirical material, they explore the key challenges and opportunities presented by the ongoing privatization of funding for gender expertise and training. Finally, Tine Davids and Anouka van Eerdewijk (Chapter 4) address some of the analytical concerns outlined in this introductory chapter, in particular the focus on individual change agents to the detriment of transformation. Their study of development institutions takes a governmentalities approach to envision change within the broader project of gender mainstreaming.

In Part II of the book, a number of critical case studies are offered to reflect in a more concrete way on the challenges of feminist knowledge transfer. First of these is Rahel Kunz's (Chapter 5) study of gender training in security sector reform, which addresses the supposed "window of opportunity" such a context provides for processes of feminist knowledge transfer. Using both documentary analysis and field research from Nepal, she shows how processes of feminist knowledge transfer may contribute to "othering processes" and thereby risk working against key principles of feminist knowledge. Thereafter, Anne-Charlott Callerstig (Chapter 6) presents her study of a mandatory gender training initiative in the public school system in Gothenburg, Sweden. Her findings show the importance of training as part of a comprehensive organizational development strategy, problematizing change strategies that rely predominantly on training and capacity building. The chapter also offers insights into how these instruments are materializing a more overarching strategy and constitute an attempt to incorporate gender mainstreaming into routinized practices. In the final substantive chapter of Part II (Chapter 7), Viviane Albenga reflects on an ongoing EU-funded project aimed at structural change towards greater gender equality in the academic sphere. A trained sociologist, Albenga's contribution to the diagnosis of gender imbalances at the university level explores conflicts of knowledge between the scholarly capital held by interviewees and the capital on gender held by the interviewer. The contribution elaborates on feminist and gender knowledge transfer as contested processes, framed by power relationships.

Finally, the concluding chapter draws together the key themes, arguments, and reflections of the diverse contributions to the book. It identifies the differences and complementarities between the chapters in this book, exploring how contributing authors engage with the broader questions and research agenda set out in this Introduction. Key reflections from this comparative analysis are posited, followed by an overarching call to reclaim the feminist nature of knowledge transfer processes and to develop professional ethics in this field. The concluding chapter culminates with a series of recommendations for moving forward with our work as gender experts and gender trainers, while sketching a tentative future research agenda.

In spite of the differences of approach to, and level of, critique of the practice of feminist knowledge transfer, we argue that a common thread runs through the chapters of this book. That is, it is an overarching commitment to finding ways of achieving feminist transformation through ongoing engagement with institutions. What we hope to contribute with this book is a better understanding of how processes of gender training and gender expertise can most effectively contribute to this goal.

Notes

1. QUING stands for "Quality in Gender+ Equality Policies in Europe" and was funded under the Sixth Framework Program of the European Commission, 2007–2011.

2. TARGET stands for "Transatlantic Applied Research in Gender Equity Training" and was funded by an EU–US Atlantis grant.
3. To access the EIGE Gender Trainers Database, please see http://eige.europa.eu/content/gender-trainers-database.
4. To access the UN Women Training Centre Community of Practice, please see http://gtcop.unwomen.org/index.php?lang=en.
5. Further information on the UN Women Training Centre and the UN Women Gender Training Community of Practice is available at https://trainingcentre.un women.org.
6. In terms of the uneven institutionalization of gender studies at the national level across EU member states, in 2012, for instance, there were approximately 50 MA degrees on gender issues available in the United Kingdom, 35 in Spain, 20 in Germany, and less than ten in France, Poland, or Italy. Of the latter, only a minority were devoted to equip future trainers with easily transferable gender knowledge. Given the scarcity or near absence of dedicated curricula, a number of gender trainers have thus gained their expertise through participation in workshops, or have learned "by doing".
7. EIGE's study provides examples of gender training initiatives, such as the German Agency for Gender Equality in the ESF (Agentur für Gleichstellung im ESF), which advises on gender mainstreaming and budgeting within the ESF and provides training to ministries and implementing bodies involved in programming and monitoring the ESF.
8. Occasionally, those activities for building qualified in-house gender equality expertise have been carried out as part of PHARE (institutional) Twinning Projects, aimed at developing the administrative capacity of national authorities in the field of gender mainstreaming.
9. "Objective 1" regions in this refer to those regions of the EU to be prioritized by regional development funds.
10. The SALAR (Swedish Association of Local and Regional Authorities) training programme enrolled over 60,000 civil servants in Sweden. For more information, see the website of the Swedish Association of Local Authorities and Regions: http://english.skl.se.

References

Alonso, Alba and Maxime Forest (2012) "Is gender equality soluble in self-governance? Europeanizing and Regionalizing Gender Policies in Spain", in Emanuela Lombardo and Maxime Forest (eds.) *The Europeanization of Gender Equality Policies: A Discursive-Sociological Approach.* Basingstoke and New York: Palgrave Macmillan.

Annesley, Claire and Alexandra Sheele (2011) "Gender, Capitalism and Economic Crisis: Impact and Responses", *Journal of Contemporary European Studies*, 19(3), Special Issue: Crises and the Gendered Division of Labour, 335, 347.

AWID (2014) *New Actors, New Money, New Conversations: A Mapping of Recent Initiatives for Women and Girls.* Toronto: Association for Women's Rights in Development (AWID). http://www.awid.org/sites/default/files/atoms/files/New%20 Actors%20FInal%20Designed.pdf (accessed 8 May 2015).

Briskin, Linda (2014) "Austerity, Union Policy and Gender Equality Bargaining", *European Review of Labour and Research*, 20(1), 115–133.

Brisolara, Sharon, Denise Seigart, and Saumitra SenGupta (eds.) (2014) *Feminist Evaluation and Research: Theory and Practice.* New York: Guilford.

Caglar, Gülay, Elisabeth Prügl, and Susanne Zwingel (eds.) (2013a) *Feminist Strategies in International Governance*. Abingdon and New York: Routledge.

—— (2013b) "Introducing Feminist Strategies in International Governance", in Gülay Caglar, Elisabeth Prügl, and Susanne Zwingel (eds.) *Feminist Strategies in International Governance*. London: Routledge, pp. 1–18.

Cornwall, Andrea, Elisabeth Harrison, and Ann Whitehead (eds.) (2007) *Feminisms in Development: Contradictions, Contestations and Challenges*. London: Zed Books.

Council of Europe (1998) *Gender Mainstreaming: Conceptual Framework, Methodology and Presentation of Good Practices*. Strasbourg (EG-S-MS (98) 2).

EIGE (European Institute for Gender Equality) (2011) *Good Practices in Gender Mainstreaming: Towards Effective Gender Training*. Vilnius: European Institute for Gender Equality. http://eige.europa.eu/sites/default/files/Good-Practices-in-Gender-Mainstr eaming-towards-effective-gender-training_0.pdf (accessed 13 May 2015).

—— (2013) *Mapping Gender Training in the European Union and Croatia. Synthesis Report*. Luxembourg: Publications House of the European Union. http:// eige.europa.eu/sites/default/files/Mapping%20gender%20training%20in%20the %20European%20Union%20and%20Croatia.pdf (accessed 13 May 2015).

European Commission (1996) "Incorporating Equal Opportunities for Women and Men into all Community Policies and Activities", COM/96/0067 Final. Communication from the Commission, 21 February 1996. Brussels: European Commission.

Ferguson, Lucy and Maxime Forest (eds.) (2011) *OPERA Final Report: Advancing Gender+ Training in Theory and Practice*. Vienna: Institute for Human Sciences (IWM). http://www.quing.eu/files/results/final_opera_report.pdf (accessed 13 May 2015).

Hancock, Ange-Marie (2007) "When Multiplication Doesn't Equal Quick Addition: Examining Intersectionality as a Research Paradigm", *Perspectives on Politics*, 5(1), 63–79.

Hay, Katherine (2012) "Engendering Policies and Programmes through Feminist Evaluation: Opportunities and Insights", *Indian Journal of Gender Studies*, 19(2), 321–340.

Hawkesworth, Mary (1994) "Policy Studies within a Feminist Frame", *Policy Sciences*, 27(2–3), 97–118.

Jacquot, Sophie (2010) "The Paradox of Gender Mainstreaming: The Unanticipated Effects of New Modes of Governance in the Gender Equality Domain", *West European Politics*, 33(1), 118–135.

Kantola, Johanna (2006) *Gender and the European Union*. Basingstoke: Palgrave MacMillan.

Kantola, Johanna and Kevat Nousiainen (2009) "Institutionalising Intersectionality in Europe: Introducing the Theme', *International Feminist Journal of Politics*, 11(4), 459–477.

Lombardo, Emanuela and Maxime Forest (eds.) (2012) *The Europeanization of Gender Equality Policies: A Discursive-Sociological Approach*. Basingstoke: Palgrave-MacMillan.

Lombardo, Emanuela and Mieke Verloo (2009) "Institutionalising Intersectionality in the European Union? Policy Developments and Contestations', *International Feminist Journal of Politics*, 11(4), 478–494.

Mayhew, Susan (ed.) (2004) "Governmentality", *A Dictionary of Geography*. Oxford: Oxford University Press.

McCall, Leslie (2005) "The Complexity of Intersectionality", *Signs*, 30(3), 1771–1800.

Podems, Donna (2010) "Feminist Evaluation and Gender Approaches: There's a Difference?", *Journal of Multi-Disciplinary Evaluation*, 6(14). http://survey.ate.wmich.edu/ jmde/index.php/jmde_1/article/view/199/291 (accessed 13 May 2015).

Prügl, Elisabeth (2013) "Gender Expertise as Feminist Strategy", in Gülay Caglar, Elisabeth Prügl, and Susanne Zwingel (eds.) *Feminist Strategies in International Governance*. London: Routledge, pp. 57–73.

Prügl, Elisabeth and Audrey Lustgarten (2006) "Mainstreaming Gender in International Organizations", in Jane S. Jaquette and Gale Summerfield (eds.) *Women and Gender Equity in Development Theory and Practice: Institutions, Resources and Mobilization*. Durham, NC: Duke University Press, pp. 53–70.

Prügl, Elisabeth and Jacqui True (2014) 'Equality Means Business? Governing Gender through Transnational Public-private Partnerships', *Review of International Political Economy*, 21(6), 1137–1169.

Seigart, Denise and Sharon Brisolara (eds.) (2002) "Feminist Evaluation: Explorations and Experiences", *New Directions for Program Evaluation*, 96, 97–108.

Shields, Stephanie A. (2008) "Gender: An Intersectionality Perspective", *Sex Roles*, 59(5–6), 301–311.

Standing, Hilary (2007) "Gender, Myth and Fable: The Perils of Mainstreaming in Sector Bureaucracies", in Andrea Cornwall, Elisabeth Harrison, and Ann Whitehead (eds.) *Feminisms in Development: Contradictions, Contestations and Challenges*. London: Zed Books, pp. 101–111.

True, Jacqui and Laura Parisi (2013) "Gender Mainstreaming Strategies in International Governance", in Gülay Caglar, Elisabeth Prügl, and Susanne Zwingel (eds.) *Feminist Strategies in International Governance*. London: Routledge, pp. 37–56.

UN Women Community of Practice (2014) *Virtual Dialogue: Knowledge on Training for Gender Equality, 3rd – 21st February 2014. Report*. Santo Domingo: UN Women Training Centre. http://gtcop.unwomen.org/images/dialogos/2014/report %20en.pdf (accessed 13 May 2015).

UN Women Training Centre (2015) "About Us: UN Women Training Centre". https://trainingcentre.unwomen.org/mod/page/view.php?id=45 (accessed 13 May 2015).

United Nations (1997) *Report of the Economic and Social Council for 1997*. A/52/3. New York: United Nations General Assembly. 18 September 1997. http://www.un.org/documents/ga/docs/52/plenary/a52-3.htm (accessed 29 July 2015).

Verloo, Mieke (2006) "Multiple Inequalities, Intersectionality and the European Union", *European Journal of Women's Studies*, 13(3), 211–228.

von Braunmühl, Claudia (2013) "Geschlechterverhältnisse in globalisierte Raümen", in Johannes Walacher, Johannes Müller, and Michael Reder (eds.) *Weltprobleme*. 7th edition. Munich: Bayerische Landeszentrale für politische Bildungsarbeit, pp. 111–125.

Wenger, Etienne (1998) *Communities of Practice: Learning, Meaning, and Identity*. Cambridge: Cambridge University Press.

——(2007) "Communities of Practice: A Brief Introduction." http://wenger-trayner.com/theory/ (accessed 22 January, 2015).

Woll, Cornelia and Sophie Jacquot (2010) "Using Europe: Strategic Action in Multilevel Politics", *Comparative European Politics*, 8(1), 110–126.

Ziffer, Alicia (2010) "Gender Training Community of Practice: Learning Through Dialogue." Paper presented at the *Fourth International Technology, Education and Development Conference (INTED)*, Valencia, Spain. http://library.iated.org/view/ZIFFER2010 GEN (accessed 29 July 2015).

Part I

Key Issues in Feminist Knowledge Transfer

1
How to Wield Feminist Power

Elisabeth Prügl

Feminism means engaging with power. Feminists have rallied against patriarchal power in order to undermine it, but they also have come together to empower themselves and challenge existing arrangements. Indeed, like all human agents, women have wielded power in various feminized roles throughout history. What is new in the contemporary era is the fact that there is not just women's power, but feminist power. That is, power that has been generated from, and is wielded through, feminist activism.

This power encompasses, on the one hand, the ability of feminist politics to produce change. On the other hand, it increasingly also comprises institutionalized power resulting from the way in which feminism has enlisted the state for its purposes. Feminists have achieved changes in laws to bring about gender equality. They also have institutionalized practices of affirmative action and, more recently, gender mainstreaming.

Such institutionalization entails a feminist knowledge transfer that meets the criteria outlined in the Introduction to this collection to different degrees. I have argued elsewhere that, for the most part, it can be interpreted as a "governmentalization" of feminist knowledge in the Foucauldian sense (Foucault, 1991, 2008); that is, feminist knowledge has been turned into expertise so that it becomes available for the government of conduct (see also Everett, 2009; Prügl, 2011a). In a related manner, scholars have suggested that the application of expertise has de-politicized feminist struggles, posturing as objective, neutral, and above the fray, while gutting feminism of its partisan passion (see, for instance, Wetterer, 2002). Yet others have taken governmental feminists to task for failing to reflect on the ethics of their practices. For example, in her assessment of the application of gender expertise in training, Bunie Sexwale (1996, p. 59) has suggested that "one of the most disturbing aspects of dominant 'gender training' is the utter refusal and lack of responsibility in adhering to any ethics and a complete disregard for ethical questions which have been debated, negotiated and by now broadly established within Women's Studies." In other words, the knowledge transfer we observe in much existing gender expertise has entailed a loss of feminist commitments.

Research summarized in this book shows that Sexwale's lament and the one-sided framing of gender expertise as a form of governmentality may be more pessimistic than warranted. Feminist ethics motivate many gender trainers; yet, gender expertise is only weakly professionalized. As a result, there are few explicit standards that orient the deployment of gender expertise, and the extensive debates about ethics in feminist research and teaching, that have animated scholars in the field of Women's/Gender studies, rarely make it into the practices of gender experts. Sexwale's warning is a reminder of the importance of thinking about gender training – and indeed of any effort to produce social change – as an exercise of power with ethical implications. And like any profession, gender experts and trainers need to develop standards of professional ethics that guide their exercise of power.

In this chapter, I take up shifting standpoints. On the one hand, I adopt the standpoint of gender experts in governmental contexts in order to explore what it would mean for them to wield power in a feminist way. In other words, I shift from the position of an observer of power as a productive force in the Foucauldian sense to that of an "empathetic cooperator" (see Sylvester, 1994) who recognizes gender experts as competent agents able to reflexively engage with their environment. In this understanding, power is not only a generative principle embedded in discourse but also a resource for agency. This orientation allows me to become normative and ask not only "how do feminists use their newly-found power?" but also "how *should* they use such power?" Following Sexwale, I recall that feminist expertise has a home in an academic discipline, that is Women's Studies or Gender Studies. I shift my standpoint to that of an academic, teaching and researching in this field, which allows me to draw on the feminist knowledge produced therein. While a minority of gender experts today have degrees in Women's or Gender Studies (Bergmann, 2006; Thompson, 2014), there is a substantial body of feminist thinking about ethics and methodology that has been developed there, and experts that self-identify as feminist often draw on such thinking. Here, I employ feminist ethics and merge this with theories of deliberative democracy to suggest a set of principles to guide the application of gender expertise.

Gender experts face highly contradictory demands that result from their position in governmental agencies, on the one hand, and their relationship to feminist movements, on the other. They gain authority by adopting a veneer of neutrality, of standing above politics, of adhering to traditional scientific standards of objectivity, of being able to provide rational solutions and offering techniques that accomplish results. They are effective as administrators and have authority as advisors precisely because they adopt these tools and style themselves as technical and detached (Abbott, 1988; Evetts, 2003; Wilensky, 1964). But, despite appearances to the contrary, expertise is inherently political as it affects people and populations profoundly and in ways that are not always predictable. Judging the effects of gender expertise, therefore, needs an ethical yardstick, and wielding feminist power requires ethical guidelines.

I argue that principles for the ethical conduct of gender experts can be derived from theories of deliberative democracy and from feminist methodology. Theories of democracy lead me to suggest that wielding feminist power should be approached as engaging in debate and struggle (see Ahikire, 2007, p. 40) that respond to principles of rational and un-coerced deliberation among equals and should produce institutional spaces where such deliberation is possible. Principles of feminist methodology and ethics complement these because they provide additional attention to hierarchies and difference and append to the democratic demand of inclusiveness a demand for reflexivity with regard to power relations.

The chapter is structured as follows: I first problematize the role of expertise in the policy process, illustrating the way in which both administration and expertise defy the image of political neutrality and are suffused with power. Second, I draw on the theory of deliberative democracy, its critiques by feminists, and insights from feminist methodology in order to develop four sets of principles for feminist conduct in government. Finally, I discuss the way in which gender mainstreaming can become an institutional site for fostering democratic deliberation and put forth a plea for more empirical research on the way gender experts already incorporate feminist principled conduct in their work.

Experts and politics

The idea that expertise can be separated from politics is intrinsic to an attitude of philosophical realism that postulates a reality beyond perception and social construction. In a policy context, this attitude translates into the understanding that expertise provides objective background knowledge which allows policymakers to take informed decisions. It assumes that the problem precedes the policy, that experts find solutions, and that policy adopts these solutions in order to respond to the problem. Critical policy studies have contested these assumptions on various grounds. Mary Hawkesworth (1988) has shown that much policy analysis relies on empiricist commitments which separate facts from values, and perception from observation, leading to a de-politicized scientism in the service of technocracy. She pleads instead for a policy science in the service of democracy. Similarly critical of positivist attitudes, Carol Bacchi (1999) has proposed that the formulation of policy problems is not neutral. The way problems are defined is already political, and the framing of the question imposes a particular solution. In this sense, the solution precedes the problem as much as vice versa, and it makes sense to approach policy processes as constant negotiations over the meaning of the policy problem.

If knowledge is an intrinsic part of the policy process, and if this knowledge is indeed constantly negotiated, then it makes little sense to hermetically separate processes of policymaking from those of policy implementation, as is the practice for part of the field of Political Science. Here, policymaking is imagined as an aggregation of private interests (in liberal theory) or an assertion of the public good (in republican theory). Democracy is imagined to reside in the quality of policymaking processes. But once a policy or law has been formulated, this apparently leaves the realm of policymaking and becomes an object of implementation, carried out by bureaucracies in a more or less rational fashion. Policy moves from the realm of democratic decision-making – and thus the play of politics – into the realm of public administration. Here, in the Weberian ideal type of bureaucracy, politics is suspended in favour of the rational application of rules. And if a distortion of rational administration is diagnosed – such as in the unthinking application of standard operating procedures or in bureaucratic politics (see Allison, 1972) – this is portrayed as an aberration from the rational ideal.

But Bacchi's Foucauldian approach to government tells us that administration is intrinsically political, that it is a site of the play of power. This is so because administration is embedded in discursive commitments that produce specific rationalities and elicit the application of certain technologies of government. Governmentality, the art of governing through the application of knowledge, produces a range of power effects including, for example, the fixing of objects, the authorization of subjects, the hemming in of options, and the normalization of identities. In this understanding, knowledge in the form of expertise constitutes the core of government, and it unfolds its power through a range of technologies, of which gender training is an example.

In the Foucauldian conceptualization of the place of knowledge in administration, the rule of experts tends to produce a self-referential logic of governmentality that cannot be captured through the language of democracy (Ferguson, 1994; Kennedy, 2005). And indeed, the expectation that experts will be objective implies that they treat scientific knowledge as a positive reflection of reality, blinding them to its political effects. For gender experts, the question thus becomes how to negotiate power in a discursive environment wedded to methodological positivism.

Feminist methodology may provide one path out of this conundrum. Feminist critiques of the pervasive biases and silences in presumably objective scholarship have led to an extensive questioning of positivist methodologies. Feminists have developed alternative approaches that distinguish themselves by the kinds of questions asked, by recognizing the positionality of the knower, by problematizing the constellation of power in research encounters, and by being explicit about the purpose of knowledge creation (for overviews, see Naples, 2003; Ramazanoglu and Holland, 2002; and Tickner, 2006). These methodological imperatives recognize the normative content of knowledge creation, generating a kind of "strong objectivity" (Harding, 1993) that problematizes the role of the knower – the academic scholar as much as the policy expert. Loath to abandon its emancipatory project to a Foucauldian imaginary of self-referential processes, feminist methodology thus postulates a responsible agent held to account by the methodological standards of the profession.

If one looks at processes of policy implementation through the lens of feminist methodology, the meaning of expertise changes. It no longer holds the status of conveying a singular truth, but encompasses a recognition and interpretation of a multiplicity of situated truths – including of truths emerging from social movements – and making them the subject of deliberation. Putting expertise at the service of deliberative processes thus requires a reformulation of the role of experts. Writing on policy processes in the environmental sphere, Frank Fischer (2009) has suggested that the role of the expert should not be that of a one-time translator of technical knowledge, but of a mediator who interprets knowledges precisely in order to facilitate public deliberation. In his understanding, the policy process should be conceived of as an ongoing cycle of deliberation, which offers an opportunity to advance democracy by providing space for authentic engagement between different political forces and discourses (see also Hawkesworth, 1988).

If one accepts Fischer's proposal, the gender experts' conundrum of exercising governmental power while conducting themselves ethically may be looked at in a different light. As facilitators of deliberation, gender experts may contribute to enhancing the democratic legitimacy of government more broadly. I am thus proposing that the work of gender experts be judged not only by the quality of its outcomes but also by the quality of the processes experts engage in and make possible. Such an approach is justified because, in complex systems, it is invariably difficult to control the way ideas proliferate and morph to produce outcomes that may or may not approximate those that were intended. Yet, such systems can be configured in ways that allow experts to conduct themselves in a principled fashion. That is, to teach, conduct research, analyse, and foster change in a way that conforms to feminist ethics and ideals of deliberative democracy. The assumption is that the democratic quality of inputs, paired with the application of principles from feminist methodology, will improve the quality of outputs.[1]

This approach can address Sexwale's complaint about the dearth of ethics in the application of gender expertise. However, it is unlikely to respond to the charge that the governmentalization of feminist knowledge de-politicizes feminist movements and/or amounts to an exercise of power.

All it can do is to make the exercise of such power more conscious by recognizing the political character of expertise. Moreover, it may make the exercise of such power more legitimate by contributing to a democratization of government. My proposal is addressed to gender experts who identify as feminists, and who look to feminism to provide them with guidance in their wielding of power. Not all gender experts share this interest – many identify as professionals in a different field, such as, for example, development economics, law, or public health. In this sense, this proposal is a political intervention in a contested space. My purpose is to develop a set of specifically feminist principles for gender experts to follow.

Principles of conduct for feminist gender experts

The meaning of democracy has become intensely contested in the context of an increasingly complex and interdependent world. Does the image of a sovereign people governing themselves still capture social reality when global constraints – from economic imperatives to political commitments – hem in political choices? How can governments remain legitimate when they appear captured by powerful interests, while failing to solve the urgent problems of our times – from climate change to financial stability? These doubts and questions have led to an extensive discussion of the meaning of democracy in an interdependent world, and of the way in which government should be reorganized to regain both effectiveness and legitimacy. The theory of deliberative democracy has proven popular in this context. On the one hand, it promises to unlink democracy from the conceptualization of a political community, the basis of a republican notion of democracy. On the other, it offers respite from the liberal idea of democracy that prescribes putting in place political institutions to achieve a compromise among individuals and interest groups.

John Dryzek describes deliberative democracy's core notion as follows: "outcomes are legitimate to the extent that they receive reflective assent through participation in authentic deliberation by all those subject to the decision in question" (2010, p. 23). The significance of this reformulation becomes visible when juxtaposing it against other formulations of democratic legitimacy. For liberal theorists, such legitimacy lies in the guarantee of the fundamental rights of the individual. For republican theorists, it derives from the assent of "the people", the ethico-political substance of a citizenry with a shared cultural background that has entered into a social contract. Against these conceptualizations, the theory of deliberative democracy locates the source of legitimacy entirely in democratic procedures. That is, "in the rules of discourse and forms of argumentation that borrow their normative content from the validity basis of action oriented to reaching understanding" (Habermas, 1996, pp. 296–297). In doing so, the theory avoids the difficulty of linking the legitimacy of government to a bounded *demos* in an increasingly globalizing world, and the difficulty of postulating abstract, universal principles of morality, which precede any empirical social and cultural interaction.

For various reasons, thinking of democratic legitimacy as a matter of procedure is attractive for the purpose of developing principles of conduct for gender experts. First, to the extent that democratic legitimacy is a matter of procedures, it is not logically attached to the institutions of democratic decision-making codified in constitutions. Instead, it also becomes applicable to the various "new state spaces" and "networks of governance" that have sprung up together with the reorganization of governmental authority. These include multilevel systems of government, such as the EU. They also encompass, for example, internationally funded projects and programmes where politics and meanings from different geographical scales intersect. Because gender expertise is often invoked as part of international efforts towards gender mainstreaming, experts frequently operate in precisely such spaces and networks (Brenner, 2004; Hajer and Wagenaar, 2003; Hooghe and Marks, 2003; Prügl, 2011b). Second, because the notion of deliberative democracy does not rest on the assumption of predefined, abstract rights, it opens up debates around "difference" and "diversity". Scholars have criticized the fact that gender mainstreaming does not have a clear definition of gender equality (True and Parisi, 2013). However, rectifying injustices requires that the meaning of equality be opened up for debate. Inclusive deliberation can be transformative precisely to the extent that it is open to unsettling accepted notions of equality (Squires, 2005, p. 380).

Finally, deliberation is a particularly appropriate path towards arriving at decisions in circumstances where expert knowledge is "contested". Such contestation has motivated a turn towards deliberative democracy in environmental studies. Here, expertise has increasingly met counter-expertise, and the impacts of expert solutions on populations have become a matter of considerable acrimony (see, e.g., Fischer, 2009). Feminist knowledge is similarly contested. Yet, whereas in the environmental arena arguments are about the validity of empirical evidence, and the effectiveness of contemporary economic organization, the problem of gender inequality ultimately amounts to a contestation of the constitutive rules of societies and cultures. As such, it garners resistance from a broad range of often unorganized social forces (see Lombardo and Mergaert in this book). Thus, perhaps more than in the case of environmental expertise, the application of gender expertise invites processes of deliberation, of a joint effort of creating meaning, rather than an encounter with positivist evidence.

A consideration of writings on deliberative democracy, paired with feminist critiques and insights from feminist methodology, leads me to propose four sets of principles. These should guide the wielding of feminist power in a way that fosters democratic deliberation and counteracts the de-politicization of feminist knowledge. These principles are: rational deliberation across difference; non-coercion, equality and feminist social criticism; inclusiveness; and reflexivity. I will now briefly discuss each principle in turn.

Rational deliberation across difference

Deliberative democracy is about reaching understanding, or arriving at decisions, in a way that relies on rational discourse and argumentation. Democratic decision-making is thus imagined not as an aggregation of individual interests (the liberal view), but as a rational exchange between individuals who have in mind broader principles or the public good. In the process of deliberation, it is expected that all are open to changing their point of view as a result of the quality of the arguments put forward.

This idea has resonated with feminist theorists, but there also have been important critiques. Iris M. Young has argued that by assuming unmarked individuals entering a deliberation, and thus denying difference, the model becomes implicitly exclusionary. It may recognize that coercion can come from economic dependencies or domination, but it ignores the "internalized sense of the right one has to speak or not to speak, and [...] the devaluation of some people's style of speech and the elevation of others" (Young, 2006, p. 122). Furthermore, Young has criticized the masculinity of a focus on rational deliberation with its implied antagonistic posturing of opposing arguments and with its elevation of reasoning over other forms of communication.

But rather than rejecting the notion of deliberative democracy, Young builds on it in order to suggest that difference does not have to be an obstacle to finding agreement. Rather, it can be a resource for public reason. She suggests an opening up to multiple forms of communication, such as, for example, narration. She also proposes a somewhat different notion of understanding than that put forward by Habermas. Understanding across differences does not imply identification; rather it means that

> there has been a successful expression of experience and perspective, so that other social positions learn, and part of what they understand is that there remains more behind that experience and perspective that transcends their own subjectivity.
>
> (Young, 2006, p. 128)

Young's proposal connects to various concepts feminist theorists have introduced to capture communication across difference – from the notion of empathetic cooperation proposed by Christine Sylvester (1994) to the world travelling described by Maria Lugones (1987). In the ideals proposed by these theorists, genuine encounters that recognize difference require that the self must be open to a change, not just of points of view but also of being.

Accounting for difference in rational deliberation would have to include this insight.

Non-coercion, equality, and feminist social criticism

According to theorists of deliberative democracy, authentic deliberation should be free of coercive influences, so that logic and reason prevail over power plays. It needs to be driven by speech that is truthful and sincere. The selective presentation and manipulative framing of issues is considered contrary to authentic deliberation. Moreover, all need to be treated as equals in making proposals, criticizing them, and giving assent.

The principles of non-coercion and equality resonate well with feminist critiques of power. Yet, feminists have noted the utopian character of these requirements in the face of the pervasive reality of women's subordination. Brooke Ackerly (2000) has discussed the matter from the perspective of Third World women. In a context full of coercion, how could environments be generated that allow Third World women to participate in an un-coerced and equal fashion? Ackerly argues that feminist social criticism logically complements a theory of deliberative democracy to the extent that such criticism is a necessary prerequisite for attacking power inequalities, and thus for creating the circumstances for un-coerced deliberation. Indeed, social criticism – as visible in Third World women's activism – has as one of its goals the promotion of deliberation. Other goals include the promotion of institutional change and the promotion of inquiry.

Ackerly proposes a methodology for social criticism that consists of three parts. Namely, it should include deliberation as a means of inquiry; foster sceptical scrutiny of elitist, coercive, and exclusionary or potentially exploitative values, practices, and norms; and develop a set of criteria for evaluating values, practices, and norms (Ackerly, 2000, p. 18). The emphasis on procedure, and specifically on deliberation, reappears here in an enlarged image of deliberative democracy. That is, one addressed not only to governance networks that link the state and civil society but one that infuses deliberation into civil society itself. And in these deliberations, critique and challenges to practices of domination take on a central role. Ackerly develops a quasi-universal set of evaluative criteria (following the work of Martha Nussbaum) that, substituting for the liberal language of rights, provide the basis of critique for existing practices and pave the way for transformation. In her interpretation, deliberative democracy becomes possible once it allows for feminist social criticism that is itself deliberative, sceptical, and follows a set of evaluative maxims.

Ackerly's insights are relevant for considering a broad range of feminist change practices, including those in government. They bring to the foreground the importance of critique, while specifying deliberation as a process and goal, and providing a set of standards by which to measure outcomes.

Her standards raise important questions for existing training practices – from making training mandatory (arguably a form of coercion) to exploring how social criticism can be included in a training context.

Inclusiveness

The principle of inclusiveness is not central to all theorizations of deliberative democracy. However, Gutmann and Thompson (2004) assert that deliberation can be understood as democratic only as long as it is inclusive. In other words, the broadest number of people affected by a decision should be consulted in deliberative decision-making.

For feminists, inclusiveness is a central value, most consistently expressed in writings on feminist methodology. Identifications of pervasive bias in mainstream scholarship have led feminists to acknowledge that all truth claims are situated, that is that they emerge from particular contexts, experiences, and political struggles (Haraway, 1988; Hartsock, 1998; Smith, 1987). From this realization, feminists have derived a strong methodological norm of inclusiveness. This norm encompasses a number of aspects. First, scholarship needs to be attentive to the diversity of knowledges that exist, and it needs to make visible and give voice to this diversity. Among the diverse knowledges which feminist scholarship pays particular attention to are those considered marginal and often silenced. Thus, feminists study from the bottom-up and look at the world through situated lenses. Second, when studying local knowledges, the norm requires a collaborative partnership with those who have such knowledge (Ackerly and True, 2010). This allows feminist research to advance practical knowledge that fosters understanding, and emancipatory knowledge that makes visible the political positions of those at the margins. Third, truth emerges from collective validations rather than positivist yardsticks. Scholarship is exercised in a community, and it is only by participating in the debates of a community that claims to truth can be ascertained, even if this is always only in a preliminary and partial fashion (Tickner, 2006, p. 27; Weldon, 2006). The principle of inclusiveness is thus indicative of a wide range of practices encompassing both the relationship of the researcher to the researched and of researchers towards each other.

In her book *Inclusion and Democracy*, Young (2000; see Chapter 3 especially) applies these feminist methodological principles to fleshing out deliberative democracy. She starts from the presumption that group-based positionality invariably gives greater power and voice to some. Accordingly, procedural rules that posture as impartial often result in bias. She therefore suggests that communicative democracy needs to go beyond inclusion, in order to also affirm the particular social group position that is relevant to an issue and to draw on the situated knowledge of people in such positions. This would allow everyone to enlarge their understanding by moving beyond parochial interests. A feminist methodological principle, that is the understanding of knowledge as situated, informs Young's proposal for a consideration of difference. She elevates this principle over reified constructions of group identities: What matters is not skin colour, or sex, or even political constructions of groups in the spirit of identity politics. Instead, what should matter in deliberative contexts are the different experiences that people derive from living different social positions. Deliberation that validates such knowledges may, on the one hand, arrive at an objectivity that overcomes the partiality of all insight. On the other hand, it may make it much more difficult to arrive at consensus. Indeed, Young questions whether the objective of deliberation needs to be consensus in the form of mutual identification. Rather, just solutions to political problems may be achieved through coordination and cooperation that allow for a continuation of difference.

The principle of inclusiveness developed in feminist methodology, and in feminist critiques of deliberative democracy, thus incorporates two distinct insights. The first links inclusiveness to difference; the second insists on the inclusiveness of individuals, and, perhaps more so, of the situated knowledge of diverse experiences. Inclusiveness, moreover, signals an attention to difference in knowledge, but also to processes of participation. That is, to the formation of partnerships that allow for better understanding and to collective validations of knowledge.

Reflexivity

Feminist methodology puts forward another principle not typically picked up in theories of deliberative democracy, that is the notion of reflexivity (nevertheless, see Dryzek, 2006). "Reflexivity" is a term with many meanings, variously associated with the current phase of modernity (Beck, 1992), social constructivism, post-positivist methodology, and emancipatory ethics. In the field of International Relations, references to reflectivism, or the "reflexive turn", often have indicated a change of ontology in scholarship that approaches international phenomena as socially constructed (Hamati-Ataya, 2012; Keohane, 1988). A reflexive world precludes the scholarly conceit of being able to identify the laws according to which this world ticks. Instead, it invites a critical interrogation of the way in which this world has come into being.

Many feminists have not stopped at recognizing the social world, and therefore gender relations, as reflexively produced, but have insisted that researchers themselves are part of the social world they study and that scholarship contributes to the construction of the world. This, in turn, has methodological implications. Feminists have insisted that reflexivity in scholarship needs to be acknowledged and fostered because of the multiple relationships of power that research is embedded in. First, scholars need to reflect on the power relations that may arise from their own location in the Global North, or their belonging to privileged status groups defined by race, class, or gender. Second, scholars need to reflect on the epistemic power they wield. This results from their ability to frame questions, define categories, and devise methods that others are asked to respond to, and from their ability to interpret and thus construct realities through their writings (Ackerly, 2008). A recognition of this power demands that those who are in the business of creating knowledge take responsibility for the effects that their truth claims make possible (Stern, 2006). Bacchi and Eveline (2010) follow this line of argument when they suggest that feminists working in policy should interrogate their representations of problems in a reflexive manner, so that they become aware of unexamined assumptions, silences in the way problems are framed, and potentially deleterious effects resulting from such assumptions and framings.

In the field of Public Administration, Cunliffe and Jun (2005) have taken a similar approach to problematize both the conduct of the administrator and the power commitments evident in the knowledge used. They distinguish an attitude of self-reflexivity from critical reflexivity. Building on a humanistic perspective, they have proposed self-reflexivity as an attitude of reflection on our ways of being and acting in the world, including our role in the construction of organizational and social life. Drawing on critical theory, post-structuralism, and post-modern ideas, they see critical reflexivity in efforts to unsettle "the assumptions underlying theoretical, moral, and ideological positions as a basis for thinking more critically about academic, organizational, and social practices" (Cunliffe and Jun, 2005, p. 228).

For experts working in bureaucracies, a reflexive attitude can help foster democratic deliberation in a context of bureaucratic rationality by self-consciously, and critically, interrogating both organizational processes and epistemic commitments. Such reflexivity helps to identify power in hegemonic discourses that stifle voices from the margins, and in bureaucratic routines that reproduce hegemonies unthinkingly. Feminist gender trainers and experts tend to be keenly aware of such power mechanisms, but are frequently alone in their posture. There is a dearth of institutional spaces that foster a collective habit of reflexivity and that counteract the various forms of power-laden common sense that invariably emerge in the formulation of expertise, and in practices of knowledge transfer.

From theory to practice

Gender mainstreaming, the projects, programmes, and policies intended to bring about gender equality, including gender training, can be approached as sites for the democratization of governance. This proposal follows the insights of Judith Squires (2005), who has encouraged an engagement of gender mainstreaming with theories of deliberative democracy. She suggests that "the emphasis that deliberative democrats place on inclusion and dialogue offers rich resources to counter the technocratic tendencies in the integrationist model of mainstreaming" (Squires, 2005, p. 381). Instead of bureaucratically absorbing the gender equality agenda into existing policies without changing these policies, Squires suggests that gender mainstreaming be transformative. It should not stop at integrating gender equality into existing power structures or at reversing these power structures to revalorize feminine values. Instead, it should produce cultural change. This would entail politicizing existing norms, and displacing existing commitments, such as the dichotomy between equality and difference. Gender mainstreaming is more likely to become transformative in this way if it is deliberative. It would approach various stakeholders as citizens, transmitting civil society debates into formal arenas of political decision-making. And rather than simply wanting to aggregate the preferences of such citizens, it would seek to facilitate transformative dialogue between them.

Given the fact that feminist ideas have been influential in developing gender mainstreaming, it is not surprising that many deliberative democratic principles already are part of the practices of gender experts and gender trainers, and that, therefore, gender mainstreaming carries within it the seeds of transformation. For example, a review of gender training manuals in the security sector shows that gender experts tend to be highly attuned to the principle of inclusiveness. Thus, many of the manuals surveyed in one project emphasize the need for the extensive participation of stakeholders (Prügl, 2010). Many gender trainers are also acutely aware of the need to recognize difference beyond superficial nods to tolerance. Thus, they strive to create training contexts that are non-coercive, and in which participants are treated as equals. Moreover, there is evidence of considerable reflexivity among feminist gender experts regarding the uses and dangers of "strategic framing", or instrumental argumentation, and indeed an explicit engagement with a commitment to reflexivity (see, for instance, Ferguson and Moreno in this book; Eyben and Turquet, 2013). Yet, not all gender experts are committed to feminist ethical principles, and even where they are, there is a dearth of institutionalized spaces that allow such principles to flourish.

The EU-funded QUING project is an exception that has explicitly served as an institutional site to foster the principles developed in this chapter. It has sought to enable reflexivity on gender training by facilitating communication among gender trainers, and the professionalization of gender training. An important outcome of this project has been the "Madrid Declaration on Advancing Gender+ Training in Theory and Practice", which evokes the language of democracy to specify the goal of such training as contributing to a "gender equal democratic society". Furthermore, it affirms the need for inclusiveness and reflexivity in the development of gender+ training. Adding a "+" to gender emphasizes a broad consideration of all types of intersectional difference.[2]

There is a need to move beyond simply critiquing the technocratic or governmental character of existing experiences with gender mainstreaming and gender training, towards recognizing complexities in practice, and assessing processes along a range of dimensions and principles. Empirical investigations should explore the way in which gender training constitutes an institutional site of democratic deliberation reflecting the principles outlined above. Such investigations would not be confined to probing the way individuals wield expertise. Perhaps more importantly, they would problematize the institutional infrastructure and discursive commitments in place, to enable conduct following deliberative and feminist principles. How does training have to be structured in order to guarantee rational deliberation across difference, encourage a non-coercive and equal environment, be inclusive, and foster reflexivity? How can projects and programmes be designed to become sites for enabling the application of these principles, and thus become conducive to unleashing feminist gender expertise? What innovative institutional sites have been generated already to accomplish these goals? The diverse institutionalizations of in-house and top-down gender training capacities, and the communities of practice described in the Introduction to this book, constitute interesting cases for assessing a feminist wielding of power along the yardsticks of feminist deliberation.

Conclusion

How can gender experts remain legitimate in the face of critiques that fear, on the one hand, a de-politicization of the feminist movement and, on the other hand, the development of a new form of power to direct the conduct of people? How can they wield power in a way that affirms their professional credibility and authority, while at the same time remaining accountable to the movement? In this chapter, I suggest that it is possible to wield power in a feminist way if this wielding of power is principled. Theories of deliberative democracy and feminist methodology suggest four sets of principles that should guide feminist conduct involved in government. They are the following:

- rational deliberation across difference that is open towards a change in being;
- ensuring non-coercion and equality in deliberation, while enabling feminist social criticism;
- inclusiveness of diverse knowledges paired with working in a participatory manner, and in partnership, for collective validation;
- reflexivity vis-à-vis both processes and epistemic commitments.

This formulation of deliberative legitimacy pertains not only to the level of individual ethical conduct but also to institutional designs. Gender experts are embedded in institutions that circumscribe their behaviour, but that can also be designed to advance the principles of gender-sensitive deliberative democracy. Institutionalizing principles of rational delibera-tion, non-coercion and equality, inclusiveness, and reflexivity may foster an application of gender expertise that produces transformation rather than administration, and that can be called democratic rather than technocratic. It can provide the conditions for a transformative practice of gender main-streaming and knowledge transfer that begins to take seriously the dangers of feminist ideas being co-opted into hegemonic state projects.

There is good reason to believe that gender experts in many places already apply the principles developed here, and creatively put in place practices to generate spaces of deliberation by which to democratize international governance. There is a strong need for the empirical documentation and exploration of such practices. Built on feminist knowledge that has long engaged with the question of power, gender experts are uniquely positioned to provide a model for the engagement of scholars and experts with the state, and for bringing expert knowledge to policy practice in a way that advances democratic principles.

Making feminist knowledge a tool of government no doubt has de-politicizing implications for feminism as a movement and an opposi-tional force. It also conveys a measure of authority to feminism that allows it to participate in shaping the rules that define the world. If feminists want to move beyond critique, they cannot help but become a part of governmen-tal power. As gender expertise is spreading and establishing itself, gender experts and academics alike are challenged to advance knowledge on how to wield governmental power in a feminist way, and release the transformative potential of feminist knowledge transfer.

Notes

1. In other words, I privilege "input legitimacy" over "output legitimacy" (Scharpf, 1999).
2. For more information on the "Madrid Declaration on Advancing Gender+ Training in Theory and Practice", please see http://www.quing.eu/files/madrid_declaration.pdf.

References

Abbott, Andrew (1988) *The System of Professions: An Essay on the Division of Expert Labor.* Chicago, IL: University of Chicago Press.
Ackerly, Brooke A. (2000) *Political Theory and Feminist Social Criticism.* Cambridge, UK: Cambridge University Press.
———— (2008) *Universal Human Rights in a World of Difference.* Cambridge: Cambridge University Press.
Ackerly, Brooke A. and Jacqui True (2010) *Doing Feminist Research in Political and Social Science.* New York: Palgrave Macmillan.

Ackerly, Brooke A., Maria Stern, and Jacqui True (eds.) (2006) *Feminist Methodologies for International Relations*. Cambridge, UK: Cambridge University Press.

Ahikire, Josephine (2007) "Gender Training and the Politics of Mainstreaming in Post-Beijing Uganda", in Maitrayee Mukhopadhyay and Franz Wong (eds.) *Revisiting Gender Training: The Making and Remaking of Gender Knowledge*. Amsterdam and Oxford: KIT Publishers and Oxfam GB, pp. 39–46.

Allison, Graham T. (1972) *Essence of Decision*. Boston: Little, Brown.

Bacchi, Carol (1999) *Women, Policy and Politics: The Construction of Policy Problems*. London: Sage Publications.

—— (2009) *Analysing Policy: What's the Problem Represented to Be?* New South Wales: Pearson Education Australia.

Bacchi, Carol and Joan Eveline (2010) "Power, Resistance and Reflexive Practice", in Carol Bacchi and Joan Eveline (eds.) *Mainstreaming Politics: Gendering Practices and Feminist Theory*. South Australia: University of Adelaide Press, pp. 139–161.

Beck, Ulrich (1992) *Risk Society: Towards a New Modernity*. London: Sage Publications.

Benhabib, Seyla (2006) "Toward a Deliberative Model of Democratic Legitimacy", in Seyla Benhabib (ed.) *Democracy and Difference: Contesting the Boundaries of the Political*. Princeton, NJ: Princeton University Press, pp. 67–94.

Bergmann, Nadja (2006) "Gender Mainstreaming als Berufsfeld", in Luise Gubitzer and Susanne Schunter-Kleemann (eds.) *Gender Mainstreaming – Durchbruch der Frauenpolitik oder deren Ende?* Frankfurt am Main: Peter Lang, pp. 221–234.

Bohman, James and William Rehg (2007) "Jürgen Habermas", in *Stanford Encyclopedia of Philosophy*. http://plato.stanford.edu/entries/habermas/ (accessed 8 May 2015).

Brenner, Neil (2004) *New State Spaces: Urban Governance and the Rescaling of Statehood*. Oxford, UK: Oxford University Press.

Cornwall, Andrea, Elizabeth Harrison, and Ann Whitehead (2007) "Gender Myths and Feminist Fables: The Struggle for Interpretive Power in Gender and Development", *Development and Change*, 38(1), 1–20.

Cunliffe, Ann L. and Jong S. Jun (2005) "The Need for Reflexivity in Public Administration", *Administration & Society*, 37(2), 225–242.

Dryzek, John S. (2006) "Transnational Democracy in an Insecure World", *International Political Science Review*, 27(2), 101–119.

—— (2010) *Foundations and Frontiers of Deliberative Governance*. Oxford: Oxford University Press.

Everett, Jana (2009) "Governance Reforms and Rural Women in India: What Types of Women Citizens are Produced by the Will to Empower?", *Social Politics*, summer, 279–304.

Evetts, Julia (2003) "The Sociological Analysis of Professionalism: Occupational Change in the Modern World", *International Sociology*, 18(2), 395–415.

Eyben, Rosalind and Laura Turquet (eds.) (2013) *Feminists in Development Organizations: Change from the Margins*. Bourton on Dunsmore: Practical Action Publishing.

Ferguson, James (1994) *The Anti-Politics Machine: "Development," Depoliticization, and Bureaucratic Power in Lesotho*. Minneapolis: University of Minnesota Press.

Fischer, Frank (2009) *Democracy and Expertise: Reorienting Policy Inquiry*. Oxford: Oxford University Press.

Foucault, Michel (1991) "Governmentality", in Graham Burchell, Colin Gordon, and Peter Miller (eds.) *The Foucault Effect: Studies in Governmentality*. Chicago, IL: The University of Chicago Press, pp. 87–104.

—— (2008) *The Birth of Biopolitics. Lectures at the Collège de France 1978–1979*. Houndsmill: Palgrave Macmillan.

Gutmann, Amy and Dennis Thompson (2004) *Why Deliberative Democracy?* Princeton, NJ: Princeton University Press.

Habermas, Jürgen (1996) *Between Facts and Norms: Contributions to a Discourse Theory of Law and Democracy.* Trans. William Rehg. Cambridge, MA: MIT Press.

Hajer, Maarten and Hendrik Wagenaar (eds.) (2003) *Deliberative Policy Analysis: Understanding Governance in the Network Society.* Cambridge: Cambridge University Press.

Haraway, Donna (1988) "Situated Knowledges: The Science Question in Feminism and the Privilege of Partial Perspective", *Feminist Studies*, 14(3), 575–599.

Hartsock, Nancy (1998) *The Feminist Standpoint Revisited and Other Essays.* Boulder, CO: Westview Press.

Hawkesworth, Mary E. (1988) *Theoretical Issues in Policy Analysis.* Albany, NY: State University of New York Press.

Halley, Janet (2006) *Split Decisions.* Princeton: Princeton University Press.

Halley, Janet, Prabha Kotiswaran, Hila Shamir, and Chantal Thomas (2006) "From the International to the Local in Feminist Legal Responses to Rape, Prostitution/Sex Work, and Sex Trafficking: Four Studies in Contemporary Governance Feminism", *Harvard Journal of Law and Gender*, 29, 335–423.

Hamati-Ataya, Inanna (2012) "Reflectivity, Reflexivity, Reflexivism: IR's 'Reflexive Turn' – and Beyond", *European Journal of International Relations*, 19(4), 669–694.

Harding, Sandra (1993) "Rethinking Standpoint Epistemology: What Is 'Strong Objectivity'?", in Linda Alcoff and Elizabeth Potter (eds.) *Feminist Epistemologies.* New York: Routledge, pp. 49–82.

Hooghe, Liesbet and Gary Marks (2003) "Unraveling the Central State, but How? Types of Multi-level Governance", *American Political Science Review*, 97(2), 233–243.

Jasanoff, Sheila (1990) *The Fifth Branch: Science Advisers as Policymakers.* Cambridge: Harvard University Press.

Kennedy, David (2005) "Challenging Expert Rule: The Politics of Global Governance", *Sydney Law Review*, 27, pp. 1–24.

Keohane, Robert O. (1988) "International Institutions: Two Approaches", *International Studies Quarterly*, 32(4), 379–396.

Lugones, Maria (1987) "Playfulness, 'World'-Traveling, and Loving Perception", *Hypathia*, 2, 3–19.

Naples, Nancy A. (2003) *Feminism and Method: Ethnography, Discourse Analysis and Activist Research.* New York: Routledge.

Prügl, Elisabeth (2010) Gender Expertise and Feminist Knowledge. Presented at the conference on "Gender Politics in International Governance;" Graduate Institute, Geneva, 6 to 8 October.

———— (2011a) "Diversity Management and Gender Mainstreaming as Technologies of Government", *Politics and Gender*, 7, 71–89.

———— (2011b) *Transforming Masculine Rule: Agriculture and Rural Development in the European Union.* Ann Arbor: University of Michigan Press.

———— (2013) "Gender Expertise as Feminist Strategy", in Gülay Caglar, Elisabeth Prügl, and Susanne Zwingel (eds.) *Feminist Strategies in International Governance.* London: Routledge, pp. 57–73.

Ramazanoglu, Caroline and Janet Holland (2002) *Feminist Methodology: Challenges and Choices.* London: Sage Publications.

Scharpf, Fritz (1999) *Governing in Europe: Effective and Democratic?* New York: Oxford University Press.

Sexwale, Bunie M. Matlanyame (1996) "What Happened to Feminist Politics in 'Gender Training/?' ", in Mary Maynard and June Purvis (eds.) *New Frontiers in Women's Studies: Knowledge, Identity and Nationalism.* London: Taylor and Francis, pp. 51–62.

Smith, Dorothy E. (1987) *The Everyday World as Problematic: A Feminist Sociology.* Toronto: University of Toronto Press.

Squires, Judith (2005) "Is Mainstreaming Transformative? Theorizing Mainstreaming in the Context of Diversity and Deliberation", *Social Politics: International Studies in Gender, State and Society,* 12(3), 366–388.

Stern, Maria (2006) "Racism, Sexism, Classism, and Much More: Reading Security-Identity in Marginalized Sites", in Brooke A. Ackerly, Maria Stern, and Jacqui True (eds.) *Feminist Methodologies for International Relations.* Cambridge: Cambridge University Press, pp. 174–98.

Sylvester, Christine (1994) "Empathetic Cooperation: A Feminist Method for IR", *Millennium: Journal of International Studies,* 23(2), 315–334.

Thompson, Hayley (2014) "Expertise in the Global Governance of Gender." Paper presented at the *International Studies Association Annual Convention,* March, Toronto.

Tickner, J. Ann (2006) "Feminism Meets International Relations: Some Methodological Issues", in Brooke A. Ackerly, Maria Stern, and Jacqui True (eds.) *Feminist Methodologies for International Relations.* Cambridge: Cambridge University Press, pp. 19–41.

True, Jacqui and Laura Parisi (2013) "Gender Mainstreaming Strategies in International Governance", in Gülay Caglar, Elisabeth Prügl, and Susanne Zwingel (eds.) *Feminist Strategies in International Governance.* London: Routledge, pp. 37–56.

Weldon, Laurel S. (2006) "Inclusion and Understanding: A Collective Methodology for Feminist International Relations", in Brooke A. Ackerly, Maria Stern, and Jacqui True (eds.) *Feminist Methodologies for International Relations.* Cambridge: Cambridge University Press, pp. 62–88.

Wetterer, Angelika (2002) 'Strategie Rhetorischer Modernisierung: Gender Mainstreaming, Managing Diversity und die Professionalisierung der Gender-Expertinnen', *Zeitschrift für Frauenforschung und Geschlechterstudien,* 20(3), 129–149.

Wilensky, Harold L. (1964) "The Professionalization of Everyone?", *American Journal of Sociology,* 70(2),137–158.

Young, Iris M. (2000) *Inclusion and Democracy.* Oxford, UK: Oxford University Press.

—— (2006) "Communication and the Other: Beyond Deliberative Democracy", in Seyla Benhabib (ed.) *Democracy and Difference: Contesting the Boundaries of the Political.* Princeton, NJ: Princeton University Press, pp. 120–135.

2
Resistance in Gender Training and Mainstreaming Processes

Emanuela Lombardo and Lut Mergaert

Introduction

Feminist knowledge transfer and gender mainstreaming are deeply interrelated. Gender mainstreaming requires that institutional and organizational cultures undergo changes to include a gender perspective – based on gender knowledge – into all public policies and processes (Council of Europe, 1998). However, policymakers generally do not have sufficient gender awareness and competence to introduce a gender perspective into all policies, and they tend to work within institutional structures that are mostly gender-blind (Roggeband and Verloo, 2006). Gender training, taken here to mean training commissioned by public institutions and targeted at public administration personnel on how to mainstream gender into their work, is a key process of knowledge transfer (Pauly et al., 2009)[1]. Not all gender trainings are necessarily processes of feminist knowledge transfer, however. While "gender" knowledge transfer refers to gender as an analytical concept concerning the socially constructed relation between women and men, the "feminist" component of training includes a "goal", a target for social change. This is of "challenging and changing women's subordination to men" (Ferree, 2006, p. 6). In feminist, rather than only gender processes of knowledge transfer, change is not expected to come smoothly but rather involves conflict and contestation.

Resistance or opposition to gender training, expressed by both organizations and participants in such trainings, is part of the contestation that accompanies processes of change. It is, indeed, a major challenge for gender training. This chapter[2] argues that analysing resistances in gender training – as part of a wider gender mainstreaming strategy – can yield useful insights into the problems arising during the implementation of such a strategy, as well as those which emerge in the politics of gender mainstreaming in general. The identification of what exactly people are resisting – whether a specific gender initiative; additional work given to a public employee

43

without sufficient training; or the goal of gender equality in itself – is an indicator of what is not working in the mainstreaming strategy. Based on such information, an organization's approach to gender mainstreaming can be refined.

Despite its role in processes of feminist knowledge transfer and change towards greater gender equality, such as gender mainstreaming, resistance is an understudied phenomenon. In this chapter, we argue in favour of recognizing the importance of resistance in the literature on gender and politics. We contribute both to the theorization of resistances in gender mainstreaming and training processes and to the analysis of forms of resistance. We relate resistance to gender training to the general issue of institutional resistance to change (Benschop and Verloo, 2006), as one of the elements that contributes to understanding the ineffective implementation of gender mainstreaming (Lombardo and Mergaert, 2013; Mergaert and Lombardo, 2014). How is resistance to gender training expressed? What are the types and forms of these resistances? And what can the analysis of resistances to gender training tell us about the problematic implementation of gender mainstreaming?

We argue that, if gender mainstreaming processes are considered opportunities for feminist – and not only gender – knowledge transfer, as this book contends, resistance can be interpreted as part of the contestation that accompanies processes of transformation towards greater gender equality. As Benschop and Verloo state, "it might even be more fruitful to conceptualise gender mainstreaming as a contestation rather than a collaboration process" (2006, p. 30). Together with these authors, we believe that the design of gender mainstreaming initiatives should include the consideration of potential conflict and resistance as part of the strategy's implementation within organizations. Our research on gender training draws on the experiences of trainers, recognizing that these are relevant to identifying the types and forms of resistance in training processes.

The information about resistance to gender training was compiled through participatory observation in trainings, expert meetings, conferences, and online forums about gender training, developed as part of the QUING and TARGET[3] research projects. We ourselves are not gender trainers, and this analysis does not, therefore, draw on our own first-hand experiences. Our main roles have been those of gender experts and consultants, either coordinating gender training programmes or organizing seminars to reflect on gender training as one important instrument in the implementation of gender mainstreaming. We participated in four formal face-to-face expert meetings on gender training between 2007 and 2009; four informal expert meetings in 2007 and 2008; three online forums in 2010, of which one focused on resistance; and one conference on gender training in 2011. This conference engaged practitioners, policymakers, and academics from European and American contexts in debates on gender training and quality criteria, with one panel specifically addressing resistances in gender training. Participants in the expert meetings mainly included gender trainers and academics, and in some cases, civil servants who commissioned trainings. Additional insight came from the coordination of two gender training programmes conducted for the European Commission's Directorate-General for Research and Innovation, through which 33 trainings were delivered in 2009–2010 and 40 trainings in 2011–2012, throughout Europe. After selecting the relevant information on resistance in processes of gender training, we processed the collected data through content analysis.

This chapter is structured as follows: the first section introduces gender mainstreaming and resistance to gender training as conceptualized in the literature and identifies different types of resistances. The second and third sections, respectively, present different manifestations of resistance to gender training and assess our findings. In the conclusions, we discuss the policy and research implications of this analysis of resistance to gender training for the implementation of gender mainstreaming.

Theorizing resistance in gender mainstreaming processes

Gender mainstreaming and gender training

Gender mainstreaming was launched in the 1990s as a key policy strategy to achieve gender equality. Governments and civil society participating in the UN's Fourth World Conference on Women in Beijing in 1995 endorsed the strategy to counter gender bias in society and policies and to produce more gender equal policies overall (United Nations, 1997, p. 1). Gender mainstreaming would challenge androcentric norms and promote gender equality in politics (Council of Europe, 1998; Jahan, 1995; Rees, 1998; Squires, 2005; Verloo, 2001, 2005; Walby, 2005). The mainstreaming strategy implies a transformation of institutional and organizational cultures, requiring changes in policy processes, mechanisms, and the actors involved (Council of Europe, 1998). Changing the policy process in gender-sensitive ways requires putting in place gender equality machinery in all governmental departments to catalyse mainstreaming work and train policy personnel in gender equality.

Scholars have discussed a variety of prerequisites for implementing gender mainstreaming. These include political will to address gender hierarchies in an organization (Charlesworth, 2005; Derbyshire, 2002; Díaz González, 2001; Mazey, 2000; Rao and Kelleher, 2005); a diagnosis of the "genderedness" of the organization as well as a plan to address this (Daly, 2005; Derbyshire, 2002; McGauran, 2009); capacity building of all actors, including the provision of resources; monitored implementation; involvement of civil society and/or experts in the process (Derbyshire, 2002; Mazey, 2000; McGauran, 2009; Verloo, 2006); and holding people responsible for the actions undertaken and their results (Hafner-Burton and Pollack, 2009; Mergaert, 2012).

One of the main problems in the implementation of gender mainstreaming is that it paradoxically requires a high level of gender awareness among policymakers who are not gender experts but suddenly find themselves "trapped in gender discourses" (Roggeband and Verloo, 2006, p. 629). Gender mainstreaming also demands specific competences and approaches for which civil servants have not necessarily been trained. The potential incompatibility between feminist and technical bureaucratic knowledge and skills thus seems to have been overlooked by early advocates of gender mainstreaming. In response, gender training emerged as a practice to build civil servants' and politicians' capacity for gender mainstreaming. By gender training we mean:

> (1) the training planned, organised or/and commissioned by public institutions; (2) targeted at public personnel, and (3) aimed at facilitating the incorporation of "a gender equality perspective in all policies and at all levels and at all stages of the policy-making process".
>
> (Council of Europe, 1998, p. 15; Pauly et al., 2009, p. 6)

The assumption behind this definition is that gender training, as an instrument of an overarching strategy to achieve gender equality through mainstreaming gender into policymaking, supports the creation of gender equality policy competences.

As gender training processes are emerging in different countries, reflections on how to improve such training is growing among trainers, consultants, and development and policy experts (Mukhopadhyay and Wong, 2007). The emergence of gender training and the introduction of gender knowledge (although not systematic) at different levels of government are indicators of gender mainstreaming's growing institutionalization. Resistances to gender initiatives, however, are to be taken seriously, as they can hinder or even block the implementation of gender mainstreaming. At the same time, resistances can open up opportunities for deliberation and the strengthening of the gender mainstreaming approach, enhancing the potential to create transformation. For these reasons, they deserve attention from gender and politics analysts.

Resistance to gender training: causes, reasons, types, and actors

We define resistance as a phenomenon that emerges in processes of change and that is aimed at maintaining the status quo, against change. This interpretation is different from the meaning of resistance that refers to the questioning of a particular dominant social order. Both concepts, however, define resistance as a form of opposition; in this case, to gender equality.

Because gender mainstreaming implies organizational change, it may – as any process of change – trigger resistance on the part of the actors involved. Processes of mainstreaming gender into organizations are likely to face particular resistance, argues Díaz González (2001), because the changes that gender mainstreaming requires challenge norms and practices concerning the relations between women and men. In processes of gender training that are part of a mainstreaming strategy, resistance is thus likely to appear, overtly or covertly, among the main actors involved in a training: policymakers commissioning the training; civil servants participating in the training; and trainers themselves.

Despite the relevance of resistance to gender equality initiatives, especially gender mainstreaming, the issue remains relatively understudied in academic works. The causes of resistance have been explored by focusing on the institutional level, arguing that a key reason for the ineffective implementation of gender mainstreaming is institutional resistance to change (Benschop and Verloo, 2006; Cavaghan, forthcoming). Organizational processes, and political and bureaucratic practices, are not gender neutral (Newman, 1995; Savage and Witz, 1992). Instead, they (re)produce gender biases that are often based on "unspoken assumptions about a traditional gendered division of labour" (Lovenduski, 2005, pp. 146–147). Resistance to change is likely to appear "when the existing organisational culture, norms, beliefs, attitudes and values are affected by the change efforts", which tends to be the case in processes of gender training and mainstreaming (Mergaert, 2012, p. 57). Within institutions pervaded by a "deeply embedded culture of masculinity" (Lovenduski, 2005, p. 48), this results in gender unequal power relations, and the transformative aim of gender equality policies to change unequal gender roles tends to evaporate (Longwe, 1995, 1997). Conflicting interests coexist within the same institution, resulting in a more or less explicit struggle in which "bureaucratic principles demand implementation", while "patriarchal principles demand evaporation" (Longwe, 1997, p. 151).

Context is important for understanding individual and institutional resistance, both to locate the phenomenon – the context we analyse here is Europe – and to keep in mind that trainees do not always have the power to enact changes. Benschop and Verloo (2006) provide an example of institutional resistance concerning a gender mainstreaming initiative with civil servants in the Ministry of the Flemish Community in Belgium. The authors found that their attempts as gender experts to work on and expose the genderedness of the institution faced resistance on the part of high-ranking civil servants. The latter controlled the agenda and preferred to downplay the need for deeper gender analysis of the organization that feminist actors invoked, to maintain the gendered status quo. In a study on gender impact assessments in Dutch ministries, Roggeband and Verloo (2006) also encountered resistance to this gender mainstreaming instrument on the part of civil servants. This resistance manifested itself when it became clear that the civil servants did not consider gender mainstreaming to be a priority in policy-making, rendering gender impact assessments both unimportant and costly to them.

Van Eerdewijk's analysis of gender mainstreaming implementation in Dutch development agencies, moreover, shows that considering institutional resistance helps to clarify why mainstreaming ends up integrating "gender, but not in a transformative way". That is, either not questioning existing unequal gender relations, or even entailing policies evaporating entirely (van Eerdewijk, 2009, p. 22). In the case van Eerdewijk analyses, institutional resistance is expressed in the "disconnection between the organisational and the operational level" (2009, p. 22) of policies , whereby "program officers are left with the responsibility to meet set gender targets, in a context that lacks the necessary strategic choices that would allow them to meet these objectives" (2009, p. 20). Such studies of resistances identify civil servants at different hierarchical levels as key actors resisting gender mainstreaming, especially its transformative goals. It is concluded that research on the ineffective implementation of mainstreaming should place civil servants' resistance centre stage and consider it both a cause and a manifestation of the ineffective implementation of gender mainstreaming.

Civil servants can express resistance to gender initiatives both by acting and by non-acting. In either case, resistance is a manifestation of power, which Lukes (2005) argues is at work not only when policymakers make decisions, but also when they refrain from doing so, or, in this case, when they do not undertake action on issues that would not benefit them. The individual and the institutional levels are interconnected because institutions are a collective of individuals and "collective non-action translates into an effective form of resistance" by holding back institutional change (Mergaert, 2012, p. 57). In this light, it is important to distinguish between implicit individual resistance and implicit institutional resistance. The former manifests itself through non-action or inadequate action, either caused by compliance with the existing gender norms or by a lack of resources (including knowledge and skills, time, financial resources, and power). The latter occurs when the mentioned incapacity is detectable at a collective level and is connected to policy decisions about resources that are taken in the higher ranks of an organization. Institutional resistance is recognized by Stratigaki (2005), who draws attention to institutions that dedicate insufficient economic and human resources to gender equality policies.

Resistance can also be expressed explicitly, such as when decisions are taken against the goal of promoting gender equality. This overt resistance can take the form of policy discourses that express ideas and aims which distance themselves from the goal of gender equality, or it can take the form of policy actions that go against that goal. An example is offered in Stratigaki's (2005) account of how EU male-dominated institutions adopted the rhetoric of gender mainstreaming to argue against gender advocates' demand for binding positive actions in decision-making. They offered the justification that, because gender was now mainstreamed into all policies, there was no more need for positive actions. Resistance in this case manifested itself through opposition to the feminist goals implied in the mainstreaming strategy.

If the causes of resistance lie in the gendered norms deeply rooted in institutions, the reasons for resistances to this kind of change vary, and analysts thus need to consider a combination of factors. One reason concerns the fact that gender mainstreaming and gender training challenge people's personal identity and beliefs. Gender mainstreaming triggers reflections about people's own gender role and assumptions, making them feel criticized or prompted to change their own personal identity. This can trigger reactions of fear and self-protection, moving people to develop attitudes of resistance (Pauly et al., 2009). Another reason can be that people resist the emphasis that gender trainers put on the political goal of transforming gender relations. This feminist goal may be rejected as excessively based on ideological arguments, rather than scientific or legal ones. Finally, a reason for resistance that is not connected to changes in gender norms, but rather to persuasion strategies, is "reactance". This is a reaction of resistance to the change advocated by a particular speaker, if one feels that the speaker is trying to steer the audience in a certain direction or manipulate them in some way (Brehm and Brehm, 1981). In sum, the combination of multiple gender specific and general reasons makes resistance a complex phenomenon that deserves more attention in the literature on gender and politics.

From existing scholarly discussions on resistance to gender mainstreaming, a number of conclusions arise. First, to understand resistance to processes of changes in gender norms, it is important to address causes, reasons, types, and actors, as well as the interactions between these aspects. Second, it is necessary to take into account the active role of civil servants, as part of both the problem and the solution. Third, there are different types of resistance: individual, institutional, implicit, explicit, gender specific, that is, resistances to gender equality issues themselves, or not gender specific, that is, resistances more generally related to processes of change. And finally, identifying different types of resistance, and considering the distinction and interrelation between the individual and the institutional levels, is important to understand resistance in gender training processes. It is also essential to finding an adequate response to it, and thus contribute to improving the implementation of gender mainstreaming.

Forms of resistance to gender training: Identification and assessment

In this section, we present and assess different forms of resistance expressed in gender training processes that can be related to the types of resistance discussed above (individual, institutional, implicit, explicit, gender specific, or not gender specific). The examples of resistance here focus on resistance on the part of the participants in gender training sessions, and also, albeit to a lesser extent, on resistance from commissioners of training. The presentation of resistances we provide is not meant to uncritically blame trainees and commissioners of training, but to offer material for analysing the phenomenon of resistance in gender training processes. We are aware that gender trainers can also be caught in the trap of blaming trainees and commissioners for their own shortcomings. This issue invites broader reflection about trainers' own resistances, which goes beyond the scope of this chapter.

Resistances from trainees

As reported by gender trainers, manifestations of trainees' resistance tend to be similar across contexts. The main forms of trainee resistance that recur in trainers' accounts are a "denial of the need for gender change", "trivialising gender equality", and "refusing to accept responsibility for solving the problem". A number of resistances appear to be targeted at gender equality as a goal. Gender trainers from contexts as different as Spain and Sweden have pointed at a form of resistance that one trainer named the "mirage of equality". This entails the feeling that, because we already live in a gender-equal society, there is no need for a change in gender norms. The perception that equality is no longer a problem is described by Agócs (1997) as "denial of the need for change". A typical manifestation of this type of resistance is a statement such as gender equality "is out of fashion" because of the perception that women and men are equally situated in employment, social life, and so a gender equality debate is useless (see Ferguson and Moreno, Chapter 3 in this book).

In relation to this manifestation of resistance, Agócs distinguishes between resistance that challenges the credibility of the change message and resistance to the change agents themselves, that is, the trainers. The former appears in situations where resisting trainees deny or undervalue the data on existing gender inequalities; claim it is exaggerated or biased; and demand trainers provide more, or different, data to persuade them of the need for change. As one trainer put it, "the most basic level of resistance is that trainees are not willing to/do not consider it possible that they can 'learn' anything about gender inequality", dismissing factual data about gender inequality presented by trainers. The trainees' contestation of factual data about gender inequality shows how complex gender training processes are. This is due to the fact that norms are hidden behind such facts as well. Even trainings that are supposedly "about transferring knowledge", and not "about attitude change", are in fact "about political positions towards gender equality".

The second kind of resistance Agócs distinguishes poses a problem for the credibility of the trainer. In the words of one trainer, this is a "resistance to learn something from a feminist". In this case, gender issues are categorized as ideological, rather than considered as scientific knowledge. This is either due to the perception of excessive politicization or due to prejudices against feminism. Gender trainers are in a difficult position, as their audience will often be ill-disposed to any message simply because of their role as gender trainers. Taking this to its paradoxical extreme, they would need to "convince the audience" of their message before even speaking their first word. Reflective studies on gender training such as Mukhopadhyay and Wong (2007) question the role of gender trainers as persuading actors. They argue that feminist epistemologies have developed more "nuanced, grounded, iterative and relationship-oriented understandings" (2007, p. 13) of processes of knowledge transfer. This idea about the role of trainers could possibly spare gender trainers ill-founded expectations about their roles. Moreover, it could put trainees and trainers on a more equal footing and create a less confrontational environment for training, although the latter often cannot avoid being perceived as persuaders.

The "denial of the need for gender change" can be articulated in trainees' resistance discourses through reference to (traditional) gender roles as natural and "innate", as reported by one trainer. During a debate on equal pay, a trainee argued that it was perfectly fair that professional sportswomen were paid less than professional sportsmen because the most important sports in the world were male sports. The examples given were football and tennis, and the argument ran that these supposedly required male physical strength, thus justifying unequal pay between women and men. Trainees can also overtly articulate resistance by directly confronting the trainer, as in the example of a participant in a session who underlined the pointlessness of gender trainings, explicitly commenting what a waste of time the gender session was, thus showing resistance through his low opinion of gender knowledge. Trainers suggest the context in which gender training occurs is extremely relevant in gauging resistance. That is, whether the trainees sign up voluntarily, which could minimize resistance, or whether the gender session is mandatory or part of a larger training initiative on issues other than gender, which could maximize resistance.

Another form of verbally manifested resistance is by "trivialising and minimising the importance of gender equality" and through the "refusal to accept responsibility" for dealing with gender equality issues (Pauly et al., 2009). Trainers report this kind of resistance manifests in utterances such as:

- "We can't afford to deal with this issue now. There are more pressing priorities."
- "It is not relevant for our work."
- "It is not my problem. I'm not responsible because I didn't create it."
- "Time will fix the problem."
- "The issue is too complex. There is no quick-fix solution."
- "It is very difficult to apply this."
- "You convinced me, but I wouldn't know how to pass on the message to my colleagues..."

While the first four quotations are overt resistances, the last three are challenges to implementation. These expressions of resistance show that equality is not a priority for the resisting person, and that nobody feels directly responsible for the problem, thus justifying non-action. They are also evidence of a perception that change will come naturally, that the natural development of society – a community based on individual merit and gender neutral capacities – will solve the problems of inequality without the need for intervention, and that introducing a gender perspective would only complicate things (Ferguson and Forest, 2011). The last two utterances of resistance – dealing with the complexity of the issue and the difficulty of transferring the message – could also be seen as an alibi for non-implementation. However, such manifestations can also be expressions of insecurity and incapacity about the trainee's advocacy skills. This possibility deserves further exploration by placing the manifestations of resistance into the training context to understand what triggers a specific oppositional attitude.

Underestimating the issue of gender equality can also occur in less discursively articulated ways, through trainees' laughter that directly derides the issue, or through reducing the discussion to more simplistic debates. In both cases, participants signal that gender cannot be considered a serious issue that needs attention. Attitudes can also communicate a lack of interest in the subject, such as when trainees continuously look at their phones and notebooks, do not participate in the discussion, or leave more motivated (often female) participants to do the work in groups.

A variation of the specific manifestation of "refusal to accept responsibility" reported by one trainer is the assumption that "gender equality is a problem owned by and thus to be solved by women, not men", thereby denying the structural aspect of the problem. The same point was raised in the evaluation questionnaire of a female participant in a (voluntary) gender training: "Even if we had some men who attended the course as well, it was still obvious that the topic is meant to be solved by women. [...] I doubt that women need the training more than men do" (Mergaert, 2010, p. 18).

According to some trainees, women are the ones who "choose" to stay off the labour market because they "want" to care for their children. They also argue that women are the ones who "choose" not to enter politics. The main reason these resisting trainees provide for the underrepresentation of women in political institutions is that political parties cannot find competent female candidates. A different example is that of trainees who believe that, as they already know everything about gender equality, they do not need to learn or do anything more. The trainer who reported the last example dubbed these resistant male trainees "cool men", who, when a trainer starts to talk about gender equality, frequently comment that they "already do the washing up" (Lombardo, 2009).

Another variation of the refusal to accept responsibility that then legit-imizes a denial of the need for change is the culturalization of the problem of gender inequality. Such resisting trainees believe, as one trainer put it, that "gender inequality only concerns other cultures, so gender inequality is alien to our domestic context/citizens". In this form of resistance, somebody else is blamed for the problem. Responsibility for the problem is shifted so that it is not "us" but "them" who have an inequality problem; it is "other" cultures, not "ours", that are at fault. This again serves to legitimize the claim that a change in gender norms is unnecessary.

These forms of resistances and the examples that substantiate them show different overlaps in the types of resistances that we have spelled out. Most of the encountered forms are individual, gender specific, and either explicitly or implicitly expressed, as shown in Table 2.1.

Table 2.1 Forms of resistance by trainees related to examples and types

Form of resistance	Example	Type of resistance
Denial of the need for gender change	Mirage of equality Disbelief about gender data (message) Refusal to learn from a feminist (agent) Challenging the trainer (agent) Defending traditional gender roles as natural (message)	Individual, explicit, gender specific
Trivializing gender equality and refusing to accept responsibility	There are more pressing priorities It is not relevant for our work It is not my problem Time will fix the problem The issue is too complex It is very difficult to apply this You convinced me, but I wouldn't know how to pass the message to my colleagues Gender equality is a problem concerning women, not men	Individual, explicit, gender specific
Trivializing gender equality	Laughter Deviating the discussion to simplistic debates Showing lack of interest (looking at phones and notebooks, not participating in discussion, free riders, etc.)	Implicit, individual, gender specific
Refusal to accept responsibility	Gender inequality only concerns other cultures, not us	Explicit, individual, gender specific

Resistances by commissioners

Many gender trainers consider support from the top levels in an organization as a condition for success in dealing with resistances when implementing gender mainstreaming and during gender training processes. The "support from higher levels gives legitimacy, as it establishes an obligation and shows commitment on the part of leaders that may help ease resistances" (Pauly et al., 2009, p. 24). Commissioners of training can be "allies in the master's house" – as one trainer put it – so that gender trainers can build networks and alliances to promote change processes within institutions (Ferguson and Forest, 2011; Lombardo, 2009). Yet it is important to be aware of the fact that the (direct) commissioners might also be caught between the different forces at play, notably when support from the highest hierarchical levels is lacking, or when "commitments" are rhetorical. It is, therefore, relevant to consider what room different actors at various hierarchical levels actually have to promote gender equality. The resistance that trainers perceive on the part of gender training commissioners might be due to these commissioners' struggle for the achievable, while the gender trainers who do not necessarily know all the institutional specifics might want to push for more.

Indeed, in working and negotiating with commissioners, trainers sometimes also experience resistance on the part of the actors commissioning gender training. As we have seen in the section on theory, implicit or explicit institutional resistance can and does occur. Institutional resistance can be expressed in several ways, ranging from dedicating insufficient funds, time, and personnel to gender mainstreaming and training, to the exclusion of non-hegemonic voices, or the refusal to make certain pieces of information public. These may pose different constraints for gender trainers, including when negotiating the training activities with commissioners, for example, when agreeing on modalities such as the length of the training.

When trainees are aware that support from top officers is merely rhetorical, and while there is no real political will behind it, they will not implement the gender initiative, or they will be more likely to resist the training (Pauly et al. 2009, p. 24). A trainer reporting on resistance on the part of commissioners gave the example of gender policy implementation being reduced to a single isolated training activity. This was done, in her view, so that "the institution can say they have done something on gender and that's it". In fact, this is only lip-service, as there is no continuity in gender training activities, and the training is not part of a broader gender mainstreaming strategy. Mergaert and Demuynck describe a similar situation that occurred when the European Commission shrunk its gender mainstreaming approach from quite a comprehensive one within the sixth RTD (Research and Technological Development) Framework Programme to a narrow approach with an isolated gender training initiative under Framework Programme 7 – a decision that was criticized by gender training participants (Mergaert and Demuynck, 2011). In the words of the aforementioned trainer:

> You can have a sense of that [merely rhetorical support by commissioners] from the beginning, because in that case it happens that any reference to transformation, processes, [and] future support that you as a trainer could offer to implement [gender equality] is considered as useless or not fitting to the needs of the organisation, or [is] simply overlooked.

While this is an example of implicit institutional resistance, we argue for the need to distinguish between institutional layers (high-, medium-, and lower-ranked personnel) and to be careful not to always uncritically blame the direct commissioners of training. The exploration of institutional resistance, however, deserves further empirical analysis of the specific institutional contexts where resistance to the implementation of mainstreaming manifests (Braithwaite, 2000; Lombardo and Mergaert, 2013; Mergaert and Lombardo, 2014; Stratigaki, 2005).

In this section, we have identified different forms of resistance that are expressed by trainees, as well as the commissioners of gender training. We argue that a careful analysis of such manifestations of resistance provides opportunities to deepen the understanding of what hinders the implementation of gender mainstreaming.

Assessing resistance to gender training

Gender training is a fruitful area to study resistances to gender mainstreaming, especially because gender trainers experience resistance daily. This daily experience has helped trainers and analysts like ourselves to detect specific types and forms of resistance. These findings allow us to distinguish between individual, explicit, implicit, and gender-specific types of resistance, meaning resistance manifested by individuals, expressed either explicitly or implicitly, and resistances that seem to be targeted at the goal of gender equality itself. The main forms of resistances encountered are the "denial of the need for gender change", "trivializing gender equality", and the "refusal to accept responsibility" for the problem of gender equality. All of these are a justification for not taking action to promote gender equality. Most of the forms of resistance that trainers encounter are strongly related with the definition of resistance spelled out above, which entails maintaining the status quo and opposing change. Given the resistance reported, any support from an institution's leaders appears crucial for trainers to legitimize the change in gender norms promoted in training practices.

Findings suggest that the analysis of resistance to gender training provides insights into what exactly it is that people and institutions are resisting, be it the message of changing gender norms, the agents of the change being promoted, gender equality as a goal, or the gender training course itself. It is important to ascertain this for diagnosing what factors are hindering the implementation of gender mainstreaming in a given context. Once the issue of resistance is located at the centre of analyses of the implementation of mainstreaming, empirical studies can explore the institutional context in which the training takes place. This can help to distinguish between individual and institutional resistance.

For example, an analysis of a specific institutional context can reveal that trainees' resistance during trainings is triggered by a feeling of incapacity, rather than by resistance to the very goal of gender equality. Such incapacity may be an indication of resistance on the part of the institution in which trainees work and a signal of insufficient resources and support for the implementation of gender mainstreaming. This distinction is helpful to identify those actors who are really resisting the principle of gender equality (often decision makers), rather than those who implement decisions in a situation of inadequate provision of skills, resources, and organizational support. It might be difficult for a trainer to empirically distinguish this kind of incapacity from "genuine" resistance to gender equality during a training session. Nonetheless, it is possible when considering the elements included at the planning stage of a specific gender mainstreaming initiative. If the resources (funding, personnel, time) or skills (training, expert consulting) needed to implement gender mainstreaming have not been foreseen in the planning of the action, actors are likely to feel ill equipped to fulfil their tasks, and thus are likely to prove resistant to gender change.

This chapter explores the issue of resistance in gender training and, by drawing mainly on the perspectives of trainers, aims to define resistance and identify the most prevalent types and forms of resistance in gender mainstreaming processes. As they do not address specific institutional contexts where gender trainings take place, our findings do not reveal the presence of the type of resistance known as "institutional", as discussed in the theory section. Future research will need to deepen the study of institutions as sites of resistance to gender mainstreaming, which is context specific (see Mergaert and Lombardo, 2014).

Our study addresses the first layer required to analyse resistance. Namely, pointing out the "problems" manifested during gender trainings that can be indicators of resistance. The second layer of analysis, going beyond the scope of this chapter, could more specifically identify what the gender training participants believe the problem is in each of the analysed training contexts. That is, whether it is the training itself that trainees oppose, for instance because of its format, or whether resistance is provoked by the gender mainstreaming strategy, or the principle of gender equality. Future empirical studies might develop more specific analyses of the different types of resistances manifested by civil servants and might differentiate between various reasons for resisting, depending on trainees' context and level in government.

Conclusions

In this chapter, we have studied resistances to gender training as part of gender mainstreaming processes of feminist knowledge transfer. We have argued that studying resistance is important for diagnosing problems in the implementation of gender mainstreaming, and for improving such implementation. By defining some of the causes, reasons, types, and actors of resistance, we have contributed to the further theorization of resistances in gender mainstreaming and training processes. We have also identified and discussed different forms of resistance to gender training. Two main conclusions can be drawn from our study. The first relates to how gender mainstreaming and training can promote feminist knowledge transfer. The second underlines the importance of taking into account the phenomenon of resistance in policy and research.

The first conclusion supports the practice of gender trainings in processes of gender mainstreaming. Gender mainstreaming is a difficult strategy to implement for different reasons. It aims to produce change within institutions, processes, and people's relationships. It questions existing gender norms, values, roles, and power hierarchies, and as a result, it challenges both personal and institutional spheres. It requires gender awareness and knowledge from civil servants who have often not been trained in these skills. Each of these elements per se is likely to raise resistance, and the combination of several individual resistances, in any case, can translate into institutional resistance. Furthermore, civil servants are likely to resist the implementation of gender mainstreaming initiatives because these challenge and upset the status quo. These combined resistances tend to result in the evaporation of gender mainstreaming objectives, as transformative change gets lost in the process. Gender training aimed at mainstreaming a gender perspective into policymaking processes is a way to work with such obstacles and resistances to change. This is because it addresses gender norms and the contestation around them and can therefore create opportunities for feminist knowledge transfer.

The second conclusion concerns the need for policymakers and researchers to pay attention to the phenomenon of resistance. The analysis conducted in this chapter proves the importance, for gender experts and policymakers, of establishing a link between the implementation of gender mainstreaming and resistance to gender training. When a problem is named, it is made visible, and this is a first step towards addressing it. There is, therefore, merit in paying more careful attention to the phenomenon of resistance. We argue that attention to the signals of resistance is needed throughout the gender mainstreaming process, from the design of gender mainstreaming strategies, to their implementation, monitoring, and evaluation.

Furthermore, analysing resistance can yield insights into how gender mainstreaming is implemented in particular contexts. For example, studying resistances in gender training can expose situations where such training is organized as a stand-alone policy instrument, rather than an indispensable element of a comprehensive and coherent gender mainstreaming strategy that requires a multiplicity of measures. Moreover, the analysis of resistance in training reveals that gender mainstreaming as a strategy tends to underestimate the internal dimension of changing institutional gender norms, focusing instead on external policy service delivery. When trainees realize rather belatedly and unexpectedly (that is, during a gender training session) that they are expected to introduce changes to gender norms within their own institution, this might cause extra resistance towards trainers. In this respect, the study of resistance provides feedback for improving the design and planning of gender mainstreaming implementation.

For researchers, this recognition implies the need to study the phenomenon of resistance or opposition to gender equality initiatives both theoretically and empirically. Theory on resistance can further conceptualize its types and forms in order to sharpen the analysis. Empirically, context- and institution-oriented studies can be developed much further than we were able to do in this chapter. We thus encourage researchers in gender and politics to conduct case studies on different resistant institutions, be they governments, academic institutions, companies, or international organizations. Such future studies could map the different types and forms of resistance in each specific context and draw a clearer picture of what hinders the effective implementation of gender mainstreaming.

Once individual and institutional resistances are documented in detail, through studies on resistances to gender training, the supposed gender neutrality of institutions is exposed, any appeal to such neutrality can easily be refuted, and evidence of policy evaporation be made more apparent. If gender mainstreaming processes are considered as opportunities for feminist knowledge transfer, resistance, despite its often unpleasant consequences for gender trainers and consultants, can be interpreted as part of the contestation that accompanies processes of transformation towards greater gender equality. Resistance is a learning opportunity for gender experts, policymakers, and scholars. If embraced with openness and preparation, it offers a chance to engage with entrenched patriarchal (and other) norms and to deal with the inevitable challenges that any process aimed at changing gender norms is bound to meet.

Notes

1. OPERA is the name of the research activity that addressed gender training issues within the European QUING project. In this project, the concept of "gender+" training was used to denote intersections with other inequalities. In this chapter, we refer to gender training rather than gender+ training because we cannot confirm that the trainings considered actually addressed intersectionality.
2. This chapter is based on research conducted within the framework of the QUING European research project (www.quing.eu) and the TARGET EU-US research project (http://www.ssc.wisc.edu/TARGET/aboutus2.htm), whose team members and the European Commission funder we wish to thank. We also thank all the gender trainers who have participated in the expert meetings and online forums, sharing their time, expertise, and experiences with us. An earlier version of this chapter was published in the *Nordic Journal of Feminist and Gender Research* (NORA).
3. For more information on the trainings, expert meetings, conferences, and online forums on gender training, developed as part of the QUING and TARGET projects, please see http://www.ssc.wisc.edu/TARGET/aboutus2.htm.

References

Agócs, Carol (1997) "Institutionalized Resistance to Organizational Change: Denial, Inaction and Repression", *Journal of Business Ethics*, 16, 917–931.

Benschop, Yvonne and Mieke Verloo (2006) "Sisyphus' Sisters: Can Gender Mainstreaming Escape the Genderedness of Organizations?"', *Journal of Gender Studies*, 15, 19–33.

Braithwaite, Mary (2000) "Mainstreaming Gender in the European Structural Funds". Paper presented at the *Mainstreaming Gender in European Public Policy Workshop*, October, University of Wisconsin, Madison. http://eucenter.wisc.edu/Conferences/Gender/braith.htm (accessed 8 May 2015).

Brehm, Sharon S. and Jack Williams Brehm (1981) *Psychological Reactance: A Theory of Freedom and Control*. New York: Academic Press.

Cavaghan, Rosalind (forthcoming) "Bridging Rhetoric and Practice: New Perspectives on Barriers to Gendered Change", *Journal of Women Politics and Policy*.

Charlesworth, Hilary (2005) "Not Waving but Drowning: Gender Mainstreaming and Human Rights in the United Nations", *Harvard Human Rights Journal*, 18, 1–18.

Council of Europe (1998) *Gender Mainstreaming: Conceptual Framework, Methodology and Presentation of Good Practices. Final Report of Activities of the Group of Specialists on Mainstreaming*. Strasbourg: Council of Europe.

Daly, Mary (2005) "Gender Mainstreaming in Theory and Practice", *Social Politics*, 12(3), 433–450.

Derbyshire, Helen (2002) *Gender Manual: A Practical Guide for Development Policy Makers and Practitioners*. London/Glasgow: DFID. http://www.dfid.gov.uk/Documents/publications/gendermanual.pdf (accessed 8 May 2015).

Díaz González, Olga Sofía (2001) *Gender and Change in the Organisational Culture. Tools to Construct a Gender-sensitive Organisation*. Eschborn: Deutsche Gesellschaft für Technische Zusammenarbeit (DTZ).

Ferguson, Lucy and Maxime Forest (eds.) (2011) *OPERA Final Report: Advancing Gender+ Training in Theory and Practice*. Vienna: Institute for Human Sciences (IWM). http://www.quing.eu/files/results/final_opera_report.pdf (accessed 13 May 2015).

Ferree, Myra Marx (2006) "Introduction", in Myra Marx Ferree and Aili Mari Tripp (eds.) *Globalization and Feminism: Opportunities and Obstacles for Activism in the Global Arena*. New York: New York University Press, pp. 3–23.

Hafner-Burton, Emile M., and Mark A. Pollack (2009) "Mainstreaming Gender in the European Union: Getting the Incentives Right", *Comparative European Politics*, 7(1), 114–138.

Jahan, Rounaq (1995) *The Elusive Agenda: Mainstreaming Women in Development*. London: Zed Books.

Lombardo, Emanuela (ed.) (2009) *Final TARGET Report for a Policy Oriented Atlantis Project*. Brussels: EACEA.

Lombardo, Emanuela and Lut Mergaert (2013) "Gender Mainstreaming and Resistance to Gender Training: A Framework for Studying Implementation", *NORA – Nordic Journal of Feminist and Gender Research*, 21(4), 296–311.

Longwe, Sara Hlupekile (1995) "The Evaporation of Policies for Women's Advancement", in Noeleen Heyzer, Sushma Kapoor, and Joanne Sandler (eds.) *A Commitment to the World's Women: Perspectives on Development for Beijing and Beyond*. New York: UNIFEM.

—— (1997) "The Evaporation of Gender Policies in the Patriarchal Cooking Pot", *Development in Practice*, 7, 148–156.

Lovenduski, Joni (ed.) (2005) *State Feminism and Political Representation*. Cambridge: Cambridge University Press.

Lukes, Steven (2005) *Power. A Radical View*. 2nd edition. London: Palgrave Macmillan.

Mazey, Sonia (2000) "Introduction: Integrating Gender – Intellectual and 'Real World' Mainstreaming", *Journal of European Public Policy*, 7(3), 333–345.

McGauran, Anne-Marie (2009) "Gender Mainstreaming and the Public Policy Implementation Process: Round Pegs in Square Holes?", *Policy and Politics*, 37, 215–233.

Mergaert, Lut (2010) *Gender in Research – Toolkit and Training Activities, Final Report for the European Commission, DG Research*. Yellow Window Management Consultants. Antwerp.

—— (2012) *The Reality of Gender Mainstreaming Implementation. The Case of the EU Research Policy*. Doctoral dissertation, Radboud Universiteit Nijmegen.

Mergaert, Lut and Katlijn Demuynck (2011) *The Ups and Downs of Gender Mainstreaming in the EU Research Policy – The Gender Toolkit and Training Activities in FP7*. Antwerp, Belgium: Policy Research Centre on Equal Opportunities.

Mergaert, Lut and Emanuela Lombardo (2014) "Resistance to Implementing Gender Mainstreaming in EU Research Policy", in Elaine Weiner and Heather MacRae (eds.) *The Persistent Invisibility of Gender in EU Policy (Special Issue 1)*. European Integration online Papers (EIoP), pp. 1–21.

Mukhopadhyay, Maitrayee and Franz Wong (eds.) (2007) *Revisiting Studies and Training in Gender and Development – The Making and Re-making of Gender Knowledge. A Global Sourcebook*. Amsterdam and Oxford: KIT Netherlands and Oxfam.

Newman, Meredith Ann (1995) "The Gendered Nature of Lowi's Typology: Or Who Would Guess You Could Find Gender Here?", in Georgia Duerst-Lahti and Rita Mae Kelly (eds.) *Gender, Power, Leadership, and Governance*. Ann Arbor: University of Michigan Press, pp. 141–164.

Pauly, Florence, Lut Mergaert, Susanne Baer, Lucy Nowottnick, María Bustelo, Emanuela Lombardo, and Mieke Verloo (2009) *QUING Deliverable No. 65: Guidelines for Curricula Standards for Gender+ Training*. Vienna: IWM.

Rao, Aruna and David Kelleher (2005) "Is There Life after Gender Mainstreaming?", *Gender and Development*, 13(2), 57–69.

Rees, Teresa (1998*) Mainstreaming Equality in the European Union*. London: Routledge.

Roggeband, Conny and Mieke Verloo (2006) "Evaluating Gender Impact Assessment in the Netherlands (1994–2004): A Political Process Approach", *Policy and Politics*, 34(4), 615–632.

Savage, Michael and Anne Witz (1992) *Gender and Bureaucracy*. Oxford: Blackwell.

Squires, Judith (2005) "Is Mainstreaming Transformative? Theorizing Mainstreaming in the Context of Diversity and Deliberation", *Social Politics*, 12(3), 366–388.

Stratigaki, Maria (2005) "Gender Mainstreaming vs Positive Action: An Ongoing Conflict in EU Gender Equality Policy", *European Journal of Women's Studies*, 12(2), 165–186.

United Nations (1997) *Report on the Economic and Social Council for 1997*. A/52/3.

van Eerdewijk, Anouka (2009) "Energies and (Dis)connections: The Practice of Gender Mainstreaming in Dutch Development Cooperation." Paper presented at the *Expert Meeting On Track with Gender*, May, The Hague, Netherlands.

Verloo, Mieke (2001) *Another Velvet Revolution? Gender Mainstreaming and the Politics of Implementation*. *IWM Working Paper No.5/2001*. IWM: Vienna.

—— (2005) "Displacement and Empowerment: Reflections on the Concept and Practice of the Council of Europe Approach to Gender Mainstreaming and Gender Equality", *Social Politics*, 12(3), 344–365.

—— (2006) "Multiple Inequalities, Intersectionality and the European Union", *European Journal of Women's studies*, 13(3), 211–228.

Walby, Sylvia (2005) "Gender Mainstreaming: Productive Tensions in Theory and Practice", *Social Politics*, 12(3), 321–343.

3
Gender Expertise and the Private Sector
Navigating the Privatization of Gender Equality Funding

Lucy Ferguson and Daniela Moreno Alarcón

Introduction

Private sector funding for gender equality initiatives is a growing phenomenon worldwide. To date, however, this issue has received relatively little attention in feminist literature. Our aim here is to map the contours of such funding and draw out the implications thereof for discussions of feminist knowledge transfer. While existing literature on the subject, as outlined below, offers a feminist critique of private sector involvement in gender equality, we suggest that our approach is original as it engages explicitly from the perspectives of those conducting feminist knowledge transfer. Drawing on the experiences of the authors and accounts from interviews, we set out the opportunities and challenges created by the increasing privatization of gender equality funding. By the "private sector", we mean medium to large enterprises operating at national and multinational levels.

The chapter engages with a number of the substantive themes of this book. In analytical terms, it explores the tensions between feminist and gender theories; resistances to gender equality; and the increased risk of co-optation when working with the private sector. Empirically, it adds to the wider contribution of the book by presenting original research on the nature and implications of the changing political economy of feminist knowledge transfer. In keeping with the terminology established in the Introduction to this book, we present engagement with the private sector as a channel for feminist knowledge transfer and explore how such a channel differs from more traditional areas, such as funding from development donor agencies and the EU. The primary instruments discussed here are gender training and gender expertise, alongside a discussion of how tools and methods can be adapted to the context of working with the private sector.

We begin by presenting a literature review of current research on the involvement of the private sector in gender equality initiatives, identifying a gap in knowledge in terms of the implications for feminist knowledge transfer. We attempt to map changes at the global level by highlighting key examples of such funding in four main areas. Namely, funding for international organizations dedicated to gender equality and women's empowerment; participation in gender equality programmes in partnership with international institutions; the development of stand-alone initiatives outside the realm of public institutions; and the integration of gender into corporate social responsibility (CSR) strategies. In the second section of the chapter, we combine interviews with gender experts and trainers with our own experiences in this field. We consider ourselves to be positioned as both insiders and outsiders in this study. By critically reflecting on our practice in feminist knowledge transfer with various private sector organizations, we aim to give a flavour of the kinds of issues and peculiarities that such a context can generate. These short case studies contribute to the body of knowledge on feminist knowledge transfer in the emerging context of private sector engagement. Next, the chapter provides a reflection on the implications of the private sector's increasing role for those working as gender experts and gender trainers. More broadly, it questions the possibilities of such engagement for leading to transformative outcomes in gendered power relations. In the concluding section, we set out how the findings fit into this volume's overall themes and suggest avenues for future research and action.

Literature review and mapping

The new "transnational business feminism" (Roberts, 2012) involves a range of actors including "feminist organizations, capitalist states, regional and international funding institutions, non-governmental organizations and transnational corporations" (Prügl and True, 2014, p. 6). These new alliances for gender equality reflect broader changes in global political economy, in which private actors are increasingly adopting concerns and practices that were previously limited to states (Prügl and True, 2014). This has been accompanied by a change in development funding, from a discourse of "aid" to one of "investment" (AWID, 2014, p. 8). This means that "the funding policies and priorities of many of these long-term allies are also shifting, and their resource base is relatively static compared to the huge funds being mobilized and deployed by the newer actors" (AWID, 2014, p. 12). These substantive changes in the political economy of gender equality funding are also accompanied by other phenomena, such as crowd funding, "impact investment", the influence of wealthy women, and the rise in celebrity involvement in gender issues (AWID, 2014, pp. 10–11).

In conceptual terms, this change needs to be contextualized within the now almost ubiquitous "business case" approach to gender equality. While some organizations, such as Catalyst, were already making the business case for "gender diversity" in the 1990s, arguably the most prominent example of this paradigm is the World Bank's focus on gender equality as "smart economics" (World Bank, 2007). This approach has been subjected to extensive critique by feminists for its tendency to present gender equality in an instrumental manner, rather than as a goal in its own right (see, e.g., Keating, Rasmussen, and Rishi, 2010, for an overview). The influence of the World Bank's smart economics approach should not be underestimated, and it has been adopted by many development organizations, such as CARE, the Norwegian Agency for Development Cooperation (NORAD), UNICEF, and the Nike Foundation (Chant, 2012). In the private sector, initiatives guided by this approach include the World Bank's Private Sector Leaders Forum and the Coalition for Adolescent Girls, as discussed below (Bexell, 2012).

The World Bank's recent *World Development Report on Gender Equality* (2012) continues to reinforce the link between gender equality and business, as exemplified by this quotation:

> Gender equality per se has grown to be a desirable trait that customers and investors look for. Corporate social responsibility is an avenue for firms to enhance competitiveness through product differentiation and capture the loyalty of women's growing market power.
>
> (World Bank, 2012, p. 36)

As Roberts and Soederberg (2012) argue, the World Development Report offers a dual approach to gender equality – as something both intrinsically valuable and also as an important component of CSR that can help to enhance a company's image, boost a firm's reputation, and garner customer loyalty (2012, p. 960).

As well as the World Bank's influential smart economics discourse, the emerging partnerships between UN agencies and the private sector should be highlighted here. The origins thereof can be traced to initiatives such as UNIFEM's cooperative scheme with Avon Products in 2008 to combat violence against women, and UNDP's 2010 partnership with Nestlé Pakistan to train female livestock workers in the country (Bexell, 2012, p. 392). However, the most high-profile example of such collaboration is the UN Global Compact/UN Women "Women's Empowerment Principles" (WEPs). Subtitled "equality means business", the WEPs are a series of principles to which private sector organizations are invited to subscribe. These portray a predominantly instrumental approach to gender equality, as set out above. The business case for gender equality is quite clearly constructed here: "Current research demonstrating that gender diversity helps business perform better signals that *self interest and common interest can come together* [emphasis added]". In former UN Women Director Michelle Bachelet's opening comments on the brochure, we are told that "empowering women is a strategy for a healthier bottom line" (UN Women/UN Global Compact, 2011). In addition, UN Women's engagement with the private sector is embedded in broader funding issues for the institution, in which external funding partnerships have become necessary for long-term financial feasibility (Interview with Expert 3, July 2014). A recently published report by the Association for Women's Rights in Development (AWID) (2014) offers the most extensive mapping to date of private sector involvement in gender equality funding. The study surveyed 170 initiatives, adding up to a total of USD 14.6 billion between 2005 and 2020. It shows that the highest prevalence of such initiatives is in Sub-Saharan Africa (50%), followed by South Asia (25%), and Latin America (20%). Twenty-five per cent of these initiatives are global in reach. The average size of these 170 initiatives is USD123 million (AWID, 2014, pp. 15–16). As Figure 3.1 shows, the vast majority focus on women's economic empowerment and entrepreneurship, followed by women's leadership and empowerment.

In addition to this overview, a handful of recent studies have explored specific examples of private sector involvement in gender equality. Elias (2013, p. 163), for example, sets out how gender equality has become a key component of many of the World Economic Forum's activities – firmly embedded within a framing of women and girls as an "investment". The Women Leaders and Gender Parity Program has three main roles – to increase the participation of women in the Forum; to produce the annual Global Gender Gap and Corporate Gender Gap reports; and to convene multi-stakeholder meetings on issues of gender equity (Prügl and True, 2014). Bexell's (2012)

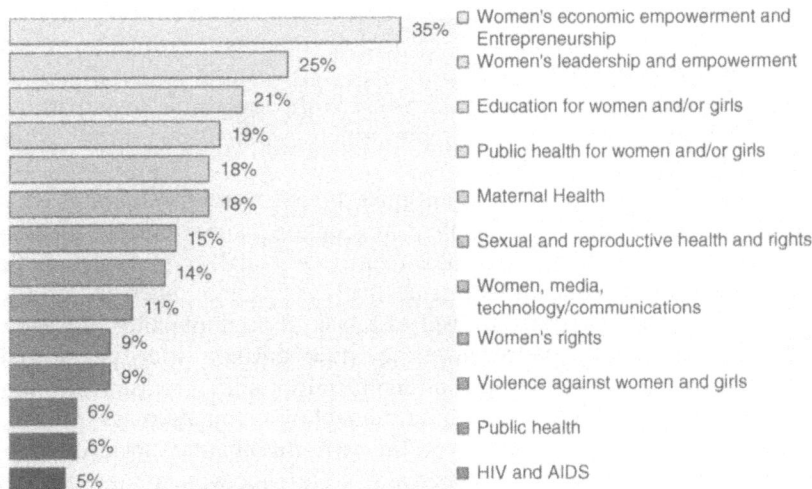

Figure 3.1 Thematic focus of private sector initiatives on gender equality

research focuses on two examples, one of which is the World Bank's Private Sector Leaders Forum, an umbrella partnership within which participating companies undertake ongoing projects to reach the overarching aims of the Gender Action Plan. The second is the Coalition for Adolescent Girls, encompassing a range of public and private actors, including the Nike Foundation, with the purpose of "unleash[ing] the untapped potential of the developing world's 600 million adolescent girls by raising awareness and driving action" (2012, p. 394). A further high-profile initiative is Goldman Sachs' 10,000 Women programme, as analysed by Prügl and True (2014). This offers training, funding, and support to women entrepreneurs worldwide. Other examples include Chime for Change, the Grassroots Girls Initiative, and the Levi Strauss Foundation (AWID, 2014, pp. 35–39).

To date, the feminist assessment of private sector involvement in gender equality has been resoundingly critical. For instance, as Roberts and Soederberg (2012) argue, this has taken place in a time of global financial crisis in which the world's most vulnerable populations – predominantly women and girls – are disproportionally affected. At the same time as companies such as Goldman Sachs are being celebrated by the World Bank and others for initiatives aimed at helping poor women, their actions are deepening inequality in many countries worldwide, all under "a veneer of corporate philanthropy" (2012, p. 965). Elias' critique of gender activities at the World Economic Forum centres around the "ahistorical and decontextualized understanding of gender equality and women's empowerment", which fails to understand the role of capitalism, and the importance of intersectionality. Moreover, it involves an "apolitical appropriation of gender issues that is distinctly postfeminist in its rejection of the language of feminism and its failure to recognize women's collective political struggles" (Elias, 2013, p. 165). Further concerns include the ways in which asymmetrical power relations are obscured in such partnerships. As Bexell argues, "friction and inequality are absent", while at the same time these partnerships "lock out certain visions of empowerment, women and gender", while favouring others (2012, p. 403).

In spite of the richness of these critiques, there is very little literature that focuses on private sector involvement in gender equality from the perspective of practice. Prügl and True (2014) provide a slightly more pragmatic critique, expressing concern with issues such as a lack of reflexivity on the part of private sector actors, as well as a lack of accountability. However, rather than dismiss the partnerships they study outright, they suggest that these "bring together the legacies of neoliberalism and feminism, with different results in different contexts, and enabling co-optations as much as new openings" (2014, p. 23). More in line with this chapter's focus on practice is the AWID report (2014), which aims to provide women's movements with guidelines and suggestions for how to engage with the private sector. Their critique expresses a number of challenges for women's movements, such as a focus on the individual; a narrow issue-focus; and the lack women's rights organizations' presence in these partnerships (2014, pp. 42–46). However, our concern in this chapter is explicitly to explore these ideas from the perspective of those working as gender experts and gender trainers in the private sector. We now go on to develop such concerns more substantively by reflecting on our own experiences in this role.

Reflections on practice

Having established a broad critique of private sector involvement in gender equality, we now set out some examples of practice. The following four short case studies illustrate examples of the authors' engagement with the private sector as gender experts or trainers. The aim here is to offer some examples of specific exchanges that such a practice can produce, in order to better understand the potential of such engagements for social transformation. The case studies highlight the difficulties involved in communicating gender issues and strategies to private sector actors and the high level of misunderstandings and miscommunications involved in such an endeavour. In each short case study, we set out the key lessons learned from the perspective of feminist knowledge transfer. The first three case studies involve predominantly negative experiences, while the final one offers a potential "good practice" that warrants further consideration.

Case study 1: Large hotel operator (name changed)

This private sector actor is one of the world's largest hotel operators and a market leader in Europe. The chain operates in 92 countries with more than 3,600 hotels, 470,000 rooms, and over 160,000 employees. We contacted this hotel group's Head of CSR and Communications in Madrid in 2013. Our motivations were many, as this hotel group had led the 2011 CSR rankings in Spain and, above all, because their CSR webpage extensively espoused the company's commitment to gender equality. Its strategy for achieving the latter entails investing in its own network of women in five continents to "reach 50% women hotel general managers with an intermediary target of 35% by 2015".

Having secured a meeting with the CSR chief, one week prior to our appointment, we researched networks (even consulting an expert to this end) and delved into the history of this hotel's CSR. At our meeting, we outlined potential areas based on gender training programmes for the tourism private sector for further work. One such area was the sexual exploitation of children in tourism. We were immediately informed, however, that this problem does not exist in its hotels in Spain, and that, as such, the hotel had signed no commitments related to this issue. A strange case of affairs, especially when Spain has the third highest rate of trafficking in women and children for sexual purposes in Europe and is a favourite destination for sex tourism (Moreno, 2014).

At several points we became aware, on the one hand, of the enterprise's interest in knowing more (they inquired about references to literature and notable projects). On the other, we observed a distinct lack of interest in certain topics. For example, when we began to expand upon a possible work plan, the head of CSR repeatedly requested that we dwell on "more practical matters", "more general" ones which would serve the entire workforce, and not just focus on gender issues. The most shocking moment of the encounter was when we were given an example of a planned activity within the network: a course to help improve the personal appearance of personnel. We attempted to redirect this line of thought, proposing courses related to emotional intelligence, or even courses from a social entrepreneurship perspective designed to improve assertiveness. The response to this last proposal was a disinclination for their staff to become entrepreneurs; "whatever for?", "so that they leave the hotel?"

Two days later, we sent the enterprise a formal proposal (which included specific gender issues). This was duly declined. The Madrid CSR Chief's last reply to us specified that he wanted "practical" and "useful" workshops not necessarily focused on gender as we had again proposed. Upon inquiring as to the possibility of meeting the Head of the Women's Network in France at the hotel's headquarters, so as to explain our work proposal and many other work possibilities in person, our request was similarly not granted.

Lessons learned:

- Private sector actors are exceptionally good at using communications to publicize their activities and enhance their corporate image. What they may state on paper in a very positive and persuasive manner is often the opposite of what is really happening, for instance in terms of CSR activities related to gender. In this case, the person in charge of CSR was also the Head of the company's Communications department, as well as one of the board members of its Women's Network.
- Substantive challenges persist in incorporating a gender perspective into CSR activities. For example, a fundamental challenge is posed by misunderstandings about what gender equality is, and why it is important to work towards it. Frequently, gender equality is claimed to be "covered" under diversity issues. The latter is exceptionally dangerous because, increasingly, diversity is being conflated with gender equality in private sector discourses (for detailed analysis, see Bear, Rahman and Post, 2010; Grosser and Moon, 2005, 2008; Fernández, Romero and Ruiz, 2012; Murphy and Schlegelmilch, 2013; Rekker, Benson, and Faff, 2014).
- Merely having a women's network does not in itself entail fulfilling gender objectives. This requires a great deal of work, alongside a clear

process, methodology, and an implicit change in a company's business management paradigm, as well as in the attitudes of the people in charge.

Case study 2: Talent and coaching agency, validated by the Ministry of Employment and Social Security of the Government of Spain (the company's sector is mentioned)

This actor is the global market leader in Talent Mobility and is represented by more than 300 offices in 65 countries worldwide. One of its values is stated as follows: "Our integrity leads to better work, better life – and to a sustainable future. We are honest and fair partners to our stakeholders at all times. Promoting fairness, diversity and equality is our corporate legacy." We were engaged by the company to teach a potential project related to CSR, which included coaching a highly esteemed and globally successful professional. We contacted one of the managers of the company in Spain, highly respected for her lectures about personal motivation and talent management for high-level professionals. She also works in depth on social innovation and entrepreneurship. She proved extremely taken with the graphics we presented to her, giving us advice about positioning, and even facilitating potentially useful contacts. Nevertheless, upon reaching the section on gender equality (an aspect vital to the project), she suggested that "we should skip this part because it's out of fashion". We were completely baffled by her comment, never having imagined that someone of such standing could make such a remark.

Lessons learned:
- The acquisition of gender awareness does not come naturally to those currently working in coaching, talent development, and innovation. Even when working on social matters, many have prejudices about gender issues and experts.
- Coaching and talent training is becoming very appealing in the corporate world, with funding coming from Education or Human Resources departments, often linked to CSR activities. Those coaching on talent, emotions, and ideas are becoming the face of innovation for companies in terms of human resources and management, mainly because such an approach improves leadership skills and teaches employees "how to be an empowered person". Such endeavours, however, only take into account business trends and the work status of the person to be coached, thereby leaving out the broader socioeconomic context in which such relations are embedded.
- This rise of coaching or talent training is potentially damaging for the profession of gender expertise, as it would be hoped that gender experts would be in charge of the Equality Business Plans in Spain. As such,

we ask whether it is necessary to "rethink gender leadership in CSR and sustainability?" (Marshall, 2007, 2011).

Case study 3: Bancobien (name changed)

This case concerns the charitable foundation of a Spanish bank which developed a programme to offer funding to women entrepreneurs in tourism across several African and Latin American countries. The programme itself was born of the first meeting of "Spanish and African Women for a Better World", held in Maputo, Mozambique, in 2006. The non-profit organization involved was dedicated to promoting employment through entrepreneurship, innovation, and the adoption of new technologies by small and medium enterprises. Due to its financing capacity, the foundation's initiative aimed to promote tourism as a tool for poverty reduction, focusing predominantly on women from developing countries. Given the merger of its parent bank with another, larger bank in 2013, however, both the foundation and the specific programme disappeared. This leaves open a number of questions concerning the fate of those women entrepreneurs who had been receiving funding.

Throughout its promotional material, the Bancobien foundation referred to the terms "gender and development" and "women's empowerment". Our engagement with the foundation commenced when we secured a meeting with its project director to discuss the programme's gender component. We were assured of their interest in a gender equality analysis of their project and their desire to ensure that appropriate criteria were included in the selection and evaluation of the initiatives to be funded. In spite of it being widely rumoured that they had "loads of money", we were never contacted to discuss this work further.

Several months later, we won a contract to work as gender experts with a large EU-funded project, of which this foundation was a leading partner. During the course of our involvement in this project, we were able to work closely with Bancobien to identify to what extent gender equality featured in their operations. It soon became clear that rather than being a fundamental concern and operational goal, gender was something of an "embarrassing" issue with which Bancobien did not want to engage. For example, while they suggested that supporting women entrepreneurs was key to their funding criteria, this did not feature at any point in their process for selecting candidates for funding. Moreover, the interviews to select initiatives for funding were conducted by Bancobien staff who had elected to volunteer with the programme during their free time.

Throughout our relationship with Bancobien, we challenged their lack of serious concern for gender equality on many occasions. These conversations were highly frustrating as we were unable to convince the project director of the need for gender expertise and training in order to arrive at gender equality outcomes or – at the very least – better outcomes for women entrepreneurs. Our concerns were echoed at public events held to promote the Bancobien project. The foundation was accused by other participants at these gatherings of not being transparent and of falsely claiming to promote gender equality and women's empowerment.

Lessons learned:

- Private sector organizations are able to claim to promote gender equality while actively resisting any calls to actually do so. This is due to the lack of public accountability for how they spend their money (see the critique by Prügl and True, 2014 as outlined above), and it demonstrates the importance of transparency and evaluation in gender equality funding.
- Claiming to promote "gender equality" and "women's empowerment" meant that Bancobien achieved high status and exposure. The project director was invited to speak as an expert at many events on gender and tourism worldwide.
- By presenting a weak, unthreatening version of gender and tourism, Bancobien was able to capitalize on their funding and promote their own initiative at the expense of other more feminist projects in this area.

Case study 4: Kuoni Travel (name used with permission)

We were invited by Kuoni Travel to offer support on integrating gender into their Human Rights Impact Assessment process. Kuoni is one of the world's largest tour operators, with destinations in nine different geographical regions. In 2013, the company was named the "World's Leading Luxury Tour Operator". Moreover, they have taken the lead in the global tourism sector by attempting to map the human rights implications of their operations. Having conducted a pilot study in Kenya and received feedback from stakeholders, they became concerned that gender issues had not been sufficiently integrated into the assessment process. As such, we were commissioned to produce and deliver a one-day training course for the CSR Manager.

In order to prepare for this, we analysed Kuoni's current Impact Assessment process and identified where gender could be incorporated. We then designed appropriate training exercises for integrating gender at each stage of the process. During the training, the manager was open, responsive, and thoughtful. We worked together to discuss which aspects were realistic/relevant, and which were not. We were able to discuss feminist research methodologies and to identify which tools and methods could be useful to the enterprise's overall Impact Assessment process.

Following this training, we remained in contact with the manager, who sent us the draft report of work conducted in India using the tools and methods discussed during the training. Rather than sideline the gender issues, the report explicitly engaged with many of the concerns we had discussed. Questions on gender equality and discrimination had been added to many sections of the assessment process, and particular care had been taken to ensure a gender balance in the interviewees and participants. We were then offered a further meeting to discuss the findings, during which we had a frank and open conversation about further improvements that could be made to the Impact Assessment process from a gender perspective. However, since the initial training – which took place some 18 months prior the time of writing – there have been no further requests from Kuoni, and it is clear that, to date, the integration of gender in the Impact Assessment process has not been accompanied by broader changes in other aspects of its work or operational practices.

Lessons learned:

- If gender expertise is actively sought out by a private sector company, far more opportunities for trainers to exert influence arise.
- Providing training on a very specific process or procedure within a company's operations offers an opportunity to integrate gender concerns, without the need to challenge the broader working practices of the company.
- Working with informed and engaged staff endowed with a clear commitment to gender issues means that the possibilities for effective and meaningful knowledge transfer are more likely.
- Working on gender equality with isolated departments, such as CSR, does not necessarily mean that changes to policy and operations will be made in other areas of a company.

Taken together, these case studies illustrate a range of our experiences of practice. In order to reflect more broadly on these issues, we now go on to further engage with the perspectives of our research participants.

Implications for feminist knowledge transfer

This final section of this chapter is based on the perspectives of three Spanish gender experts who work both in Spain and internationally. These in-depth semi-structured interviews were conducted in Madrid in July 2014 and have been translated from Spanish. While we are not suggesting that such interviews are representative of all gender experts working in diverse contexts, we believe they give a flavour of different experiences of working with the private sector. In order to preserve anonymity, we have not named the experts, but rather give an outline of each one's profile. "Expert 1" has not worked directly with the private sector, but has a profound understanding of the private sector's involvement in gender and development issues. She has worked as a lawyer in the Inter American Court of Human Rights; as programme director for Gender and Development Cooperation in Peru, Costa Rica, and Spain; and is a member of the Spanish Gender Group. "Expert 2" is currently working as a gender expert in her own consultancy and collaborates extensively with the private sector, as well as with other organizations. She is one of the most recognized gender consultants in Spain, with over 15 years' experience in the field, both nationally and internationally. During this time, she has worked with a number of organizations, including as the Director of an international programme run by the Spanish Development Agency and UN Women. She is also a member of the Spanish Gender Group. Finally, "Expert 3" worked extensively with the private sector in her capacity as Director of the UN Women Spain office, formerly UNIFEM Spain. She held this role from 2007, until the office was closed in December 2012. During her time with UNIFEM and UN Women, she was involved directly in ongoing engagements with the private sector to seek opportunities for collaboration and funding.

The findings of the interviews can be grouped broadly into challenges and opportunities for feminist knowledge transfer. In terms of challenges, we highlight the importance of language and image; the role of feminism; and the limited scope of private sector intervention. We then set out some potential opportunities or strategies for working on feminist knowledge transfer with the private sector, touching on the following points: the importance of context; potential criteria for engagement; and next steps.

Challenges

The first issue to explore is the misunderstandings and miscommunications that regularly occur between gender experts and the private sector. This is embedded in a more problematic clash of cultures and discourses – those of the gender experts, on the one hand, and, on the other, those of the private sector working on CSR within a paradigm of modern management techniques and approaches. This mismatch has been apparent in a number of instances in the experiences of the experts interviewed. It should also be noted that gender experts are not necessarily well informed or trained on the goals and values of the private sector organizations with which they engage. This can generate a further set of issues, as discussed in more detail below. For example, when UN Women staff began holding meetings with representatives from the Spanish private sector, they found that many individuals did not understand what UN Women is and what it represents. Moreover, in the words of one expert:

[...] many simply were not familiar with the UN, including multinationals based in different countries around the world who should have known a great deal about international law. It was quite an obstacle to have to inform them about the United Nations as it meant nothing to them.

As such, even basic assumptions we may hold as gender experts about the private sector's knowledge on gender need to be questioned. Throughout the course of these meetings, the UN Women representatives experienced a range of responses – "absurd dialogue, candidness, shocking language", and so on. Some private sector representatives claimed that gender was not important and that "society does not demand a focus on such matters". Several times – even when data on gender inequality was provided – they claimed that these statistics did not reflect their business or sector (Interview with Expert 3, July 2014).

This raises some clear challenges for gender experts about how we are perceived by the private sector. Due to the lack of knowledge on gender issues, gender expertise is not perceived as a *profession*. Consequently, the claims of gender experts can be easily dismissed and ignored, even when made by representatives of a UN organization. It is worth reflecting on whether such blatant disregard would be shown for other international institutions, such as the International Monetary Fund, for example. Related to this, the experts reflected on the way the language used in their encounters with the private sector has changed. As Expert 1 notes, "language is power" and it explicitly affects "how we position ourselves". However, according to Expert 2, the traditional language of feminism and gender expertise "does not connect with the reality of life for the private sector". This raises some methodological challenges for feminist knowledge transfer, such as "how does one connect a gender perspective to the reality of a company director who lives in a system of privilege?" (Interview with Expert 2, July 2014).

Tying in with the broad themes of this book, a second set of challenges concerned the fact that "when we discussed equality, this was understood to be synonymous with diversity" (Interview with Expert 3, July 2014). In Expert 2's experience, the equality plans of corporations are no longer primarily about gender, but instead tend to focus on disability. As a consequence, "enterprises are not inclined to hire gender experts". As Expert 3 argues, this is a direct consequence of the hasty and superficial ways in which gender has been incorporated into private sector operations. While they may adhere to a discourse about gender equality, in general, they have "not yet incorporated it throughout their structures and policies or worked to overcome obstacles". Where a gender approach has been addressed, this has largely been in terms of corporate image. This is of concern for an analysis of feminist knowledge transfer as many enterprises "believe they exist in a post-gender equality discourse" (Interview with Expert 3, July 2014).

To engage with the book's focus on tensions between gender and feminism, it should be noted that when working with the private sector, "sometimes one even has to defend the gender perspective itself, it is now no longer about defending feminism" (Interview with Expert 2, July 2014). As such, gender experts need to consider these issues carefully when working with the private sector. Other pertinent reflections on this theme include

Expert 2's observation that she has had more success with the private sector since setting up her own company as a gender expert, as compared with working as a freelancer. However, this comes with its own challenges, as feminist organizations are now less inclined to work with her, perceiving her as "a businesswoman who wants to take away their money". These kinds of tensions between gender experts who engage with the private sector and feminist organizations are extremely interesting and merit further research and attention in the future.

Finally, there are substantive challenges related to the limited scope of private sector interventions in, and understandings of, gender inequality. As shown in Figure 3.1, drawn from AWID's research, the private sector is primarily concerned with a narrow range of issues based around economic empowerment and leadership. Moreover, these are tackled "in a feminized context intended to enable women to have some degree of power" (Interview with Expert 1, July 2014). This is a problem, however, for gender experts concerned with key matters such as reproductive and sexual rights. As Expert 1 described it, this leads to "having to camouflage these themes as maternal and child health, child mortality, and similar issues". This demonstrates a lack of coherence within the private sector when working on gender equality, and a disregard therein for feminist analysis and feminist approaches. More broadly, this raises concerns about agenda-setting and the definition of priorities for gender equality funding. If the private sector is free to determine the content and focus of gender equality initiatives, what are the implications for transformation through feminist knowledge transfer? We now turn to some more practical reflections on how to tackle these issues.

Opportunities and strategies

Undoubtedly there are some clear challenges for working with the private sector on gender equality. However, in order to assess the possibilities for engagement, it is first necessary to understand the context in which different companies operate. As Expert 2 pointed out, "I would not discriminate against companies just for being companies. Everything depends on the type of business they conduct and the criteria they strive to meet." This echoes our own positive experiences with Kuoni Travel outlined above. As such, how might we develop feminist criteria for working with the private sector? Expert 2 set out some possible conditions to be met by a private sector entity, such as: promoting gender equality and providing a thorough explanation thereof; engaging in ethical debate about the sources of funding; understanding to what extent a company can undo its good work in other areas; and determining the level of consistency between the intentions and operations. In addition, a general assessment can be undertaken as to whether a company is politically conservative in nature, as this is likely to affect its potential for engaging in feminist knowledge transfer.

The issue of the different discourses and language of gender experts, on the one hand, and the private sector, on the other, requires reflexivity and strategizing. Cultural differences encompass how meetings are conducted, how priorities are set, and how the understanding is constructed of what is "worth doing", "efficient", and "practical to do". Moreover, there are substantive gaps between knowledge and perceptions of gender equality, feminism, and gender expertise. This involves gender experts having to adopt a "business case" approach which highlights "the key factors that will prompt enterprises to understand the benefits gender equality and equity hold for them" (Interview with Expert 2, July 2014). As Ferguson (2014) reflects, often in our work as gender experts, we are required to present our arguments using a "business case" approach, whether or not that chimes with our political convictions and understanding of feminist transformation. However, as Expert 2 advises, "viewing private enterprises as enemies is a waste of energy that might otherwise be used to study businesses and better understand them".

In terms of practical steps, we as a collective of actors working on feminist knowledge transfer need to regroup and reflect substantively. Expert 3 suggests that more attention needs to be paid to "formulating and deconstructing the gender perspective". Other priorities to be addressed collectively include: how to secure meetings with the private sector; how to approach such meetings; how to plan what to say; and how to define the most effective tools and methods for gender training with the private sector. We now turn to an analysis of the overarching conclusions of the chapter.

Conclusions

In this chapter, we have explored the implications of increasing private sector involvement in gender equality initiatives and funding. We are concerned explicitly with what this means for gender experts and gender trainers, as well as for feminist knowledge transfer more broadly. After setting out current feminist critiques of private sector funding, we highlighted the gap in such literature as regards reflections on practice by gender experts and gender trainers. We follow the concerns of such critiques and the implications that engagement with such initiatives is merely helping to foster "rational economic woman" (Rankin, 2002). Nevertheless, we posit that by refusing to engage with private actors working on gender equality, we are restricted to what Bergeron and Healy refer to as "the perspective of the critic who can only voice their ethical concerns in relation to a lamentable inevitability" (2013, p. 7). In contrast, we follow AWID's more practical concern of "whether to engage, how to engage, who to engage with, and where not to step in" (2014, p. 12). Neatly summed up by Expert 2, if we were to succeed in instilling a gender approach within the private sector it would be "wonderful". While caution is necessary, we call for the collective presently working on feminist knowledge transfer to find ways to make the private sector "allies and actors who work towards equality" (Interview with Expert 2, July 2014).

In order to unpack these questions more substantively, we propose that Prügl and True's criteria (2014, pp. 7–8) for working with private sector could be of use to gender experts. These offer a framework of four criteria for assessing private sector initiatives. First, "inclusiveness and mechanisms to deal with exclusions or biases in the programs enabled by the partnerships". Second, the "degree of public transparency and accountability of the partnerships, especially to those groups who are intentionally and unintentionally affected by their programs". Third is a concern with reflexivity, "of being attentive to the way in which a program exercises power including gendered power, affecting subject-participants sometimes in unintended, negative ways". Fourth, they suggest that partnerships should be evaluated for their "operational effectiveness". These criteria might serve as a valuable basis for questioning the value of engagement with the private sector, and, moreover, the potential for feminist knowledge transfer in terms of any given initiative.

In addition to these criteria, in this chapter, we have suggested a number of strategies for gender experts and trainers to adopt when working with the private sector. We argue that it is necessary to reframe our thinking, and adapt our methods and tools, if we are to meet the challenge of changes in gender equality financing, while finding a way to retain a feminist approach. To quote Lydia Alpizar, "we have to learn to talk to the other side and develop allies, while respecting our authenticity [and] values" (AWID, 2014, p. 41). This involves taking the time and space to "learn each other's language (and the intention behind it)" in order to forge meaningful and effective partnerships (2014, p. 47).

In order for this to be successful, gender experts need to acknowledge more explicitly the discursive disjunctures involved in working with the private sector on gender equality and develop strategies for addressing this. This will require engaging with contemporary management practices as well as dedicating more time and resources to researching the values and cultural practices of different private sector institutions. Moreover, it is useful to recognize public–private sector partnerships for gender equality as part of a "neoliberalization of feminism with open outcomes" (Prügl and True, 2014, p. 7). More work needs to be done to understand what this might mean more concretely in terms of feminist knowledge transfer. We hope that in this chapter, we have contributed to these debates by sketching an outline of some of the key issues to consider and envisioning what a future research agenda in this area might entail.

References

AWID (2014) *New Actors, New Money, New Conversations: A Mapping of Recent Initiatives for Women and Girls.* Toronto: Association for Women's Rights in Development (AWID). http://www.awid.org/sites/default/files/atoms/files/New%20Actors %20FInal%20Designed.pdf (accessed 8 May 2015).

Bear, Stephen, Noushi Rahman, and Corinne Post (2010) "The Impact of Board Diversity and Gender Composition on Corporate Social Responsibility and Firm Reputation", *Journal of Business Ethics*, 97(2), 207–221.

Bergeron, Suzanne and Stephen Healy (2013) "Beyond the 'Business Case': A Community Economies Approach to Gender, Development and Social Economy". Paper presented at the *United Nations Research Institute for Social Development (UNRISD) Conference on Potential and Limits of Social and Solidarity Economy*, May, Geneva. Cited with permission.

Bexell, Magdalena (2012) "Global Governance, Gains and Gender: UN–Business Partnerships for Women's Empowerment", *International Feminist Journal of Politics*, 14(3), 389–407.

Chant, Sylvia (2012) "The Disappearing of 'smart economics'? The *World Development Report 2012* on Gender Equality: Some Concerns about the Preparatory Process and the Prospects for Paradigm Change", *Global Social Policy*, 12(2), 198–218.

Elias, J. (2013) "Davos Woman to the Rescue of Global Capitalism: Postfeminist Politics and Competitiveness Promotion at the World Economic Forum", *International Political Sociology*, 7(2), 152–169.

Ferguson, Lucy (2014) "'This Is Our Gender Person': The Messy Business of Being a Gender Expert in International Development", *International Feminist Journal of Politics*, DOI 10.1080/14616742.2014.918787 (accessed 8 May 2015).

Fernández-Feijoo, Belen, Silvia Romero, and Silvia Ruiz (2012) "Does Board Gender Composition Affect Corporate Social Responsibility Reporting?", *International Journal of Business and Social Science*, 3(1), 31–38.

Grosser, Kate and Jeremy Moon (2005) "Gender Mainstreaming and Corporate Social Responsibility: Reporting Workplace Issues", *Journal of Business Ethics*, 62(4), 327–340.

——— (2008) "Developments in Company Reporting on Workplace Gender Equality? A Corporate Social Responsibility Perspective", *Accounting Forum*, 32(3), 179–198.

Keating, Christine, Claire Rasmussen, and Pooja Rishi (2010) "The Rationality of Empowerment: Microcredit, Accumulation by Dispossession, and the Gendered Economy", *Signs*, 36(1), 153–176.

Marshall, Judi (2007) "The Gendering of Leadership in Corporate Social Responsibility", *Journal of Organizational Change Management*, 20(2), 165–181.

——— (2011) "En-gendering Notions of Leadership for Sustainability", *Gender, Work & Organization*, 18(3), 263–281.

Moreno Alarcón, Daniela (2014) "El camino hacia la igualdad: el caso de Cartagena de Indias, Colombia', *Memorias*.

Murphy, Patrick E. and Bodo B. Schlegelmilch (2013) "Corporate Social Responsibility and Corporate Social Irresponsibility: Introduction to a Special Topic Section", *Journal of Business Research*, 66(10), 1807–1813.

Prügl, Elisabeth and Jacqui True (2014) "Equality Means Business? Governing Gender through Transnational Public-private Partnerships", *Review of International Political Economy*, 21(6), 1137–1169.

Rankin, Katherine N. (2002) "Social Capital, Microfinance, and the Politics of Development", *Feminist Economics*, 8(1), 1–24.

Rekker, Saphira A. C., Karen L. Benson, and Robert W. Faff (2014) "Corporate Social Responsibility and CEO Compensation Revisited: Do Disaggregation, Market Stress, Gender Matter?", *Journal of Economics and Business*, 72, 84–103.

Roberts, Adrienne (2012) "Financial Crisis, Financial Firms ... and Financial Feminism? The Rise of Transnational Business Feminism and the Necessity of Marxist-Feminist IPE", *Socialist Studies/Études socialistes*, 8(2), 85–108.

Roberts, Adrienne and Susanne Soederberg (2012) "Gender Equality as 'Smart Economics'?: A Critique of the World Bank's 2012 World Development Report", *Third World Quarterly*, 33(5), 949–968.

UN Women/UN Global Compact (2011) *Women's Empowerment Principles: Equality Means Business*. 2nd edition. New York: UN Women/UN Global Compact Office. http://www.unglobalcompact.org/docs/issues_doc/human_rights/Resources/WEP_EMB_Booklet.pdf (accessed 8 July 2014).

World Bank (2007) *Gender Action Plan: Gender Equality as Smart Economics*. Washington, DC: World Bank. http://go.worldbank.org/FSV68RJ1F0 (accessed 8 July 2014).

World Bank (2012) *World Development Report 2012: Gender Equality and Development*. Washington, DC: World Bank.

4
The Smothering of Feminist Knowledge: Gender Mainstreaming Articulated through Neoliberal Governmentalities

Tine Davids and Anouka van Eerdewijk

Introduction

In this chapter, we reflect on feminist expertise and knowledge in relation to feminist engagement with the broad field of international development and development institutions, in particular. Gender mainstreaming is one prominent practice of such feminist engagement, and we look at it as a primary vehicle for feminist knowledge transfer. Whereas gender mainstreaming envisioned policy transformations and, in addition, societal transformation, there has been widespread disappointment about actual practice not living up to this transformative promise (Eerdewijk and Davids, 2014; Lombardo et al., 2010; True and Parisi, 2013; see also Cornwall et al., 2004; 2007; Sweetman and Porter, 2005; Sweetman, 2012). This chapter reflects on how gender and change are conceptualized, framed, and transferred in both the process of gender mainstreaming and in feminist critiques of it. In line with the Introduction to this book, we conceptualize this knowledge transfer as an inherently political and contested process. Its political character becomes apparent in processes of meaning giving that are not neutral, but loaded with power. We conceptualize these power dimensions with the Foucauldian concept of "governmentalities", in order to capture how they seek to govern conduct, and how this is informed by knowledge, rationalities, and belief systems. We draw attention to how gender and change are not pre-given and stable terms in this process, but are the very site of the political and power struggle over meaning giving.

In our exploration of the challenges, dangers, and opportunities of governmentalities in feminist knowledge transfer, we point to three different but interrelated sides of this feminist engagement. In this chapter, we are interested in identifying and unpacking which techniques of governance are deployed. As such, we approach gender mainstreaming as a governmentality that intersects with other (neoliberal) governmentalities. Our first observation is that in this intersection, two related techniques of governance appear: individualization and externalization. We argue that gender mainstreaming became a constitutive component of the international neoliberal context in which a process of individualization manifests itself in a narrow understanding of change agents, be it women or policy actors, as free agents. Gender mainstreaming techniques make the integration of gender an individual, rather than an institutional, affair. Furthermore, the neoliberal framing of development as manageable and measurable directs change outside development agencies, while leaving the gendered nature of organizations and institutions themselves out of sight.

Second, in these techniques of individualization and externalization, gender expertise and training, rather than voice and social movement, have gained a prominent place. Third, in these intersections, specific meanings and understanding of gender and change are being produced; the hegemonic gender narratives on smart economics, smart politics, and smart justice celebrate women as change agents. These narratives inscribe a disruption between feminist knowledge and gender. Our central argument in this chapter is that, in the interlocking articulation of feminist knowledge and neoliberal mentalities, the feminist understanding of gender difference as unequal and structural is being "smothered". We therefore call for reconsideration of how change itself is understood.

The chapter starts by explaining what we understand by governmentality perspective and its intersection with other governmentalities. Next, we illustrate that the articulation of gender mainstreaming governmentalities with neoliberal governmentalities has resulted in techniques of individualization and externalization. That brings us to considering the central role of training and expertise in the context of these techniques and to our observations on the smothering of feminist knowledge on gender. In the final section, we reflect on the problematic dimensions of this smothered gender knowledge and suggest how to recast change and agency.

Our analysis is based on the findings of the *On Track with Gender* initiative, in which various organizations engaged in a process to reflect on the policy, practice, and theory of gender mainstreaming in order to take it to the next level. These were the Centre for International Development Issues Nijmegen (CIDIN), the Netherlands' Ministry of Foreign Affairs, Hivos International, Oxfam Novib, ICCO, Cordaid, and the Royal Tropical Institute (KIT). The five papers written in the "Taking Stock" phase, the accompanying Expert Meeting, and the special issue "Rethinking Gender Mainstreaming", published in the *International Journal of Development Studies* in 2014, form the basis for this chapter, together with additional literature.

Applying a governmentalities perspective to gender mainstreaming

Gender mainstreaming strategies opt for sensitizing policies and policymaking for their consequences on gender inequality (Squires, 2005; Verloo, 2005). With its early roots in the 1980s, and full emergence in the first half of the 1990s, gender mainstreaming gained prominence as a concept and strategy that addresses and challenges the inherently gendered character of policymaking in its many manifestations (Goetz (2006 [1995], 1998). Because the gender bias and exclusionary character of policy processes has material consequences for women and men in many parts of the world, gender mainstreaming identifies the level of structures and systems, of which policymaking is a core dimension, as its object of change (Beveridge and Nott, 2002). Mainstreaming strategies for gender equality by definition imply the purposeful integration of gender equality concerns and objectives into a particular and contextual policy practice, which is not neutral (Benschop and Verloo, 2006; Ely and Meyerson, 2000). Not neutral indicates that these contextual practices of policymaking impose their own mechanisms and technologies on these strategies for gender equality.

In these discursive practices, feminist knowledges and ideals transform into something else. Once feminist goals and strategies are deployed in different policies, organizations, and institutes, they become part of those practices that seek to govern, and as such, part of governmentalities. This governing is directed at regulating the conduct of those involved or targeted within the development field, whether it concerns the members of an organization, institute, partner organizations in development, or the general public. Gender mainstreaming processes are hence both technologies of governance and become embedded in the apparatus of gender policies and practices. As Caglar, Prügl, and Zwingel note:

> Thus in becoming part of international institutions, feminist strategizing develops its own rationality: to govern through subtle and indirect means. In this context feminist strategizing is turned from a mode of resistance into an instrument of power.
>
> (2013, pp. 5–6)

This is in particular the case since development institutions and organizations pretend to contribute to development and, in that sense, aim at instigating change. In function thereof they adopt, produce, and frame narratives that "speak about the world in ways that lend political convictions the sense of direction that is needed to inspire action" (Cornwall et al., 2007, p. 5). Every organization tries to impose, in its own small, local, particular, or large-scale and international way, policies, goals, projects, and world views, which it envisions to be true and in the best interest of its partners and clients.

This is the way in which feminist knowledge, goals, and ideals have become part of institutional power. Power here is conceptualized in a Foucauldian way as disciplining power, seeking to control and manage the conduct of people, not so much as a direct and repressive governing from above, but in the way people govern themselves into being moral agents and law-abiding citizens. This disciplining of people into moral agents happens with the guidance of mentalities that, in turn, are informed by knowledge and belief systems. These mentalities direct agents to act according to what is considered righteous and normal within specific contexts. Knowledge thus is paramount to the workings of power; knowledge informs worldviews and political convictions that are needed to inspire change and action. It is also knowledge that defines and informs what is desirable and normal in a particular context. When applied to the practice of gender mainstreaming, this means that gender experts

> [...] produce policy relevant knowledge, which – in Foucault's words – "induces effects of power". In other words, knowledge makes things governable and regulates the conduct of others by constantly drawing the boundaries of acceptable behaviour in a specific policy field.
>
> (Caglar et al., 2013, p. 5)

Feminist knowledges thus transform and are transformed into becoming a governmentality itself. But this is also brought about through the articulation with other mentalities at stake in particular policies, organizations, and contexts, as we illustrate below. As a consequence, governmentalities that seek to govern gender relations are not only informed by feminist knowledges. In a neoliberal context, gender mainstreaming, and with it gender knowledge, intersects and articulates with neoliberal governmentalities and knowledge.

In this sense, we consider gender mainstreaming to be deeply intersectional. Not only intersectional in the sense that the concept of gender can be conceptualized as intersecting with other differences, such as those of class and ethnicity, but intersectional in the sense that gender mainstreaming as a governmentality intersects with other governmentalities. In understanding this intersecting, we draw upon the way La Clau and Mouffe (1985 [2001]) define articulation between discourses. That is, as a particular practice of meaning giving in which different (competing) discourses meet in a battle over the meaning of different words, concepts, metaphors, or signs. The outcome of this encounter is the (temporary and partial) fixation of a specific meaning (or web of meanings) and is determined by the character of the encounter itself. Thus,

[...] any practice establishing a relation among *elements* such that their identity is modified as a result of the articulatory practice, while a discourse is the structured totality resulting from this articulatory practice.

(La Clau and Mouffe (1985 [2001]), p. 105)

An *element* is a sign within a discourse on which meaning has not yet been fixed. It is through the practice of articulation that a temporary fixation or closure is established, since "the transition from the 'elements' to the 'moments' is never entirely fulfilled" (Laclau and Mouffe, 1985, p. 110). Articulation, thus, is about a struggle for meaning; it is the ongoing struggle between different discourses to fix the meaning of signs. Elements, which are particularly open to different ascriptions of meaning, are labelled as "floating signifiers" (LaClau and Mouffe (1985) [2001], p. 113). When we translate this to intersecting governmentalities within gender mainstreaming, we could say that gender is one such element (a floating signifier), which through the intersection with different governmentalities (as the "structured totalities resulting from this articulatory practice") acquires a certain and different meaning. What meaning this might be is determined by the struggle itself.

Scrutinizing gender and feminist knowledge transfer as part of power instruments consequently entails scrutinizing the meaning of gender as an outcome of the struggle over meaning between different gendered governmentalities. As Repo puts it:

Rendering gender an object of analysis by theorising it in this manner does not entail making assumptions of what it "is", but rather involves examining the rationalities of power through which it emerges in the first place as a discourse amenable for deployment in governmental processes to govern the life and labour of human populations.

(Repo, 2014)

However, gender is not the only "floating signifier" here. Since both feminist ideals of transforming society and the development practice itself are change driven, the correlated struggle over the meaning ascribed to the notion of change is also at stake. Such rationalities of change are at stake in the strategic deployment of gender mainstreaming as a governmentality and in the way it intersects with other governmentalities.

Gender mainstreaming's transformative potential "lost in translation"

In the second half of the 1990s, gender mainstreaming was readily adopted in the arena of international development by multilateral organizations, such as the World Bank and UN organizations; donor governments in the

"Global North"; international organizations such as the European Union; national governments in the "Global South"; and non-governmental (development) organizations in different parts of the world. It did not take that long before the disappointment with how gender mainstreaming was being implemented became apparent. In the Introduction to a special issue of the *Journal of International Development*, in which we revisit the disappointment and critique surrounding gender mainstreaming, we observe how the practice of gender mainstreaming is based on, and (re)produces, a problematic notion of agency. Therein, change agents are cast as free individuals. This can be observed in relation to hegemonic ideas of gender, empowerment, and women's role in realizing gender equality in society as well as in relation to policy actors who are assumed to be able to transform policymaking and institutions. In both cases, the emphasis is on the individual as a free agent, making choices, and changing practice. In both cases, structures and gender relations are under-conceptualized and left out of sight (van Eerdewijk and Davids, 2014). This means that feminist understandings of gender, that lie at the foundation of gender mainstreaming as a governmentality, have evaporated in its practice. This happens through mechanisms and practices at many levels and locations, through a "dispersed set of techniques" (Prügl, 2011, p. 76). We will illustrate this individualization by highlighting two examples, drawing on our earlier work on gender mainstreaming in Dutch and international development cooperation.

A first observation is that the change that gender mainstreaming is aiming for has been located outside the donor organizations in international development. Both development NGOs and the Dutch Ministry of Foreign Affairs maintain relations with so-called counterparts in the Global South. These are presented as being on equal footing, despite the fact that funding is a key characteristic of these relationships. Partner organizations engage in dialogue with their donor organizations to discuss their financial and administrative matters, but this dialogue does not extend to debating donor's policymaking and priorities themselves. The necessary change is hence located at the receiving end, in this case the partner organizations; the institutional biases of the donor organization itself are left out of sight (Roggeband, 2014; *cf.* Ferguson, 2014). This one-sided dialogue and focus on accountability of the partner organization to the donor occurs in a time increasingly characterized by managing large grants and pressure from funding agencies on NGOs to focus more on realizable goals and less on grassroots activism (Mitra, 2011 in Roggeband, 2014; see also Kamstra, forthcoming). The Paris Declaration and subsequent aid reforms are a case in point here, with their rationale of harmonization, alignment, efficiency, results management, ownership, and accountability; management *for* results has turned into management *by* results (Holvoet and Inberg, 2014, p. 324).

Secondly, gender mainstreaming has come to rely on specific instruments to achieve its goals; these technocratic and de-politicized tools carry specific effects with them. In Dutch development NGOs, gender targets and gender assessments have been key instruments in implementation. Both instruments are expected to contribute to the integration of gender in partners' portfolios, projects, and programmes. Whereas in their design, gender assessments and, to a lesser extent, gender targets embody a profound understanding of gender inequality and women's empowerment, this potential evaporates in actual practice. A close inspection of the micro-politics of evaporation reveals that these gender mainstreaming instruments bypass the gendered nature of the development agencies themselves, because the mainstreaming of gender has to take place against already set priorities that continue to go unquestioned. In addition, their implementation relies on the conceptual and strategic judgements of individual staff members. "Such tools tend to individualize the responsibility for transformation and mainstreaming, while leaving the priority setting as well as the organizational values untouched" (van Eerdewijk, 2015). Gender mainstreaming becomes an individual rather than an institutional affair and overestimates the agency of staff members in organizations (van Eerdewijk, 2014).

Gender mainstreaming strategies in international development indeed embody a "focus on personal change of individuals", rather than "deeper structures of gendered oppression" (Parpart, 2014, p. 391). Although gender mainstreaming policies and strategies have taken different shapes in different institutes and locations, gender mainstreaming policies (and evaluations) have tended to look for solutions in all the same places, that is, "within established institutional structures and practices" (2014, p. 386). Namely, more resources, improved accountability, better coordination, more regulation from the top, and above all, gender focal points, and more gender training for senior as well as other staff in organizations. These solutions carry an optimistic undertone on policymakers' agency, "a policy-oriented, can-do language" (2014, p. 384). Whereas gender mainstreaming is based on a diagnosis of a structural problem, the solutions tend to be defined in terms of free agency. In this diagnosis/prognosis paradox, the possibilities of individuals to transform deep and unequal social relations and institutions are overemphasized (Roggeband and Verloo, 2006; see also Ferguson, 2014). Individuals come to be constituted as the key agents of change, while at the same time institutional prioritization and biases of policymaking and the institutions itself are pushed out of sight.

Training and the demand for expertise

In this setting, a profound trend in gender mainstreaming strategies in diverse organizations has been the reliance on trainings, manuals, checklists, and tools (Kothari, 2005; Mukhopadhyay, 2014; Parpart, 2014; Roggeband,

2014). Knowledge and knowledge transfer to individual staff have become key mechanisms in transformation for gender equality. In international institutional contexts, gender training has been employed to produce the right inclination among bureaucrats towards the governance of gender, by seeking to increase the technical and administrative skills of professionals so that they become better programme administrators (Prügl, 2011, p. 83).

Expertise refers to a complex mix of professionals, truth claims, and technical procedures that makes it possible for authorities (governments, multilateral institutions, donor bodies, and international NGOs) to make their version of gender reality operable (Mukhopadhyay, 2014). Gender training has become a disciplining mechanism, building new selves that have internalized these mentalities of difference to such an extent that external controls, oversights, and incentives are no longer necessary. Gender training has tended to take a specific form in this context, one that aims at transmitting a set of skills that asks participants to focus on checklists and frameworks. "The most common standardized form of training [...] is a short, event-oriented and workshop bounded form presenting 'gender' as a set of skills, which can be straightforwardly delivered and reproduced" (Mukhopadhyay, 2014, p. 362). These formats are to rely on frameworks and checklists that can be easily applied, and they push for the condensation of complex theories and context-specific analysis into easy and digestible terms (*cf.* Ferguson, 2014, pp. 5–9). The design of gender training has been heavily influenced by demand from the development sector, requesting short-term, condensed formats that focus on the "what", rather than the "knowing how". Gender training has become a normalizing technology that has installed itself as a rapidly growing profession.

Interestingly, the demand for gender expertise has been accompanied by the decay of gender infrastructure. This has manifested itself in an almost contradictory dynamic in which gender mainstreaming has gotten caught. On the one hand, there is an increasing reliance on expertise and experts, at the expense of social movement voices and activists – in that sense, gender professionalized (see also Kothari, 2005; Alvarez, 2009). Simultaneously, an undermining of internal gender infrastructures has taken place. Whereas gender mainstreaming encompassed both a mainstreaming and a stand-alone track, the adoption of gender mainstreaming was often at the expense of the latter. Gender units were dissolved or weakened, gender focal points were under resourced or absent, and the number of gender specialists went down (Roggeband, 2014, p. 340; see also van Eerdewijk and Dubel, 2012). There was both an assumption and a need for everyone to do gender; and that is also where gender training comes in, with the assumption that this set of technical skills of gender analysis, planning, and programming can be transferred to "everyone".

This contradictory dynamic entails a "yes, but" mechanism that both asserts and denies feminist knowledge and actors (do Mar Pereira, 2012;

see also van Eerdewijk, 2015). The "yes" captures the ready adoption and seeming openness to feminist knowledge and a gender equality agenda. The "but" points to "a dismissive recognition [...] through which feminist work is simultaneously replenished and contained" (do Mar Pereira, 2012, p. 296). Gender is accepted and taken in as relevant and important, but "can be better done with non-feminist theories" (2012, p. 292) and with non-feminist actors. As a consequence of this dismissive recognition, "gender has been institutionalized in development organizations, although not in the way that gender and development theorists and practitioners would have liked" (Mukhopadhyay, 2014, p. 357). In the next section, we turn to what kind of gender knowledge and narratives have been produced.

Articulation and smothering

The adoption of gender mainstreaming has been accompanied by specific understandings of gender, more specifically by a range of hegemonic, win-win narratives. The instrumentalist frames of gender as smart economics, smart justice, and smart politics have been subject to feminist critiques (see, e.g., Batliwala, 2007; Caglar et al., 2013; Chant, 2012; Parpart, 2014; Roggeband, 2014). One example is the recent World Bank discourse on gender (World Bank, 2012), that according to Chant and Sweetman (2012, p. 512) seeks to use women and girls to fix the world, without acknowledging that such a win-win scenario in which poverty is alleviated, economic growth is assured, and gender equality attained, is very far from the truth that women in poor households and communities experience. Such gender narratives have been questioned widely, amongst others for the uncritical belief in globalization, accompanied by a neglect of the effects of the global crisis on gender relations, and, for instance, unpaid care work (Parpart, 2014).

In terms of gender knowledge, the emphasis on practical, reachable, and unthreatening measures and goals, striving to integrate women in different kind of forums and arenas, does define women's positions in terms of disadvantages, but without problematizing them. At the same time, this reproduces positions held by men as the norm (Benschop and Verloo, 2006, p. 21; Parpart, 2014). Gender myths have become problematic barriers in policymaking and implementation, such as the idea that the access of poor women to economic resources "leads to their overall empowerment" (Batliwala and Dhanraj, 2004, p. 11). Thus, as Batliwala and Dhanraj argue:

> The myth of women as the best anti-poverty agents and investments, and the mass-scale creation of women's self-help groups [in India], seems to be nurturing a form of depoliticised collective action that is completely non-threatening to the power structure and political order.
>
> (2004, p. 17)

Ironically, these win-win and efficiency gender narratives have opened up space for a celebration of women as change agents, either as gender experts in bureaucracies, NGOs, or grassroots organizations or as girls and women in their own families and communities. It is assumed that the disempowered will empower themselves, and meanwhile the power holders in the status quo are left off the hook (see, for instance, Jakimow and Kilby, 2008, pp. 390–396). And not only that, these power relations are obscured:

> [...] this impressive global process [of winning support for gender main-streaming] was paralleled by a shift from state-oriented towards market-driven development policies that had a negative impact on the living situations of the poor, and of poor women in particular. Thus, the irony was that during a phase of high level sensitization regarding gender hierarchies worldwide, the living conditions of many women deteriorated.
>
> (Caglar et al., 2013, p. 9)

Batliwala and Dhanraj argue that "religious fundamentalism and neo-liberal economic reforms are converting grassroots women in India into both agents and instruments in a process of their own disempowerment" (2004, p. 11). As a result of how gender mainstreaming ties into broader technologies and mechanisms of neoliberal signature, the burden to change unequal gender relations is placed on women. Simultaneously, however, they are detached from the power relations in which they are and become subjects.

This representation of gender as something other than structural inequality has had consequences for how development programmes address inequality. Poor women and women at the grassroots level are targeted, and in this way, standardized and categorized into subjects in need of training and "whose needs and rights are expertly understood" (Mukhopadhyay, 2014, p. 358; see also Mohanty, 1991). This has made policy blind to real life women and to the actual social relations and norms in which they live and give meaning to their lives and aspirations:

> [...] knowing about gender is about skills and performance, and gender inequality is dissociated from structural inequalities. Because this reality is created by powerful institutions that govern development, its normativity obstructs activist efforts to bring about structural change. The use of language in government [...] not only shapes the domain to be governed, but also operates as intellectual technology to construct action. And so the normalised versions of the gender reality give rise to programmes targeting symptoms rather than the malady of gender inequality.
>
> (Mukhopadhyay, 2014, p. 361)

By narrowing down the conceptualization of gender to women, and to women as change agents, the feminist knowledges that lie at the foundation of gender mainstreaming are watered down.

This has not only come with a price, it has been rather ineffective in promoting gender awareness and sensitiveness among staff and beneficiaries. It also serves another purpose than the challenging of gender inequalities: "to reconstitute the mainstream mandate of the organization, which is the technical mandate" (Mukhopadhyay, 2014, p. 362). The process of institutionalization of gender mainstreaming has been marked by governmentalities through which gender knowledge is inscribed in a way that interrupts the relationship between feminism and gender:

> [...] the dissociation in the language of gender from structural inequalities that generate it, has also made it more acceptable to institutions since "doing gender" does not entail addressing structures producing inequalities in general, not only gender inequalities.
>
> (Mukhopadhyay, 2014, p. 360)

The interruption of the relationship between feminism and gender occurs at certain points, places, and phases of the organization. Instead of a mentality of gender difference as unequal power relations and institutional bias, as gender mainstreaming governmentalities set out for (see also Prügl, 2011), an unproblematic version of gender difference is installed. That mentality contributes to reproducing rather than challenging gender inequalities.

Gender mainstreaming was launched at a moment in time in which neoliberal economy and ideology were gaining ground (Harcourt, 2006; Sen, 2005). Technocratization, standardization, instrumentalization, as well as the result-based management, upward accountability, and professionalization are manifestations of neoliberal management techniques through which gender mainstreaming has been articulated. Over the past 20 years, the feminist informed governmentalities of gender mainstreaming intersected and were articulated with, and through, other neoliberal (and other)[1] governmentalities that it did not necessarily set out for. Consequently, the eventual shape of gender mainstreaming and the conditions of power (and in the end, of options for change) it produces are more varied and cannot be reduced to one particular gender mainstreaming governmentality. We use the notions of intersection and articulation to underline the nature of embeddedness and the interlocking processes in the dynamic interface between feminist politics and mainstream institutions. That articulation with and through allows for understandings of the politics of feminist engagement with institutions and policymaking at another level.

The effect of the interlocking articulation of feminist knowledge and neoliberal mentalities is that the feminist understanding of gender difference as unequal and structural is smothered. We purposively use the term "smothering" here, which means to die or kill by lack of air, to cover (too) thickly, to suffocate. It carries a connotation of being overwhelmed and can also be understood in terms of preventing a fire from burning by covering it thickly. Interestingly, it is also used in expressions such as "smothering with kisses" or love. This smothering of those gender mainstreaming governmentalities that call attention to the negative consequences of unequal gender relations contributes to the reproduction and the masking, whether unwillingly or indirectly, of masculinist cultures and governmentalities of politics and policymaking. In the process of intersecting governmentalities, feminist knowledge gets individualized, and the problematic and restricting structural aspects of gender power relations remain under-conceptualized. In the final section of this chapter, we argue that this not only entails transfers of feminist knowledge on gender as a category of analysis into the rationality of, and belief in, women as change agents. It also entails a correlated transfer of the beliefs, rationalities, and knowledge on change.

By way of conclusion: Recasting change

What we have tried to make intelligible so far is how feminist knowledges, in the very process of mainstreaming itself, have been articulated in different techniques of governance. We have illustrated how gender training and gender expertise became key in the context of two related techniques: externalization and individualization. The overemphasis on gender training and gender expertise resulted in the constitution of individual staff and policymakers as change agents, in an institutional context of externally directed policies that push the genderedness of development agencies themselves out of sight.

The interlocking articulation of feminist knowledge and the neoliberal mentalities of individualization and externalization results in, as explained above, the smothering of feminist understandings of gender difference as unequal and structural, and thus political. The emphasis on gender equality, as a neoliberal value or something that can be "fixed" by a change agent, projects gender as an easy changeable category. It is this rationality of change, this belief in change agents, and in effective and individual agency, that gained a comfortable place within policy circles (Zalewski, 2010, p. 12). In the final section of this chapter, we want to draw attention to how these mentalities account for the construction of subjects as moral agents. In so doing, they obscure the normalizing and disciplining side of gender, and thereby the view of how deeply rooted gender is in all layers of society, including within ourselves. In other words, these governmentalities obscure and smother an understanding of gender as embodied, structural, and tenacious, and therefore not that easily changeable.

The result of the intersecting governmentalities of gender mainstreaming and neoliberalism – as the "structured totality resulting from this articulatory practice" (Laclau and Mouffe, 1985, p. 105) – is a normalization based on an understanding of gender as cultural and social and, thus, changeable. Gender as the "floating signifier" (1985, p. 113) in this struggle over meaning is separated rather radically from sex, fixing the latter as natural and biological. As such, sex is not considered a construction but (almost) an absolute reality, that is not (that easily) changeable and, consequently, not the object of change (see also Davids et al., 2014). Put differently, the underlying meaning of neoliberal individualization in constructing change agents as the way to reach gender equity is an understanding of individuals as having a particular sex that has no connection to gender. This would imply that people are not gendered, so to speak, or at least that their sex has no bearing on their capacity to make choices (Repo, 2014, p. 13). While gender is projected as a set of contextual and cultural factors that can hamper or facilitate people's choices (which needs to be fixed), it is projected outside the individual itself.

The political character of feminist knowledges (see also the Introduction to this book) is then smothered twice, not only in externalizing the gendered character of institutions but also in externalizing the gendered character of individuals. Sex is not only framed as separate from gender, but also as a neutral biological given that has no connection to gender, or bearing or influence on gender (see also Repo, 2014). This understanding of gender in a binary opposition to sex is rather problematic (Delphy, 1993; Jauhola, 2010; Zalewski, 2010) because the detachment of gender from sex makes it possible to position gender outside the subject (Baden and Goetz, 1998). This then makes it possible to consider women as the best change agents to fight gender inequality. It results in making women appear as if they are not gendered themselves and active agents in (re)producing unequal gender relations, or, for as far as they may be gendered, as if they possess only "good gender".

The way in which a gender mainstreaming governmentality itself hence conditions some form of (neoliberal) individual freedom for women is not unproblematic. Both Halley (2006) and McRobbie (2009) criticize the binary oppositions in which gender gets framed in gender mainstreaming, leading to diverse and even disastrous consequences for women, turning a blind eye at how men suffer from gender regimes and producing heteronormativity (see also Zalewski, 2010). The dichotomy between sex and gender depicts the possibility of change as something that can be accomplished by the subject, and that is simultaneously situated outside the subject. It reduces gender to contextual and socio-cultural factors that can be relatively easily managed or fixed in order to enhance individual choices. It does not acknowledge the political character, nor does it cast these choices as embedded in power relations. This means that change can be conceptualized as revolutionary, in the sense of a total and clear break with the past. This change is utopian in the way that it promises something radically new, as if one could be liberated from the power relations of oppression and of the contamination of "bad gender" (Butler, 2000).

It is exactly this revolutionary promise of getting beyond gender in a, as Zalewski (2010, p. 23) puts it, gender-free world that also informs the critique of gender mainstreaming. This assumption of revolutionary change lies at the basis of the disappointment about gender mainstreaming not living up to this transformative promise. Yet, we would like to argue that if we want to advance a research agenda on gender mainstreaming from a governmentalties perspective, we have to let go of this notion of change. Or as Wendy Brown (2005) says, we have to mourn the loss of this notion of revolutionary change to be able to let go of the idea of the subject of Enlightenment (and modernity) as rational and autonomous, which corresponds to this idea of change. This calls for a different understanding of agency. If we accept that power works "in and through" the subject, as a Foucauldian approach suggests, then agency both displays the way in which an actor upholds a certain discourse and subverts it (see also Davids, 2011). In trying to bring about change, we have to acknowledge that women as well as men are actors and barriers of oppressive systems. Their agency is neither totally free nor autonomous, but also consists of, sometimes unconscious, sometimes willing, repetition and reproduction of dominant discourses and the upholding of patriarchal norms (see also Ferguson, 2014).

Reworking these norms is a tenacious and long process, and not something that can be easily fixed by adjusting contextual factors, as neoliberal mentalities suggest. Actors can oppose some of these norms while coinciding with others. Resistance is not, therefore, always total – a new start, breaking with the past. Nor is it as coherent as Western Enlightenment thinking often suggests. Resistance can also be more subtle and small scale. Every moment that repeats norms is also a moment of instability for these same norms, as Butler (2000) and Foucault (1972) suggest. In repeating the norm, slight changes may occur which open up the possibility for subversion. Indeed, governmentalities are "doing their jobs" but might not be as totalitarian as imagined. They often also work in contradictory ways, and this leaves room for ambiguity that opens space and possibility for contestation (Prügl, 2014). This contestation might at times be radical, but can also be manifested in small and subtle ways. We therefore think that if change is to be reached while different governmentalities are in place, this change will most often not be sudden, total, or revolutionary, but slow and partial. Some implementations of gender mainstreaming might offer spaces for contestation while others do not, or do so only very partially. A feminist interest could consequently be to address such room for subversion and contestation, in order to search for different styles of subversions, other than, but within existing power hierarchies. This implies that we have to assess gender mainstreaming instruments for their capacities of opening up different spaces for contestation.[2]

Notes

1. In our analysis here, we focus on how gender mainstreaming is articulating with neoliberal governmentalities. Van Santen (2014) offers an analysis of how gender mainstreaming intersects with, and articulates with, Islamic governmentalities.
2. See also Prügl in this book, who explores deliberative democracy as a strategy for wielding feminist power.

References

Alvarez, Sonia E. (2009) "Beyond NGO-ization? Reflections from Latin America", *Development*, 52(2), 175–184.

Baden, Sally and Anne Marie Goetz (1998) "Who Needs [Sex] When You Can Have [Gender]? Conflicting Discourses on Gender at Beijing", in Cecile Jackson and Ruth Pearson (eds.) *Feminist Visions of Development, Gender Analysis and Policy*. London: Routledge, pp. 19–38.

Batliwala, Srilatha (2007) "Taking Power out of Empowerment", *Development in Practice*, 17(4 and 5), 557–565.

Batliwala, Srilatha and Deepa Dhanraj (2004) "Gender Myths that Instrumentalize Women: A View from the Indian Frontline", *IDS Bulletin*, 35(4), 11–18.

Benschop, Yvonne and Mieke Verloo (2006) "Sisyphus' Sisters: Can Gender Mainstreaming Escape the Genderedness of Organizations?", *Journal of Gender Studies*, 15, 19–33.

Beveridge, Fiona and Sue Nott (2002) "Mainstreaming: A Case for Optimism and Cynicism", *Feminist Legal Studies*, 10(3), 299–311.

Brown, Wendy (2005) "Feminism Unbound: Revolution, Mourning, Politics", in Wendy Brown (ed.) *Edgework, Critical Essays on Knowledge and Power*. Princeton and Oxford: Princeton University, pp. 98–115.

Butler, Judith (2000) *Gender Turbulentie*. Amsterdam: Boom/Parrèsia.

Caglar, Gülay, Elisabeth Prügl, and Susanne Zwingel (2013) "Introducing Feminist Strategies in International Governance", in Gülay Caglar, Elisabeth Prügl, and Susanne Zwingel (eds.) *Feminist Strategies in International Governance*. London: Routledge, pp. 1–18.

Chant, Sylvia (2012) "The Disappearing of 'Smart Economics'? The *World Development Report 2012* on Gender Equality: Some Concerns about the Preparatory Process and the Prospects for Paradigm Change", *Global Social Policy*, 12(2), 198–218.

Chant, Sylvia and Caroline Sweetman (2012) "Fixing Women or Fixing the World? 'Smart Economics', Efficiency Approaches, and Gender Equality in Development", *Gender and Development*, 20(3), 517–529.

Cornwall, Andrea, Elisabeth Harrison, and Ann Whitehead (2004) "Introduction: Repositioning Feminisms in Gender and Development", *IDS Bulletin*, 35(4), 1–10.

—— (2007) "Gender Myths and Feminist Fables: The Struggle for Interpretive Power in Gender and Development", *Development and Change*, 38(1), 1–20.

Davids, Tine (2011) "The Micro Dynamics of Agency: Repetition and Subversion in a Mexican Right-wing Female Politician's Life Story", *European Journal of Women's Studies*, 18(2), 155–168.

Davids, Tine, Francien van Driel, and Franny Parren (2014) "Feminist Change Revisited: Gender Mainstreaming as a Slow Revolution", *Journal of International Development*, 26, 396–408.

Delphy, Christine (1993) "Rethinking Sex and Gender", *Women's Studies International Forum*, 16(1), 1–9.

do Mar Pereira, Maria (2012) "'Feminist Knowledge Is Proper Knowledge, But? ...' The Status of Feminist Scholarship in the Academy", *Feminist Theory*, 13(3), 283–303.

Ely, Robin J. and Debra E. Meyerson (2000) "Advancing Gender Equity in Organizations: The Challenge and Importance of Maintaining a Gender Narrative", *Organization*, 7(4), 589–608.

Ferguson, Lucy (2014) "'This Is Our Gender Person': The Messy Business of Working as a Gender Expert in International Development", *International Feminist Journal of Politics*, DOI 10.1080/14616742.2014.918787.

Foucault, Michel (1972) *The Archaeology of Knowledge*. New York: Pantheon Books.

Goetz, Anne-Marie (2006 [1995]) "Institutionalizing Women's Interests and Accountability to Women in Development (Introduction)", *IDS Bulletin*, 37(4), 71–81.

———— (ed.) (1998) *Getting Institutions Right for Women in Development*. London: Zed Books.

Halley, Janet (2006). *Split Decisions: How and Why to Take a Break from Feminism*. Princeton and Oxford: Princeton University Press.

Harcourt, Wendy (2006) *The Global Women's Rights Movement: Power Politics around the United Nations and the World Social Forum*. Civil Society and Social Movements, Programme Paper 25. Geneva: UNRISD.

Holvoet, Nathalie and Liesbeth Inberg (2014) "Gender Mainstreaming in the Context of Changing Aid Modalities: Insights from Two Paris Declaration Champions", *Journal of International Development*, 26(3), 317–331.

Jakimow, Tanya and Patrick Kilby (2008) "Empowering Women: A Critique of the Blueprint for Self-Help Groups in India", *Indian Journal of Gender Studies*, 13(3), 375–400.

Jauhola, Marjaana (2010) "Building Back Better? – Negotiating Normative Boundaries of Gender Mainstreaming and Post-tsunami Reconstruction in Nanggroe Aceh Darussalam, Indonesia", *Review of International Studies*, 36, 29–50.

Kamstra, Jelmer (forthcoming) "What Causes Homogenization of NGOs across Continents? The Case of Democracy Promoting NGOs in Ghana and Indonesia".

Kothari, Uma (2005) "Authority and Expertise: The Professionalisation of International Development and the Ordering of Dissent", *Antipode*, 37(3), 425–446.

Laclau, Ernesto and Chantal Mouffe (1985 [2001]) *Hegemony and Socialist Strategy: Towards a Radical Democratic Politics*. London: Verso.

Lombardo, Emmanuela, Petra Meier, and Mieke Verloo (2010) "Discursive Dynamics in Gender Equality Politics: What About 'Feminist Taboos'?", *European Journal of Women's Studies*, 17(2), 105–123.

McRobbie, Angela (2009) *The Aftermath of Feminism: Gender, Culture and Social Change*. London: Sage Publications.

Mohanty, Chandra Talpade (1991) "Under Western Eyes: Feminist Scholarship and Colonial Discourses", in Chandra Talpade Mohanty, Ann Russo, and Lourdes Torres (eds.) *Third World Women and the Politics of Feminism*. Bloomington: Indiana University Press, pp. 51–80.

Mukhopadhyay, Maitrayee (2014) "Mainstreaming Gender or Reconstituting the Mainstream? Gender Knowledge in Development", *Journal of International Development*, 26, 356–367.

Parpart, Jane L. (2014) "Exploring the Transformative Potential of Gender Mainstreaming in International Development Institutions", *Journal of International Development*, 26, 382–395.

Prügl, Elisabeth (2011). "Diversity Management and Gender Mainstreaming as Technologies of Government", *Politics and Gender*, 7, 71–89.

—— (2014) "Neoliberalising Feminism", *New Political Economy*, DOI 10.1080/1356 3467.2014.951614.

Repo, Jemima (2014) "Gender Equality as Biopolitical Governmentality in a Neoliberal European Union", *Social Politics*, DOI 10.1093/sp/jxu028.

Roggeband, Conny (2014) "Gender Mainstreaming in Dutch Development Cooperation: The Dialectics of Progress", *Journal of International Development*, 26, 332–344.

Roggeband, Conny and Mieke Verloo (2006) "Evaluating Gender Impact Assessment in the Netherlands (1994–2004): A Political Process Approach", *Policy and Politics*, 34(4), 617–634.

Sen, Gita (2005) *Neolibs, Neocons and Gender Justice: Lessons from Global Negotiations.* Occasional Paper 9. Geneva: United Nations Institute for Social Development.

Squires, Judith (2005) "Is Mainstreaming Transformative? Theorizing Mainstreaming in the Context of Diversity and Deliberation", *Social Politics*, 12(3), 366–388

Sweetman, Caroline (2012) "Introduction", *Gender and Development*, 20(3), 389–403.

Sweetman, Caroline and Fenella Porter (2005) "Editorial", *Gender and Development*, 13(2), 2–10.

True, Jacqui and Laura Parisi (2013) "Gender Mainstreaming Strategies in International Governance", in Gülay Caglar, Elisabeth Prügl, and Susanne Zwingel (eds.) *Feminist Strategies in International Governance*. London: Routledge, pp. 37–57.

van Eerdewijk, Anouka (2014) "The Micropolitics of Evaporation: Gender Mainstreaming Instruments in Practice", *Journal of International Development*, 26, 345–355.

—— (2015) "Gender Mainstreaming: Views of a post-Beijing Feminist", in Wendy Harcourt (ed.) *The Palgrave Handbook on Gender and Development: Critical Engagements in Feminist Theory and Practice*. London: Palgrave Macmillan.

van Eerdewijk, Anouka and Ireen Dubel (2012) "Substantive Gender Mainstreaming and the Missing Middle", *Gender and Development*, 19(3), 491–504.

van Eerdewijk, Anouka and Tine Davids (2014) "Escaping the Mythical Beast: Gender Mainstreaming Reconceptualised", *Journal of International Development*, 26(3), 303–316.

van Santen, José (2014) "'Educating a Girl Means Educating a Whole Nation': Gender Mainstreaming, Development and Islamic Resurgence in North Cameroon", *Journal of International Development*, 26(3), 368–381.

Verloo, Mieke (2005) "Displacement and Empowerment: Reflections on the Concept and Practice of the Council of Europe Approach to Gender Mainstreaming and Gender Equality", *Social Politics*, 12(3), 344–365.

World Bank (2012) *World Development Report 2012: Gender Equality and Development.* Washington, DC: World Bank.

Zalewski, Marysia (2010) "'I Don't Even Know What Gender Is': A Discussion of the Connections between Gender, Gender Mainstreaming and Feminist Theory", *Review of International Studies*, 36(1), 3–27.

Part II

Critical Case Studies of Feminist Knowledge Transfer

5
Windows of Opportunity, Trojan Horses, and Waves of Women on the Move: De-colonizing the Circulation of Feminist Knowledges through Metaphors?

Rahel Kunz

Introduction

The passing of UN Security Council Resolution 1325 and subsequent resolutions launched the Women, Peace and Security (WPS) agenda to mainstream gender into matters of conflict and peace building.[1] Advocates hail gender mainstreaming as a window of opportunity for global feminist knowledge transfer in order to promote the transformation of gender relations, particularly in post-conflict societies. Critics have challenged this optimism, arguing that gender works as a Trojan horse, whereby gender mainstreaming initiatives are used instrumentally to legitimize liberal peace building. These two metaphors have come to dominate the debate on "feminist knowledge transfer" in the WPS agenda. So far, most feminist critiques have focused either on the inadequate translation and implementation of the WPS agenda or on the problematic tendencies of the underlying (liberal) feminism, such as de-politicization or bureaucratization (for an overview, see Ferguson, 2014, p. 2). I argue that we need to ask more fundamental questions regarding ways of conceptualizing the circulation of feminist knowledges.

Taking seriously the power of metaphors, this chapter[2] analyses how these metaphors shape the ways we think and act about feminist knowledges and their circulation. In order to do this, I draw on a three-part framework to analyse the meaning-making and identity-making function of metaphors and their power implications. The two metaphors above disagree in their assessment of the implications of feminist knowledge transfer in the context of post-conflict interventions. My analysis shows that despite their disagreement, they contribute in similar ways to meaning- and identity-making and have converging power effects. I argue that these metaphors

99

and the broader discourse within which they are embedded reproduce a particular understanding of the circulation of feminist knowledges: the feminist knowledge transfer scenario. This reproduces power hierarchies between different actors and forms of feminist knowledges, and processes of in/exclusions, which render solidarities difficult. More broadly, I suggest that this scenario enacts forms of coloniality understood as "the hidden process of erasure, devaluation, and disavowing of certain human beings, ways of thinking, ways of living, and of doing in the world" (Mignolo in Gaztambide-Fernández, 2014, p. 198).

Instead, I propose to take seriously alternative metaphors – such as the queered gender advisor, waves of women on the move, and ethical encountering – as starting points to reconceptualize the circulation of feminist knowledges and to allow for different sorts of encounters based on de-centring, mutual learning, and possibilities for self-questioning. More broadly, this chapter warns about the continued complicity of feminism in colonial endeavours and opens up space for decolonizing the circulation of feminist knowledges.

Here I use the term "feminist knowledges" to include diverse forms of knowledge that agree broadly with objectives of women's rights/emancipation/empowerment and/or gender equality/justice. The advantage of this broad understanding is that it allows us to consider the variety of forms of knowledge that exist and circulate around these topics, without a priori exclusion or hierarchization. The drawback is that this definition includes the knowledges of (women's and men's) groups that either do not self-identify as feminists or explicitly distance themselves from the label for various reasons. These reasons could include, for instance, feminism being associated with Western ideology or with bra-burning women. Moreover, a broad understanding cannot do justice to the specific terminology associated with particular forms of knowledge. Indeed, the point here is not to propose a universally useful definition nor to label particular groups and their forms of knowledge as feminist against their will. Instead, this broad definition is a useful starting point to make space for a broad variety of knowledges.

The chapter draws on the analysis of key international documents on gender mainstreaming, complemented with fieldwork material from Liberia for illustrative purposes. The fieldwork material includes over 60 interviews and focus group discussions with international and Liberian gender experts; representatives of UN organizations and regional and Liberian (women's) civil society and community organizations; security sector personnel; government representatives; and donor institutions.[3] Liberia is an interesting context for the study of the circulation of feminist knowledges. As part of the UN peace operation in Liberia, a large gender mainstreaming machinery has been established, with a "significant level of external intervention in gender-related policies" (Fuest, 2008, p. 218). Yet, Liberia also has a long-standing vibrant women's movement that has been active across the pre-conflict, conflict, and post-conflict periods. The movement interacts in complex ways with this gender mainstreaming machinery (Alaga, 2011; Moran, 2011).

After introducing the two key metaphors that have been used internationally to talk about feminist knowledge transfer in the context of the WPS agenda, the third section analyses the metaphors to argue that they have similar power implications, constituting a particular understanding of the circulation of feminist knowledges. The fourth section sketches a number of alternative metaphors. It analyses their potential to challenge or transform power relations associated with feminist knowledge transfer, in an effort to decolonize the understanding of the circulation of feminist knowledges.

Women, peace, and security metaphors

Within the WPS agenda, two key metaphors have been used to talk about the circulation of feminist knowledges: the window of opportunity and the Trojan horse. The first is used mainly in international policy documents as well as in some feminist writings. The latter can be found mainly in (academic) feminist critiques.[4]

Window of opportunity

The early 1990s saw the emergence of what has been called the "liberal peace project". In short, this project advocates the promotion of liberal democracy, the rule of law, and market economies in post-conflict countries, based on the assumption that the successful transfer of these liberal norms will bring peace, stability, and economic development (Campbell et al., 2011). With the introduction of the WPS agenda, gender mainstreaming has become part of liberal peace interventions. Thus, gender projects are "included in the standard package of postconflict programming" (Moran, 2010, p. 266). This contains initiatives such as gender-sensitive security sector reform (SSR), and disarmament, demobilization and reintegration (DDR) programmes, as well as gender training for peacekeepers and security sectors agents in target countries.

For example, in the case of Liberia, the UN post-conflict intervention was marked from the beginning by a strong gender mainstreaming component, with the appointment of a senior gender advisor as part of the Office of the Special Representative of the Secretary-General.[5] This gave rise to an extensive gender mainstreaming machinery, involving many western, regional, and national gender experts. Initiatives focused on reforming Liberia's security sector laws; formulating gender policies; recruiting and promoting women in the security sector; establishing gender quotas and new institutions; and conducting gender training and awareness-raising campaigns (Aisha, 2005; Fuest, 2008).

Optimism related to the transfer of liberal norms as part of the liberal peace project has spilled over into some of the feminist literature and gender activism. This has led to the emergence of "international conflict feminism", whose advocates subscribe to shared norms regarding gender equality and a shared lexicon such as gender mainstreaming and capacity building (Nesiah, 2012, p. 141). International conflict feminism is based on the assumption that women's physical insecurity necessitates the promotion of liberal governance to restore security and order. The latter promises to "transport a country away from the gendered brutality of war into the folds of an international legal order that respects women's rights" (Nesiah, 2012, p. 143). It is acknowledged that UNSCR 1325 "does not necessarily carry a torch for liberal statecraft or free market economics", but "to the extent that these vehicles offer it wide scope for engagement with peace processes and nation-building efforts, international conflict feminism works with those ideologies and institutions and makes them its own" (Nesiah, 2012, p. 157).

This is the backdrop against which ideas about feminist knowledge transfer in the field of security have been developed. Post-conflict peace operations are perceived as a key moment of transformation and a "window of opportunity" for mainstreaming gender concerns and transferring feminist knowledge (Alden, 2010; Meintjes et al., 2001; Schroeder, 2005; Smet, 2009; Valasek and Bastick, 2008). For example, Smet argues that "the international community does have a window of opportunity to impact positively on gender relations in post-conflict societies" (2009, p. 147). This window of opportunity has been particularly referred to by policy literature focusing on gender and SSR. Thereby, SSR is perceived as a key moment of transformation, and thus a window of opportunity, for integrating gender concerns and feminist knowledge transfer (Alden, 2010). For example, a joint UNDP and UNIFEM publication on *Gender Sensitive Police Reform in Post Conflict Societies* claims:

> Post-conflict contexts can offer special opportunities for attracting larger numbers of women recruits to the police, because of the way conflict may have changed traditional gender roles, with women taking on new roles as community leaders and even combatants.
>
> (UNDP and UNIFEM, 2007, p. 9)

Similarly, FemLINK explains:

> The transition from violent conflict to peace is a pivotal moment. It opens a unique window of opportunity in which institutions, structures and relationships within society can be transformed and the root causes of violent conflict can be analyzed and addressed.
>
> (FemLINK, 2007)

In my interviews in Liberia, I found similar references to the window of opportunity. For example, when a gender advisor of a regional organization stated: "In the post-conflict moment, there are a lot of reforms being done. You take advantage of those reforms to mainstream gender in the Security Sector Reform. It actually offers an opportunity" (Interview with representative of regional organization, Liberia, 2013). The window of opportunity metaphor and the international conflict feminism discourse more generally tend to legitimize interventions in the name of liberal peace building.

Trojan horse

The metaphor of the "Trojan horse" has been used in various ways in the feminist literature. On the one hand, it has been argued that feminism can or should actively use gender mainstreaming and gender experts as Trojan horses to get into institutions and reform their processes. Thus, Woodward (2001) argues that gender mainstreaming holds a promise of a Trojan horse in policy processes. Prügl suggests that gender experts "could be considered the Trojan horses of feminism in governmental processes" (2013, p. 60). Thus, through the gender mainstreaming activities of gender experts, particular types of knowledge are created and smuggled into the reform processes of particular institutions (see also the Introduction to this book). The concern, therefore, has been with what happens to feminist knowledge in the process of being transferred in this particular way.

On the other hand, the metaphor has been employed to refer to the ways in which particular forms of feminist knowledge are themselves being used as a Trojan horse, resulting in the instrumentalization and co-optation of feminism. In this context, the metaphor has not always been used explicitly, but sometimes more indirectly, or through similar metaphors. Fraser (2009) argues, for instance, that feminism has become complicit in entrenching and embedding neoliberal agendas that are detrimental to feminism itself. In the field of security, the Trojan horse metaphor is used mostly by scholarly critiques of international conflict feminism. These have expressed concern about the ways in which (a particular type of) feminism has become linked to liberal peace building (Harrington, 2006). Thus, for example, Hudson claims that:

> Critiques of the liberal peace have grown, but the mutually formative relationship between the liberal peace and a type of peace that might be described as liberal-feminist has been largely overlooked in both mainstream and critical literature. The liberal peace project uses gender discourses as a tool to help enforce its norms.
>
> (Hudson, 2012, p. 444)

Thereby, gender mainstreaming is seen as the Trojan horse of the liberal peace project, as Nesiah argues in her critique of international conflict feminism in the context of Sri Lanka:[6]

[T]he quest inspired by Resolution 1325 for representation in peace building is often a Trojan horse for far-reaching commitments to globally hegemonic economic and political choices. While Resolution 1325 advocacy presents itself as a transformative expansion of the peace process and a challenge to inherited hierarchies, the Resolution often works seamlessly with local and global processes that endorse and legitimise dominant ideologies.

(2012, p. 155)

Thus, for example, market-friendly gender inclusion policies linked to privatization and deregulation have been promoted in the context of the implementation of 1325 in Sri Lanka. These have endorsed neoliberal state-building practices, despite widespread feminist critique of such policies in terms of their detrimental impacts on (particular groups of) women (Nesiah, 2012, p. 155).

Thereby, the Trojan horse metaphor serves to challenge the transfer of feminist knowledge understood as instrumental in achieving the diffusion of Western liberal norms and peace-building interventions. This metaphor portrays feminist knowledge as being instrumentalized to smuggle in liberal norms and to marginalize and delegitimize local feminist knowledges. This metaphor, and the critical discourse within which it is embedded, serve as an important critique of international conflict feminism. So too does it serve as a reminder of the potential of feminist complicity in coloniality. Yet, through buying into the transfer scenario, it risks homogenizing and reifying liberal peace building, as well as reinforcing certain meanings, identities, and power relations regarding feminist knowledges constituted by the window of opportunity metaphor it seeks to critique. I argue that it is not enough to fault the instrumentalization of liberal feminism. Instead, we need to interrogate the understanding of the circulation of feminist knowledges underlying both metaphors.

Analysing metaphors

Metaphors are intimately linked to politics. Two main approaches to conceptualize metaphors in political science can be identified (Carver and Pikalo, 2008). On the one hand, the substitutive approach understands metaphors as "verbal cosmetics" (Boys-Stones, 2003, p. 4, quoted in Mottier, 2008, p. 183) or stand-in words used instrumentally to describe social reality. Thereby, the metaphorical is understood as in opposition to the literal (Carver and Pikalo, 2008, p. 2). On the other hand, the interaction or cognitive approach challenges the idea that metaphors have a merely substitutive function. Instead, this approach suggests that metaphors constitutively organize and transform. According to this view, "those metaphors which turn out to be successful establish a privileged perspective on an object or constitute 'the' object and, by doing so, disappear *as* metaphors" (Maasen, 1995, pp. 14–15). Here, metaphors are central to thought and action (Mottier, 2008, p. 184).

Based on such an interaction approach, Mottier (2008) develops an analytical framework that includes three elements of metaphors. These are: "how metaphors construct meanings"; "how metaphors work as mini-narratives which construct identities and identity boundaries, involving naming and labelling processes"; and "the ways in which metaphors reproduce, challenge or transform relations of power" (Mottier, 2008, p. 192). The first element relates to the ways in which metaphors are constitutive of meaning. Secondly, through naming and labelling, metaphors construct particular identities. The third element investigates the complex ways in which metaphors are implicated in power relations. This last element shows the dual importance of analysing metaphors. It highlights the ways in which metaphors contribute to reproducing power relations, yet also harbour the possibility to challenge or transform these relations. Drawing on this framework, my analysis shows that, despite their opposed positions, the two metaphors discussed above work in similar ways to contribute to a particular conception of feminist knowledges and their circulation. In this way, they also contribute to create particular desirable and marginalized identities, with particular power implications.

Meaning-making

Metaphors constitute a certain meaning by emphasizing some details and de-emphasizing others (Carver and Pikalo, 2008). Here, I highlight two elements. First, both the window of opportunity and the Trojan horse metaphors focus on the post-conflict moment, suggesting a clear break between the pre-conflict, conflict, and post-conflict periods. Yet, post-conflict is often not a clear-cut moment, but rather a continuum between conflict and peace (Cockburn, 2001). Moreover, as Vigh notes, "the focus on *post*, implying as it does a notion of crisis as an interruption of 'normal' life, seems to obscure the fact that a great many people find themselves caught in prolonged crisis" (2008, p. 8). Feminist scholars have highlighted that the distinction between periods of conflict and post-conflict obscures the fact that gender-based violence often continues, or even increases, after a conflict has officially ended (Meintjes et al., 2001; Moser and Clark, 2001). The notion of post-conflict fails to take into account the complexity of these realities.

As a result of this focus on the post-conflict moment, there is a danger of silencing initiatives of circulating feminist knowledges that span the pre-during-post conflict continuum. In addition, the window of opportunity metaphor risks assuming that there were no (or lesser) opportunities for the transformation of gender relations before or during the conflict. Thereby, it risks silencing the various ongoing struggles for women's rights that run across the pre-post divide. Thus, for example, the Liberian women's involvement in the peace struggle emerged out of long-standing women's activism (Moran, 2011) and involved transnational links and the circulation of women and feminist knowledges between Liberian women and (diaspora) women in Ghana (Alaga, 2011). There is also a tendency to fail to recognize the conflict itself as a potential opportunity of empowerment, even though this has been documented in various contexts (Alison, 2009; Gautam et al., 2001; Sjoberg and Gentry, 2007).

Focusing only on the post-conflict moment implies focusing on an instance in which the circulation of feminist knowledges often takes a very specific character, involving international gender experts. This then becomes understood as *the* instance of feminist knowledges circulation. Both metaphors narrow perceptions of what counts as an instance of circulating feminist knowledges, whereas adopting a pre-during-post continuum approach allows us to broaden this.

Secondly, both metaphors are based on an understanding of post-conflict societies as "clean slates". This is illustrated by the following statement from a key BRIDGE publication on gender and armed conflict:

> The destabilisation of gender relations that frequently accompanies armed conflict and its aftermath also opens up potential opportunities. Following the upheaval of war, we have a clean slate to start again and ask some fundamental questions about what kind of society we want and how gender relations will function within it.
>
> (El Jack et al., 2003, p. 6)

Similarly, in an interview with an international gender expert working in Liberia, I was told: "I was quite surprised because they are so willing to learn more. I think they are quite open to everything and I never had someone who say 'No this is all stupidity. I don't want to hear about it.'" (Interview with international gender expert, Liberia, 2013).

Admittedly, the "clean slate" assumption is stronger for the window of opportunity metaphor, which portrays the post-conflict moment as a time when gender dynamics can be radically reconstructed, assuming that somehow existing power relations have been suspended, which creates limitless possibilities for "entering the window". Post-conflict societies are presented as open, easy to access, and willing to change. There is a belief that "progressive outsiders can guide the survivors to a new, neoliberal paradise" (Moran, 2010, p. 267). This contributes to legitimize feminist knowledge transfer linked to external interventions. Yet, even the Trojan horse metaphor subscribes to the idea that post-conflict societies have been "intervened upon", although in this discourse, intervention has violent conflict connotations, as illustrated by the Trojan horse. Ultimately, both metaphors portray processes of the circulation of feminist knowledges in terms of transfer and intervention.

Identity-making

The meaning-making dimension analysed above is linked to the creation of particular desirable, silenced, or marginalized identities, with implications for the understanding of the circulation of feminist knowledges. The analysis here focuses on a number of key identity-making elements of WPS metaphors (for a more detailed analysis, see Kunz, 2014). Put in a slightly simplistic way, both metaphors constitute a situation whereby the post-conflict moment is associated with the arrival of external gender/feminist experts to implement gender mainstreaming initiatives, in cooperation with local organizations and experts. In this scenario, the gender expert symbolizes the "centre" from which feminist knowledge is being transferred and who is involved in translating and localizing feminist knowledge. In the window of opportunity metaphor, women's organizations, women victims, or security agents in post-conflict societies are portrayed as either the implementers or beneficiaries of the feminist knowledge that is transferred to bring progressive change. Local (gender) experts are formed and involved in translating and localizing feminist knowledge.[7] This plays out similarly in the Trojan horse metaphor, apart from the more pessimistic evaluation of the transfer and its implications. International (gender) experts smuggle in feminist knowledge through a linear transfer from the external gender experts to the internal context where the recipients are situated. The main difference is that this metaphor highlights the problematic effects of the scenario of feminist knowledge transfer, including the window of opportunity metaphor.

The key characteristic of identity-making here is the way in which both metaphors portray the dichotomy between the sender and the receiver of feminist knowledges. Thereby, they contribute to discursive mechanisms of in/exclusion which marginalize particular identities that do not fit this dichotomy. One example is the "wo/man troublemaker", who questions 1325 implementation activities, or the process of the circulation of feminist knowledges in the metaphor scenario. Actors labelled as troublemakers are often either side-lined or co-opted, as has been shown in other contexts. For example, Gibbing reports how Iraqi women activists invited to speak to a group of gender experts at the UN were labelled as "angry" because they did not "speak positively about women's efforts in the reconstruction of Iraq and the role the UN could play" and instead condemned the US invasion and used terms like "imperialism" (Gibbings, 2011, p. 525; Hudson, 2012; Nesiah, 2012). This echoes racialized stereotypes of the "angry brown woman", who is not taken seriously and side-lined or disciplined (Razack, 2004). This scenario of feminist knowledge transfer marginalizes subjects who resist or subvert the process, or who choose to engage on their own terms, or not to engage at all.

Power implications

The meaning- and identity-making processes of metaphors are implicated in reproducing, challenging, and transforming relations of power, some of which have been mentioned above. I argue here that both metaphors contribute to reproduce power hierarchies among feminist knowledges as a result of their understanding of feminist knowledges circulation as a transfer scenario. In this scenario, the authority of knowledge is located with international gender experts or the Western feminist knowledge to be transferred, or with local gender experts trained by internationals. This establishes a hierarchy of feminist knowledges and ways of legitimate thinking and acting on WPS. This builds pressure on women's and civil society organizations to adapt to this scenario. For example, as Nesiah describes in the context of the implementation of UNSCR 1325 in Sri Lanka:

> Historically, the global circulation of feminist solidarities and agendas has been enriching for many Lankan women's NGOS and contributed to critical, counterhegemonic interventions. Yet the interpenetration of new governance modalities into these transnational flows has had many contradictory implications for the trajectories of feminist initiatives.
> (Nesiah, 2012, p. 150)

Certain "decades-old social change agendas have been repackaged in terms that resonate with the resolution", in order to be visible and gain financial and political support in international circles (Nesiah, 2012, p. 155). Thus, national women's groups have been pressured to renegotiate their activities "to concede to global agendas that determine which projects are viable" (Nesiah, 2012, p. 154). This contributes to the demobilization of local social movements, a narrowing of feminist political vocabularies, and the marginalization of alternative feminist agendas.

In the context of Liberia, similar developments can be observed. Interview respondents report that they need to reformulate their objectives and activities in line with the WPS agenda to be visible and receive funding from the international community (Interviews with Liberian women's and civil society organizations, Liberia, November 2013). They also report a trend towards an increasing specialization of women's organizations and the proliferation of (women's) NGOs focusing on the implementation of 1325 projects. This recalls the idea of feminist knowledge transfer outlined above and in the broader literature on the NGO-ization of feminist movements (Alvarez, 2009). The scenario of feminist knowledge transfer marginalizes subjects who resist or subvert the process, who choose not to engage, or to engage on their own terms. The result is a restrictive understanding of the agenda and the forms of circulation of feminist knowledges, as well as who can legitimately be involved therein.

More broadly, the two metaphors regarding scenarios of feminist knowledge transfer reproduce coloniality. That is, "the hidden process of erasure, devaluation, and disavowing of certain human beings, ways of thinking, ways of living, and of doing in the world" (Mignolo in Gaztambide-Fernández, 2014, p. 198). What transpires here are colonial assumptions about expertise and knowledge circulation, what Shepherd has termed the "imperial logic of a 'trickle-down' theory of expertise" (Shepherd, 2011, p. 516). Simply put, the idea is that "locals" do not have the necessary specific knowledge – for example, pertaining to security and gender – and therefore there is a need to bring in external experts – for example, to carry out gender training. "Other" feminist knowledges are portrayed as lacking, and therefore in need of assistance and intervention. Moreover, these metaphors tend to conceptualize feminist knowledge as a form of expertise, disavowing gender as a category of critical analytics for disruption and contestation, as discussed below. This displaces the debate regarding gender inequalities from the realm of politics into the realm of expertise, which risks shrinking the political space to debate gender issues, and reinforcing the appearance of the technicality of peace building (Kunz, 2014).

The analysis so far shows how these two metaphors reproduce existing hierarchies and colonial power relations among feminist knowledges. These power relations are problematic because they act to exclude and marginalize ways of being and doing that do not conform to the expertise and knowledge transfer logic. Moreover, they also have implications in terms of broader questions around the possibility of solidarity. The scenario of the position of the "clever" outsider – for example, the international gender expert – who is in a privileged position vis-à-vis national women's groups, in terms of knowledge and access to funding and networks, makes it difficult to imagine a situation of solidarity across this divide (Bhambra and Margree, 2010). Yet, this is exactly what some of my respondents call for, as analysed in more detail in the following section.

Decolonizing the circulation of feminist knowledges through metaphors?

So far, I have focused on the ways in which metaphors reproduce power relations and enact coloniality. Yet, metaphors also harbour the "potential for creativity in politics" (Carver and Hyvarinen, 2013, p. 6). As such, I suggest that they can be mobilized productively in an attempt to decolonize the understanding of the circulation of feminist knowledges analysed above. This process can be described as follows:

Thinking and doing decolonially means unveiling the logic of coloniality and delinking from the rhetoric of modernity. Knowledge and truth in parenthesis, epistemic geopolitics beyond absolute knowledge, restitution of colonised subaltern knowledges, and diverse visions of life are some of the keystones of decolonial thinking and doing.

(Mignolo, 2012, p. xvii)

In this spirit of delinking, I now consider a few alternative metaphors, not with the aim of elaborating a single, universally valid metaphor, but to suggest that there are multiple ways of understanding the circulation of feminist knowledges that go beyond the transfer scenario of the dominant metaphors.

Queered gender advisor (and researcher)

One starting point could be to reconceptualize the meaning and identity of gender experts (and researchers) and expertise, as well as the ways in which they are involved in the circulation of feminist knowledges. The figure of the gender expert epitomizes many dilemmas, such as the urgency of action paradox, the instrumentalization trap, and the dilemma of imperialism versus anti-feminism. If we want to move away from some of these dilemmas and paradoxes, it might be useful to build on Jauhola's "queered gender advisor", who, "instead of 'knowing gender', would have the task of interrupting the processes of knowing and subverting the normalised understandings of gender" (Jauhola, 2013, p. 174). This leads away from an understanding of feminist knowledge as expertise towards gender as a critical analytic category for disruption and contestation. This metaphor also allows us to move away from an understanding of feminist knowledge as a form of "possessive" knowing, that is as capturing, controlling, and imposing, towards an activity of deconstruction, disruption, and permanent provocation (Jauhola, 2013, p. 30). It could also open up space to recognize the potential for solidarity in our experiences and encounters.

Such an understanding of feminist knowledges does not require expert knowledge on feminist theory or gender issues, but can take a variety of actions or inactions. In this sense, queered gender advisors and researchers could play a potentially disruptive and contesting role in the WPS agenda. Yet, this requires resisting the colonial urge to "change the other", as well as a critical (self-)reflection on the position of advisors and researchers. Jauhola proposes that the researcher's position be recognized as political and situated:

[…] seeing, listening, recording and interpreting the struggle over meanings is a conscious feminist process of making the negotiated gender-norm-making visible, yet remaining cautious of the western (feminist, academic) desire to be the one who knows and determines authenticity".

(Jauhola, 2013, p. 29)

As feminist researchers, we also need to be more self-reflective of our own involvement in the circulation of feminist knowledges and their conceptualization (Ferguson, 2014; Jauhola, 2013).

Waves of women on the move

I was just in South Africa for the African Union meeting and I was announcing to them that there's a revolution on right now and it's moving and there are waves of it, and they're not seeing it, and it's going to hit them, it's the waves of women wanting to move. Women of the world are making decisions, they are no longer going to be silent... As you see more and more violence in the world you see more and more women standing up against it. It's happening and if the other women of the world would just support them in it, I think we will see a complete revolution that has occurred really. They will just sit there stunned. ... You can support it or you can get out of its way but it's going to happen. We are on a move and that's important.

(Interview with ABIC representative, Liberia, 2013)

These are the words that a representative of the Angie Brooks International Centre (ABIC), a Liberian women's organization, used to describe the current circulations of feminist knowledges in Africa. The metaphor of waves symbolizes movement coming from, and going in, various directions. Waves are organic, things are happening, and there is no call for external intervention, although support is welcome. As part of these waves of women on the move, she refers to the initiative by her organization called the Women's Situation Room (WSR), launched during the 2011 Liberian elections.[8] The aim of this initiative is to mobilize the experience of women in preventing and mitigating conflict through a space for consultations with various parties during electoral processes, including women and youth groups, the media, and public and private sector representatives. WSRs are a site for dialogue and the exchange of experiences between women's and other civil society groups from different countries (Interview with ABIC representative, Liberia, 2013). This initiative has been replicated subsequently in other countries, such as Senegal, Sierra Leone, and Nigeria.[9]

In the context of this initiative, feminist knowledges circulate in many different ways and directions, defying the simplistic, linear top-down version of the transfer scenario. As an ABIC representative emphasized, "One of the things, I think, about the Women Situation Room that is powerful is we never turn up unless we are invited. We don't go unless we are asked" (Interview with representative of ABIC, Liberia, 2013). The emphasis on dialogue and "being invited" are two characteristics of this initiative that distinguish it from the transfer scenario, which is perceived as unsolicited and top-down. The waves of women on the move metaphor and the WSR also defy the sender–receiver dichotomy underlying the transfer scenario. Here, the circulation of feminist knowledges goes in many directions, and there is room for exchange and mutual learning. The circulation of the WSRs to other West African states and beyond promotes the circulation of feminist knowledges, women's organizations, and solidarity. It also allows for the possibility of engaging in the circulation of feminist knowledges on various terms.

Ethical encountering

The metaphor of the "ethical encounter" (Ahmed, 2013) could be helpful in reconceptualizing the circulation of feminist knowledges as an encounter. This allows us to step away from gender as expert knowledge and might go some way towards opening up space for contestation and mutual learning. Such encounters involve a contact between the self and the other that goes beyond colonial moments, as described by Inayatullah and Blaney:

> We read them [these encounters] to suggest that the elemental motive for travel, discovery, and contact is not the drive for relative or absolute gains, but the working out of inner projects, fears, and myths that require contact with the other.
>
> (Inayatullah and Blaney, 2004, p. 66)

Based on the recognition of the co-constitution of the self–other relationship, this might be a starting point for alternative ways of interaction that attempt to resist the colonial impulse of changing the other. Thereby, "the challenge is to expose the very vulnerability and insecurity of the self, to make possible the ethical encounter with the other" (Masters, 2005, p. 130). In addition, such ethical encounters are understood as a process of "becoming" for everybody involved, and the mode and terms of encountering are not determined in advance (Colebrook, 2008, p. 30). Such encounters suggest a meeting that involves surprise and conflict (Ahmed, 2013). The waves of women on the move and the Women's Situation Rooms initiative are examples of attempts to move towards such encounters.

In my own research, I experienced various forms of encounters. For example, when asking Liberian gender experts, somewhat provocatively, whether they thought that the whole gender mainstreaming endeavour as part of the peace-building intervention was a form of neo-imperialism, many responded by saying that they did not always perceive the situation in that way. In some instances, they had experienced encounters of feminist knowledges circulation as an opportunity for the exchange of experiences and mutual learning.

For instance, they recalled sessions of gender training where participants shared the particular forms of gendered socialization and gender discrimination they experience in their respective countries and cultures. As a result, they asked me about gender relations and women's rights in Switzerland (e.g. how many women police officers do you have in Switzerland?), for which I was not fully prepared during my first interview. But I realized the opportunity for a different sort of encounter that my various interview partners were pushing for. This illustrates the ways in which such encounters can be a possibility for mutual learning and self-questioning for both gender advisors and researchers, despite constraining structural power differences. Yet, in our attempts to decolonize the circulation of feminist knowledges, we must also acknowledge that any encounter, any circulation of feminist knowledges, involves a certain degree of untranslatability. Moreover, we must allow for the possibility of non-circulation, non-engagement, and inaction.

Conclusion

This chapter highlights the implications of the ways in which existing metaphors on WPS conceptualize the circulation of feminist knowledges in terms of transfer. These metaphors reproduce existing hierarchies and colonial power relations among feminist knowledges. Thereby, they act to exclude and marginalize ways of being and doing that do not conform to the knowledge transfer scenario. Moreover, these metaphors tend to conceptualize feminist knowledge as a form of expertise, disavowing gender as a category of critical analytics for disruption and contestation. This displaces the debate regarding gender inequalities from the realm of politics into the realm of expertise, shrinking the political space to debate issues related to gender injustice/inequality, and reinforcing the appearance of the technicality of peace operations.

Yet, taking seriously the power and political potential of metaphors, I have suggested a number of starting points to decolonize the WPS agenda and challenge the peace-building paradigm, such as the queered gender advisor and researcher, waves of women on the move, and ethical encountering. These metaphors and initiatives not only challenge the transfer scenario but also point towards broader questions of the production of knowledges. They hint at the possibility of the co-construction of feminist knowledges and different ways of thinking about the links between the construction and circulation of feminist knowledges. This warrants further thought and engagement.

The analysis raises questions regarding the broader implications of the transfer scenario for the possibility of solidarity on issues linked to gender equality/justice. The transfer scenario creates the position of the (external) gender expert who is in a privileged position vis-à-vis national women's groups, in terms of knowledges and access to funding and networks. Such asymmetry makes it difficult to achieve a situation of solidarity (Bhambra and Margree, 2010). Yet, this is exactly what the ABIC representative interviewed suggests in her call for support for the waves of women on the move. To what extent can such counter-metaphors contribute to opening space for various forms of "feminist" solidarities and ethical encounters that do not require expert knowledge? Beyond the queered gender advisor, there is a need to further reflect on the potential role of the feminist researcher in this endeavour.

Notes

1. Subsequent Resolutions on Women, Peace and Security are 1820 (2008), 1888 (2009), 1889 (2009), 1960 (2010), 2106 (2013), and 2122 (2013).
2. Research for this chapter was carried out in the context of a collaborative research project on gender experts and gender expertise (PA00P1_145335 and 100017_143174). I am grateful for stimulating discussions with my project colleagues Katarzyna Grabska, Françoise Grange, Elisabeth Prügl, Feyneke Reysoo, Hayley Thompson, and Christine Verschuur at the Graduate Institute in Geneva. Special thanks go to my Liberian research partner, Kou Gbaintor-Johnson, for our stimulating cooperation, and to Mohamed Sesay for his helpful comments. Funding by the Swiss National Science Foundation is gratefully acknowledged. I would also like to thank the editors of this volume for their constructive comments on earlier versions of this chapter.
3. Special thanks go to my respondents for taking time to talk with me. This research would not have been possible without you. The interviews were carried out during 2012–2013 and respondents have been cited anonymously to guarantee confidentiality.
4. The window of opportunity metaphor has also been used in other contexts: by local women's groups in particular post-conflict settings; in the context of post-authoritarian transition in Southern Europe and Latin America; in post-communist transformation in Eastern Europe; and in the context of EU accession processes (Forest, 2006; Lombardo and Forest, 2012).
5. See http://unmil.unmissions.org/Default.aspx?tabid=3937&language=en-US
6. Similarly, Charlotte Gage asks in her blog post regarding the Global Summit to End Sexual Violence in Conflict: "Is sexual violence in conflict a new Trojan horse?" See: http://blogs.lse.ac.uk/gender/2014/06/23/is-sexual-violence-in-conflict-a-new-trojan-horse/.
7. This recalls writings on the NGO-ization of feminist movements (Alvarez, 1999, 2009).
8. For more information on the Liberian Women's Situation Room (WSR) initiative, see http://www.angiebrookscentre.com/what-we-do/our-actions/the-womens-situation-room/.
9. For more information on the replication of the WSR initiative in other countries, see http://www.unwomenwestandcentralafrica.com/womens-situation-room.html.

References

Ahmed, Sara (2013) *Strange Encounters: Embodied Others in Post-Coloniality.* Abingdon and New York: Routledge.

Aisha, Fatoumata (2005) "Mainstreaming Gender in Peace Support Operations: The United Nations Mission in Liberia", in Festus Aboagye and Alhaji Bah (eds.) A Toruous Road to Peace: The Dynamics of Regional, UN and International Humanitarian Interventions in Liberia. Pretoria: Institute for Security Studies, pp. 147–163. http://www.issafrica.org/uploads/TORTUOUSCHAP7.PDF (accessed 8 May 2015).

Alaga, Ecoma (2011) "Security Sector Reform and the Women's Peace Activism Nexus in Liberia", in Funmi Olonisakin and Awino Okech (eds.) Women and Security Governance in Africa. Cape Town: Pambazuka Press/Fahamu Books, pp. 68–88.

Alden, Amie (2010) "A Continuum of Violence: A Gendered Analysis of Post Conflict Transformation", *POLIS*, 3, 1–37.

Alison, Miranda H. (2009) *Women and Political Violence: Female Combatants in Ethno-National Conflict*. London and New York: Routledge.

Alvarez, Sonia E. (1999) "Advocating Feminism: The Latin American Feminist NGO 'Boom'", *International Feminist Journal of Politics*, 1(2), 181–209.

——— (2009) "Beyond NGO-ization?: Reflections from Latin America", *Development*, 52(2), 175–184.

Bhambra, Gurminder K. and Victoria Margree (2010) "Identity Politics and the Need for a 'tomorrow'", *Economic and Political Weekly*, 45(15), 59–66.

Campbell, Susanna, David Chandler, and Meera Sabaratnam (2011) *A Liberal Peace?: The Problems and Practices of Peacebuilding*. London: Zed Books.

Carver, Terrell and Jernej Pikalo (2008) *Political Language and Metaphor: Interpreting and Changing the World*. London and New York: Routledge.

Carver, Terrell and Matti Hyvarinen (2013) *Interpreting the Political: New Methodologies*. London and New York: Routledge.

Cockburn, Cynthia (2001) "The Gendered Dynamics of Armed Conflict and Political Violence", in Caroline N. O. Moser and Fiona Clark (eds.) *Victims, Perpetrators or Actors?: Gender, Armed Conflict and Political Violence*. London: Zed Books, pp. 13–29.

Colebrook, Claire (2008) "How Queer Can You Go? Theory, Normality and Normativity", in Noreen Giffney and Myra J. Hird (eds.) *Queering the Non/human*. Aldershot and Burlington: Ashgate, pp. 17–34.

El Jack, Amani, Emma Bell, Lata Narayanaswamy, and BRIDGE (2003) *Gender and Armed Conflict*. Brighton: BRIDGE.

FemLINK (2007) "What is UN SCR 1325?" http://www.femlinkpacific.org.fj/index.cfm?si=main.resources&cmd=forumview&cbegin=0&uid=content&cid=23 (accessed 8 May 2015).

Ferguson, Lucy (2014) "'This Is Our Gender Person': The Messy Business of Being a Gender Expert in International Development", *International Feminist Journal of Politics*, DOI 10.1080/14616742.2014.918787.

Forest, Maxime (2006) "Emerging Gender Interest Groups in the New Member States: The Case of the Czech Republic", *Perspectives on European Politics and Society*, 7(2), 170–184.

Fraser, Nancy (2009) "Feminism, Capitalism and the Cunning of History", *New Left Review*, 56, 97–117.

Fuest, Veronika (2008) "'This Is the Time to Get in Front': Changing Roles and Opportunities for Women in Liberia", *African Affairs*, 107(427), 201–224.

Gautam, Shobha, Amrita Banskota, and Rita Manchanda (2001) "Where There Are No Men: Women in the Maoist Insurgency in Nepal", in Rita Manchanda (ed.) *Women, War, and Peace in South Asia: Beyond Victimhood to Agency*. London: Sage Publications, pp. 214–251.

Gaztambide-Fernández, Rubén (2014) "Decolonial Options and Artistic/AestheSic Entanglements: An Interview with Walter Mignolo", *Decolonization: Indigeneity, Education & Society*, 3(1), 196–212. https://decolonization.org/index.php/des/article/view/21310 (accessed 8 May 2015).

Gibbings, Sheri Lynn (2011) "No Angry Women at the United Nations: Political Dreams and the Cultural Politics of United Nations Security Council Resolution 1325", *International Feminist Journal of Politics*, 13(4), 522–538.

Harrington, Carol (2006) "Governing Peacekeeping: The Role of Authority and Expertise in the Case of Sexual Violence and Trauma", *Economy and Society*, 35(3), 346–380.

Hudson, Heidi (2012) "A Double-Edged Sword of Peace? Reflections on the Tension between Representation and Protection in Gendering Liberal Peacebuilding", *International Peacekeeping*, 19(4), 443–460.

Inayatullah, Naeem and David L. Blaney (2004) *International Relations and the Problem of Difference*. London: Routledge.

Jauhola, Marjaana (2013) *Post-Tsunami Reconstruction in Indonesia: Negotiating Normativity Through Gender Mainstreaming Initiatives in Aceh*. Abingdon and New York: Routledge.

Kunz, Rahel (2014) "Gender and Security Sector Reform: Gendering Differently?", *International Peacekeeping*, 21(5), 604–622.

Lombardo, Emanuela and Maxime Forest (eds.) (2012) *The Europeanization of Gender Equality Policies: A Discursive-Sociological Approach*. Basingstoke and New York: Palgrave Macmillan.

Maasen, Sabine (1995) "Who Is Afraid of Metaphors?", in Sabine Maasen, Everett Mendelsohn, and Peter Weingart (eds.) *Biology as Society, Society as Biology: Metaphors*. Dordrecht: Kluwer Academic Publishers, pp. 11–35.

Masters, Cristina (2005) "Bodies of Technology", *International Feminist Journal of Politics*, 7(1), 112–132.

Meintjes, Sheila, Meredeth Turshen, and Anu Pillay (2001) *The Aftermath: Women in Post-Conflict Transformation*. London: Zed Books.

Mignolo, Walter D. (2012) *Local Histories/Global Designs: Coloniality, Subaltern Knowledges, and Border Thinking*. Princeton, NJ: Princeton University Press.

Moran, Mary H. (2010) "Gender, Militarism, and Peace-Building: Projects of the Postconflict Moment", *Annual Review of Anthropology*, 39(1), 261–274.

——— (2011) *Liberia: The Violence of Democracy*. Philadelphia: University of Pennsylvania Press.

Moser, Caroline N.O. and Fiona Clark (eds.) (2001) *Victims, Perpetrators Or Actors?: Gender, Armed Conflict and Political Violence*. London: Zed Books.

Mottier, Veronique (2008) "Metaphors, Mini-Narratives and Foucauldian Discourse Theory", in Terrell Carver and Jernej Pikalo (eds.) *Political Language and Metaphor: Interpreting and Changing the World*. London: Routledge, pp. 182–194.

Nesiah, Vasuki (2012) "Uncomfortable Alliances: Women, Peace and Security in Sri Lanka", in Ania Loomba and Ritty A. Lukose (eds.) *South Asian Feminisms*. Durham, NC: Duke University Press, pp. 139–161.

Prügl, Elisabeth (2013) "Gender Expertise as Feminist Strategy", in Gülay Caglar, Elisabeth Prügl, and Susanne Zwingel (eds.) Feminist Strategies in International Governance. London: Routledge, pp. 57–73.

Razack, Sherene H. (2004) *Dark Threats and White Knights: The Somalia Affair, Peacekeeping, and the New Imperialism*. Toronto: University of Toronto Press.

Schroeder, Emily (2005) "A Window of Opportunity in the Democratic Republic of the Congo: Incorporating a Gender Perspective in the Disarmament, Demobilization and Reintegration Process", *Peace, Conflict & Development*, 6(6), 4.

Shepherd, Laura J. (2011) "Sex, Security and Superhero(in)es: From 1325 to 1820 and Beyond", *International Feminist Journal of Politics*, 13(4), 504–521.

Sjoberg, Laura and Caron E. Gentry (2007) *Mothers, Monsters, Whores: Women's Violence in Global Politics*. London and New York: Zed Books.

Smet, Stijn (2009) "A Window of Opportunity – Improving Gender Relations in Post-Conflict Societies: The Sierra Leonean Experience', *Journal of Gender Studies*, 18(2), 147–163.

UNDP and UNIFEM (2007) *Policy Briefing Paper: Gender Sensitive Police Reform in Post Conflict Societies*. New York: UNDP and UNIFEM. http://www.unwomen.org/~/media/headquarters/media/publications/unifem/gendersensitivepolicereformpolicybrief2007eng.pdf (accessed 8 May 2015).

Valasek, Kristin and Megan Bastick (eds.) (2008) Gender & Security Sector Reform Toolkit. Geneva: DCAF, OSCE/ODIHR, UN-INSTRAW. http://www.dmeforpeace.org/learn/dcaf-gender-and-security-sector-reform-toolkit (accessed 8 May 2015).

Vigh, Henrik (2008) "Crisis and Chronicity: Anthropological Perspectives on Continuous Conflict and Decline", *Ethnos*, 73(1), 5–24.

Woodward, Alison E. (2001) "Gender Mainstreaming in European Policy: Innovation or Deception?" Discussion paper. Wissenschaftszentrum Berlin für Sozialforschung, Forschungsschwerpunkt Arbeitsmarkt und Beschäftigung, Abteilung Organisation und Beschäftigung, No. FS I 01–103. http://core.ac.uk/download/pdf/6496779.pdf (accessed 8 May 2015).

6

Gender Training as a Tool for Transformative Gender Mainstreaming: Evidence from Sweden

Anne-Charlott Callerstig

Introduction

Gender training is widely seen as necessary for non-gender experts to be able to conduct gender impact analysis and to suggest adequate measures for gender mainstreaming (Council of Europe, 1998). Gender training is also considered key to minimizing the risk of resistance in terms of the implementation of gender equality policies (Halford, 1992). Major training efforts have subsequently been common in connection with gender mainstreaming initiatives. The heavy reliance on gender training as a driver for change in gender mainstreaming strategies, together with reports of difficulties in achieving envisioned policy and organizational changes, raises questions about the potential of gender training as a policy instrument for implementing gender equality policies.

This chapter explores gender training as way of achieving the changes envisioned in one equality strategy, namely the strategy of gender mainstreaming, which seeks to create more gender sensitivity in all phases and all areas of policy implementation. This chapter explores the underlying assumptions of why gender training is understood to be necessary in order to succeed with the gender mainstreaming strategy and discusses the potential of gender training for creating more gender-sensitive policies and practices. This is done by focusing on the results of a study concerning a gender mainstreaming initiative in a large Swedish municipality, wherein gender training was the main instrument for change. The initiative was funded by the programme for gender mainstreaming in local authorities, run in Sweden between 2008 and 2013. Under this programme, local authorities could apply for funding to support their work in terms of gender mainstreaming in public services. Resources distributed for gender training activities made up a large part of the activities supported, amounting to up to 25% of the total budget of the programme (EUR 25 million).

This chapter discusses the effects and impact of gender training both on individuals and on polices and the organizations, as well as on the relationship between them. This relates to the more general ambition discussed in this book that gender training should ideally entail a transfer of knowledge which aims at being "transformative". The transformative goal signifies that participants should not only come to better understand gender but also that, as a consequence of training, participants will begin to acknowledge, challenge, and change existing inequalities. In the case of gender mainstreaming, it means that training should lead to participants starting to change the way they undertake their daily work. The underlying assumption within this transformative ideal is thus that a change in understanding can lead to a change in behaviour, and furthermore that change in individuals can lead to change on an institutional level and impact existing policies and practices. The discussions in this chapter relate to the broader discussion of whether this assumption is valid, and if so, under what conditions this is likely to happen. Different types of tensions, dilemmas, and conflicts in and around gender mainstreaming are highlighted with respect to how they relate to gender training. Also discussed is how they impact and can or cannot be influenced through gender training.

The main questions that will be raised in relation to the case study are: In what way was gender training understood to be important for achieving the objectives of the gender mainstreaming initiative studied? What factors impacted the implementation process and why? And, in what way was gender training instrumental for the results of the initiative? These questions form the basis for a wider discussion in the chapter on gender training as a policy instrument more generally, as well as on gender training's potential impact on the outcomes of gender mainstreaming initiatives, in line with the broader concerns of this book. In the following section, some theoretical starting points concerning the potential for gender training to lead towards change, not only in the understandings of individual persons but also in their behaviour, will be addressed. Following this, some reflections from different perspectives will be shared on how changes in individual behaviour can be related to changes on an institutional level.

Gender training and gender mainstreaming – Some theoretical starting points

Training is a popular tool in many policy areas, but research shows that it is not always effective in influencing people's actions. For example, it is difficult to reach all employees of an organization though training, and studies have shown the tendency to only reach those who are already knowledgeable about, and interested in, the subject of the training (van der Doelen, 2005). In addition, some research suggests that people tend to absorb information that supports their already existing views and values. New knowledge does not, therefore, automatically change people's attitudes and insights (van der Doelen, 2005). There is a danger that existing "knowledge gaps" will widen as a result of training. Those who already "can" and "want to" will learn more, whereas those who "cannot" or "do not want to" absorb new knowledge in a way that challenges their existing views will either decide not to take part in training courses or will relate to the training in such a way that their negative attitudes will be strengthened.

Gender training can also become an alibi, for instance when gender lectures are provided for staff but there is no real intention of promoting change on an organizational level. Furthermore, commissioners of gender mainstreaming initiatives often claim that it is possible to see changes in the behaviours of individuals due to gender trainings, in terms of how people act and speak in new ways. This, they argue, helps to strengthen efforts to work with gender mainstreaming. However, this has been shown to be very difficult to measure (Callerstig and Lindholm, 2013). Moreover, there is still little research on the impact of gender training as a policy implementation instrument beyond largely general discussions, such as whether harder policy instruments offer better results than softer ones (Hafner-Burton and Pollack, 2009), or whether permanent organizational functions are better than temporary or voluntary initiatives (Timmers et al., 2010).

Gender training as a means for gender equality

Studies of policy implementation and policy instruments have generally long history and have generated immense insight into how to understand and control implementation processes. General prerequisites for policy implementation have been identified as the importance of staff "know how", that is staff having the knowledge, capacity, and resources for the work in question; "willingness" to realize the objectives; and "understanding", that is knowledge about, and an understanding of, what is to be achieved (*cf.* Sannerstedt, 2001). Implementation processes have been found to be complicated in all policy areas.

Yet, some problems are particularly common in terms of gender mainstreaming. These may be summarized as: gender equality is seldom prioritized in an organization; there is often a lack of support from management and a lack of adequate resources; existing organizational gender regimes might hinder implementation; and that the work is largely driven by enthusiasts (Callerstig, 2014). A general lack of understanding about gender inequalities is still a widespread problem. Earlier studies have, for example, shown that gender equality as a concept is seldom defined or is defined in different ways (Lombardo et al., 2009). Gender equality issues are complex and it is usually difficult to find simple solutions, which in turn puts greater demands on the change process. Unawareness about the way we all "do" gender is, furthermore, also widespread (Andersson et al., 2009; Martin, 2006). From this perspective, it is easy to see that different forms of knowledge transfers (gender training, coaching, expertise, etc.) have been understood as essential in the implementation of the gender mainstreaming strategy.

Discussions about gender training as an instrument for gender main-streaming relate to theories on the role of policy instruments in understanding policy implementation. Different forms of policy instruments or policy tools are often used in implementation processes to achieve intended goals (Schneider and Ingram, 1990; Lascoumes and Le Gales, 2007). Sometimes these will be prescribed in the policy itself, such as in the case of policies on quotas. At other times, their design will be left more to the implementers of the policy, such as in the case of gender mainstreaming.

Policy instruments have come increasingly into focus in research. Today, they are seen as interesting in themselves, unlike in earlier studies where they were often analysed from a functionalist perspective. It has been recognized that policy instruments are not neutral devices and that they produce specific effects, independent of the objectives pursued (Lascoumes and Le Gales, 2007). Studying the choice of instruments can reveal a more or less explicit understanding of the relationship between those governing and the governed, as well as social control and ways of exercising it (Lascoumes and Le Gales, 2007, p. 3). The choice of policy instruments more specifically uncovers what is understood to be the problem presented by the policy, and how it may be solved, including an understanding of the objective to strive for.

There are many different theories on policy instruments and what constitutes the most effective means of steering an implementation process (Bemelmans-Videc et al., 2003). There are also different perceptions about the role that gender training plays as a policy instrument for gender equality, which relates to the key theme of this book concerning theories of change and transformation. In simple terms, it can be summarized as a more positive or a more negative approach, or rather, top-down versus bottom-up. One perspective emphasizes an incremental (i.e. gradually increasing) transformation process, where gender equality is seen as something that gradually emerges over time and through increased knowledge. In line with this perspective, the use of "soft" control measures, such as training, is an important means of achieving change. The other perspective is based on a more radical change theory and stresses the need for "harder" control measures. From this perspective, existing inequalities are part of a societal stratification process with domination and control mechanisms. It is felt that these must be challenged with policy instruments, such as quotas, laws, and regulations, in order to be effective. Gender training can, of course also, be part of this strategy, but not as the sole driver for change.

Table 6.1 Two perspectives on change

	The incremental model	The fast track model
Problem	Personal attitudes and values	Structural inequality
Primary solution	Information, training, and public debate	Laws, regulations, and sanctions
Change approach and expected outcomes	Positive change perspective Formal equality (*de jure*)	Negative change perspective Actual/real equality (de facto)

Source: Adapted from Dahlerup and Freidenvall, 2005.

The two perspectives, furthermore, imply different understandings of what constitutes gender equality; formal equality (non-discrimination) versus actual or real equality (substantive). The latter model has been referred to as the "fast track model" and the former as an "incremental model" for gender equality. These are presented in Table 6.1 (Dahlerup and Freidenvall, 2005).

From this perspective, gender training as a policy instrument, or a driver for change, can be related to different understandings of the relationship between increased knowledge, on the one hand, and a shift in attitudes and behaviours, on the other. The political scientist Evert Vedung (1991) has described how policy instruments can be related to different theoretical assumptions which influence the choice of these policy instruments. They are portrayed below in two different models. The first emphasizes the necessity of knowledge for attitudes and values that are believed to explain how people will act and is referred to as the "theoretical learning model". The second model instead stresses that, as a person's behaviour changes, they will acquire new attitudes and values that support their new way of acting. In this way, they will acquire the knowledge they need. This model is known as "dissonance theory".

In essence, the theoretical learning model (Figure 6.1) is based on the influence of each individuals' knowledge, attitudes, and values; something that is expected to lead to reflection, which in turn gives rise to the individual changing his or her actions. This approach has been criticized for being too individualistic, rationalistic, and unrealistic (Vedung, 1991). Even if individuals know what is right and proper, they do not always act on the basis of the knowledge they possess to this effect. Relations like power, interests, resources, and other factors, more to do with organizational and institutional relations, are neglected in this perspective. If knowledge and insight do not lead to gender equal behaviour, then what is the alternative?

One alternative is to apply a strategy that builds on external control. The idea here is that the behaviour of individuals should be influenced, rather

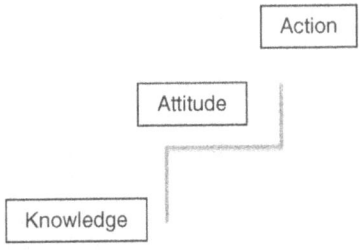

Figure 6.1 Theoretical learning model
Source: Adapted from Vedung, 1991.

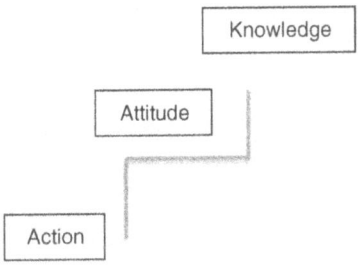

Figure 6.2 Dissonance theory
Source: Adapted from Vedung, 1991.

than their insights as to why they should behave in a certain way. The starting point for this perspective is that action comes first and insights follow (see Figure 6.2). The individual will avoid dissonance (contradictions) and instead strive towards views that agree with the reason for the action. According to dissonance theory, reflection arises as a result of changed behaviour. When managers and staff begin to work in new ways, this will also gradually affect their knowledge, attitudes, and values. There is a parallel here with ideas about the normative effect of laws, that is that people's attitudes and values can be changed with the aid of legislation that determines what is right and what is wrong. Knowledge is acquired when it is "needed" to change actions. There is also a flipside and limit to this strategy, namely that it evokes resistance, and that it initially makes it difficult for those concerned to understand the value of the changed behaviour.

The two models are, furthermore, based on different assumptions about the possibility of finding the "right" solution to a problem. The theoretical learning model starts out from a rational point of view; in that, by gathering enough information, a decision about the "best" solution can be made. The dissonance model starts from a perspective of there being no clear-cut or "correct" solutions, but instead takes the view that we usually regard the "right" solution as that which we are currently engaging in. When we begin to act in new ways, we often change our view of what is "right".

But is it so easy to make a clear choice between these two change approaches? A third perspective is to focus on the aim of gender mainstreaming, which is not only to adapt policies to existing rules and regulations on gender equality but to transform them. This makes a strictly top-down perspective problematic. This, in turn, is because solutions to the problems of gender inequality are not pre-set, unlike in other cases, such as in policies on quotas, where it is more clear what the problem is and what should be done about it. In gender mainstreaming, both discovering the causes of and the solution to the problem should be achieved through the implementation process. Jahan (1995) explains how the gender mainstreaming strategy aims at a transformation process that entails a change of policy. The transformation achieved by gender mainstreaming can mean:

> [...] prioritising gender objectives among competing issues, reorienting the mainstream political agenda by rethinking and re-articulating policy ends and means from a gender perspective.
>
> (Jahan, 1995, p. 13)

This ambition to "re-orient/think/articulate" policies is similar to what has been described as a process of policy learning by Sabatier (1993), namely, "a relatively enduring alteration of thought or behavioural intentions that are concerned with the attainment (or revision) of the precepts of a policy belief system" (Sabatier, 1993, p. 19). In addition, this should be made with specific objectives and perspectives in mind. The learning in gender mainstreaming, therefore, includes adjusting and correcting current processes and practices in line with existing rules and regulations on gender equality, known as "adaptive" learning (Ellström, 2010; Ellström et al., 2008). However, actors also need to reflect on and develop new solutions, known as "innovative" or "developmental" learning, which would entail more profound change (Ellström, 2010; Ellström et al., 2008). It is mainly developmental learning that has been emphasized to enable deeper change processes in organizations (Dewey, 1989; Elkjaer, 2001; Ellström, 2010; Engeström, 1996). However "changes in thinking" do not always lead to or preclude a change in policy (Kemp and Weehuizen, 2005, p. 3). Nor do they necessarily entail the organizational changes needed to implement the "new" policies. Mechanisms for adaptive learning often need to be present to achieve specific aims (Ellström, 2010; Ellström, et al., 2008).

Before discussing the results from the case study, the management training initiative and the programme for gender mainstreaming of which the initiative was part are outlined in more detail in the following section.

The Swedish programme for gender mainstreaming in local authorities (2008–2013) and gender training

Sweden is often portrayed as one of the world's most gender equal countries. There are, however, still many remaining problems in society from a gender perspective. Gender-based inequalities persist both in Sweden and elsewhere (Hearn, 2012). The institutionalization of gender equality politics in Sweden is simultaneously strong in comparison to many other countries, including other Nordic countries (Borchorst, 1999; Sainsbury and Bergqvist, 2009), and it has been argued that Sweden is therefore a likely context for gender mainstreaming to be successful. Expectations have accordingly been high regarding its implementation (Daly, 2005; Rubery et al., 2004; Sainsbury and Bergqvist, 2009). However, similar to research findings from other countries, the results in the Swedish case have been disappointing to a certain degree. Studies conducted in Sweden have revealed problems such as weak steering and support for gender mainstreaming; a lack of understanding of how to relate a gender perspective to specific policy areas; and general a lack of interest in the matter, partly because it is widely believed that Sweden is already a gender equal country (Callerstig, 2014; Olofsdotter Stensöta, 2009, 2010; Sainsbury and Bergqvist, 2009).

Gender mainstreaming, together with specific initiatives, has been the main strategy for the national gender equality policies in Sweden since the mid-1990s.[1] In order to succeed with the strategy, gender training has been emphasized as one of the most important instruments for its implementation both in Sweden and elsewhere (see, e.g., Council of Europe, 1998; and Government of Sweden, 2007). In Sweden, the support manual for gender mainstreaming contains a "ladder" model that shows how work surrounding gender mainstreaming could best be organized (Government of Sweden, 2007). The bottom step of the ladder stipulates "fundamental understanding". In the description of this step, the manual explains:

> Before gender mainstreaming work begins, the entire organization – from the management down – is offered training in gender equality and gender and in what Swedish gender equality policy and the gender mainstreaming strategy mean.
>
> (Government of Sweden, 2007)

In 2008, the programme for gender mainstreaming was set up by the Swedish Association of Local Authorities and Regions (SALAR), following a decision of the Swedish government. The initiative was originally planned for 2008–2010 but was endorsed for two additional periods. With funding totalling EUR 25 million until 2013, it has been one of Sweden's largest ever initiates on gender equality. Over the years, the programme has funded 87 initiatives on gender mainstreaming in Swedish municipalities and county councils.

Different types of training activities have been conducted for project leaders and process leaders in the programme. In addition, some 66,000 politicians, managers, and civil servants have participated in gender training at the local level until 2010, and an additional 17,500 until 2012. During the whole programme, some 83,500 persons took part in gender training activities up until 2012.

The training and capacity-building activities in the programme had different target groups and were conducted in different ways, with variations in terms of length and depth. Key features of the programme's gender training philosophy include a flexible and interactive approach; orientation towards key processes in public service organizations (in particular, steering and accountability mechanisms); developing project leader skills among gender equality professionals; and sensitizing and ensuring commitment among top-level managers and politicians.

The Management Training Project in Gothenburg City

In this chapter, the findings of one case study will be discussed. This initiative was funded by the programme in the City of Gothenburg, wherein the main activity was a training course called "Management Training in Gender". For the sake of simplicity, the initiative will be referred to as "Management Training" throughout the section. The case study was carried out between Spring 2009 and Spring 2010. The results are based on semi-structured interviews (Kvale, 1997) with project management – specifically, the project leader in the municipality and the gender expert engaged for the Management Training – as well as departmental managers and school principals. Eight longer interviews were conducted with managers from the department and principals within the municipality. In addition, central documents in the project – such as the application, project description, consultancy report, final report, and other documents – were examined, as was the project's web blog. An analysis seminar was held with participants (informants and project management) shortly after the longer interviews were conducted to discuss the results.

The initiative was close to its conclusion, but not completely finished, at the time that the case study ended. For example, when the longer interviews were conducted, the work to develop action plans was still in progress. The case study was conducted using an interactive research approach. In interactive research, the creation of a joint learning process between researchers and practitioners is a central feature (Svensson et al., 2007). The interactive method developed for the research study has been thoroughly described elsewhere (Callerstig, 2014; Callerstig and Lindholm, 2011).

Gothenburg City is one of the largest municipalities in Sweden, with 13 municipal upper secondary schools, some 25 independent upper secondary schools, and 2,000 employees responsible for working within the education system of the City's Education Department. The Management Training initiative was a part of a larger gender mainstreaming initiative entitled "A school for all". The purpose of the training was to equip managers to "be able to make assessments, analyses and decisions that contributed to increased gender equality". The training course broadly followed the model developed for gender mainstreaming by the Swedish government (Government of Sweden, 2007). The training was made compulsory for all managers in the Education Department as well as all school principals. Key people working with quality development and planning issues also took part in the training.

The training consisted of a series of traditional lectures – to which one whole day and five half-days were devoted – and six working sessions, lasting three hours at a time. The lecture series involved topics such as basic knowledge about gender equality politics; gender patterns and power dynamics in society and in schools; and gender mainstreaming in practice. The working sessions had the specific aim to "convert knowledge into practical action". According to the application for the programme, this meant that "the school managers would determine how a gender perspective could be incorporated in the school's everyday educational activities". In these sessions, the gender expert engaged for the session worked together with the managers. The "gender scan" method was also used during the working sessions.[2]

Key findings

In the following section, I will discuss the developments which followed the initiative, as well as some of the issues raised in the interviews and analysis seminar in relation to the implementation process. Below, some of the key findings relating to the questions addressed in this chapter are highlighted.

Lack of interest among the city's school staff a prevailing problem

According to several informants, when the new initiative began, gender equality was marginal and barely visible issue in the Department, and gender equality objectives had low priority. The informants argued that the Department's existing gender equality objectives were vague and that work in the area was slow. This had previously largely been driven by "enthusiasts", and work with gender equality issues was mainly assigned to those who showed interest in it. There was no clear understanding about what constituted a gender equality problem among staff or how it might be solved. Moreover, there seemed to be little incentive to work with the issue. Gender equality as a whole did not appear to be given priority, but was instead addressed, if at all, out of a sense of duty.

Apart from the prevailing lack of knowledge about gender and gender mainstreaming, another obstacle to progress was that there seemed to be a general lack of awareness about gender equality problems among the Department's managers and staff. This lack of awareness was thought to contribute to a lack of engagement by school managers and to negatively affect the attitudes of schools' staff. One of the Department's managers confirmed this:

> It is not a group or a function that is the biggest gender equality problem. The biggest problem is that people – including myself – have so many deep seated ideas and if the management isn't interested then nothing happens.
>
> (Interviews conducted as part of the Management Training initiative, 2009–2010)

New focus prompted by the gender mainstreaming initiative, and newly appointed director, sparked life into work on gender equality

According to the informants, the gender mainstreaming initiative and the Management Training initiative were seen as an opportunity to infuse new life into work in this sphere. Whereas in the past, work had focused more on gender equality plans from a personnel (HR) perspective, the emphasis was now on daily activities performed in schools. Several of the informants said that this perspective made gender equality issues more interesting for staff. Emphasizing the actual work done in the classroom also seemed to reduce resistance to addressing gender equality as a topic, which had previously been observed. Fewer people protested and, as a result of the new perspective, more were able to understand why gender equality was important. A new departmental Director was also appointed at more or less the same time as the new project began. His experience of gender mainstreaming in another district within the municipality was regarded as successful and applauded by politicians and civil servants alike.

A "two-pronged" change strategy focused on training managers to assume responsibility for the work

A project manager and a process manager were also employed in connection with the Management Training project. Both had previous experience of working with gender equality issues in the municipality. The project manager had also been involved in gender equality work from a personnel perspective within the Department. According to both the project manager and the process manager, an important key strategy in gender mainstreaming was to foster enthusiasm and engagement among managers and school principals. The Management Training project was an important part of this focus. However, the two managers noted that engagement and willingness should come from the managers themselves, which meant that they had to understand and believe in the importance of gender equality issues.

In the interviews, the project manager and process manager explained how a discussion between them concerned how much they should steer and drive gender mainstreaming, at least in the start-up phase, and how long they should wait for the individual managers to assume responsibility for it.

It was considered that the managers' engagement would increase dramatically if they themselves created action plans and then acted to implement them in their schools, even though for this they would need additional knowhow. This change strategy was regarded by the project manager and the process manager as "two-pronged": partly geared towards the managers acquiring new knowledge, and partly with the help of a gender expert, towards their converting this knowledge into action plans which they would then implement.

Engaging school managers to increase the interest of staff

In order for the gender mainstreaming initiative to succeed, it was necessary for all staff members to become engaged, not just the managers. According to the project manager, it was important to get the managers to promote gender equality in the organization and take responsibility for the process. The reasoning used was that getting managers to initiate gender mainstreaming themselves was vital to prompting other staff members to recognize gender inequalities. For the Department's managers, this meant a personal learning process and developing new gender equality objectives for the Department in tandem with the development of action plans for the schools. Working systematically in this way meant a new approach for many managers, as one pointed out:

> It's the first time that we've worked with this in this way, [before there] had been mainly isolated measures. For me, it's the first time we've worked in more detail and that all the managers are involved.
>
> (Interviews conducted as part of the Management Training initiative, 2009–2010)

The "transfer of ownership" – setting new objectives

Getting the Department's managers and administrators to formulate gender equality objectives was regarded as central by the project management in the initial work. As indicated above, an earlier problem was that gender equality had often been driven by enthusiasts. In order to ensure success, the first step was to "transfer the ownership", in the words of the project manager, from enthusiasts to school managers. This would be done by letting the managers work to create new operational objectives for the action plans with the help of the gender expert in the training's working sessions.

Furthermore, the existing vague overarching Departmental objective was not considered a good starting point for developing action plans for the city's schools, and thus needed to be revised. This had also been highlighted by an organizational consultant whom the Department had engaged prior to the gender mainstreaming initiative. That the managers of the Education Department, and not the gender equality experts, should formulate the new objective was regarded as something that would increase engagement in gender mainstreaming. The majority of informants considered that the gender equality objectives needed to reflect their actual work and activities in order to be seen as relevant. As the Department manager pointed out:

> Gender mainstreaming is dependent on the management breaking the objectives down so that they are clear. Politicians and top management have to make these big decisions and grassroots bureaucrats need to make sure that they reflect the reality.
>
> (Interviews conducted as part of the Management Training initiative, 2009–2010)

The experience of breaking down gender equality objectives, however, was felt to be difficult by many managers, and the work undertaken in the working sessions was sometimes felt to be too theoretical and abstract. The participants often started out from their own personal experiences of the work rather than from the national or municipal gender equality objectives.

Gender inequality was seen as an individual and not an organizational problem but not all can become gender experts

A common view among both the school principals and Education Department managers was that the staff influenced whether conditions were "equal" or not in schools. "Gender-neutrality" in the classroom was therefore regarded by the majority of the informants as an important objective. A common argument was that girls and boys should be treated equally, and not on the basis of traditional gender roles. This "treatment" must also be as obvious as it is unconscious.

While the actions of school staff were seen as important for gender equality, according to several informants, it was not considered possible to expect all staff to be gender experts. As one manager put it, "We can't expect all the staff to be gender experts, although we can insist on equal treatment" (Interviews conducted as part of the Management Training initiative, 2009–2010). The project manager further argued that all staff could not be expected to have the same knowledge about gender. She also wanted a shift of focus from an emphasis on personal values and ideas to practical guidelines and routines, noting that, "People should not need to decide whether they are feminists or not. At work you should do as you are told" (Interviews conducted as part of the Management Training initiative, 2009–2010). Both the project management and the managers emphasized the importance of improving knowledge and awareness and of incorporating a gender perspective in routines and guidelines.

Gender mainstreaming was still seen as "optional" after the compulsory training

According to the informants, the Management Training had not convinced all the managers. When the interviews took place, the action plans were not complete and not all the principals were equally motivated. How would the Department's managers handle the fact that so many of the municipality's school principals still, despite the compulsory Management Training, regarded gender mainstreaming as "optional"? As the personnel manager pointed out, "A lack of interest and a lack of knowledge are the main obstacles. And as gender equality competes with everything else [...] adopting such a perspective is not always possible" (Interviews conducted as part of the Management Training initiative, 2009–2010).

Too many priorities and a lack of time were the main reasons for lack of results

A lack of time and a number of different priorities were regarded as the main risk factors with regard to the continuation of gender mainstreaming when the training period ended. A common view among the informants was that they prioritized work with deadlines and with some kind of central monitoring. With regard to sustainability, the project's approach was, therefore, increasingly seen as a risk factor, because focus, time, and resources disappeared when the initiative came to an end. Several managers said that the creation of a sustainable change process required more than simply establishing a new understanding and awareness of gender equality issues. One school principal argued: "There is a great danger that when this project is over it'll all be forgotten and that something else will be prioritized", while another indicated that, "If the management is serious about this initiative it will take root, otherwise it will simply be a passing fancy" (Interviews conducted as part of the Management Training initiative, 2009–2010).

A shift from creating prerequisites to demanding results

The overarching objective for gender mainstreaming in the Education Department was later changed from "everybody should have the necessary knowledge" to "all activities should be gender mainstreamed". Work on gender mainstreaming was also included as a question in the regular personal follow-ups between school principals and the Head of the Education Department. This development reflected the beliefs of the Department's new director. As the Head of the Education Department argued:

> The ideal is that you have very good objectives and are also prepared to follow them up. The task has to be made clear [...] You also have to measure. Measure, measure, measure!
>
> (Interviews conducted as part of the Management Training initiative, 2009–2010)

The results of the gender mainstreaming initiative and the Management Training included changes in routines, such as during the production of statistics. Many new methods for gender mainstreaming were also tested as a result of the initiative. In addition, a new system for gender budgeting was presented in autumn 2010. As a result of the initiative, a "challenge" was formulated by the Department of Education: "The world's most gender equal upper secondary school is in Gothenburg City! It is part of our vision and our goal. Challenge us!"

Gender training and different perspectives on learning and change: Findings from the analysis and reflection seminar

How, then, should the potential of gender training to reach the objective of gender mainstreaming be understood, according to the participants in the initiative? In the case study, this was discussed in an analysis and reflection seminar held shortly after the interviews. The dilemmas encountered in working with gender mainstreaming were highlighted and discussed in relation to the findings as ideological dilemmas in gender equality initiatives. This meant that they cannot be resolved in practice but must instead be handled or "balanced" in practical work (Billig et al., 1988; Callerstig and Lindholm, 2013; Nentwich, 2006). The purpose of the seminar was to let participants reflect on the findings and discuss how to develop practical work (see Callerstig and Lindholm, 2013, for a detailed description of the interactive approach methodology used).

Changes in behaviour do not follow automatically from new knowledge

The question of how to handle the dilemma inherent in the need to transfer knowledge and the need to control behaviour – as outlined above in terms of the theoretical learning model and the dissonance model – was taken up during the analysis seminars. One conclusion from the discussions was that both perspectives and the practical approaches developed from them were important. Both strategies were seen to have their advantages and disadvantages. A one-sided focus on the theoretical learning model was regarded by participants as problematic because it is easy to place responsibility for change entirely on individual employees. The organization too must support change if there is to be any real result. The danger is also that this can lead to an understanding of gender inequality as something that people "bring into" the organization and that insufficient attention is paid to organizational structures and processes in the process of (re)producing inequalities (also shown by Abrahamsson, 2000). Furthermore, it was seen as important to problematize all suppositions that people automatically change their behaviour when they acquire new knowledge. A strictly controlled and top-down approach would, however, meet resistance according to the participants. Furthermore, it was problematic because without "proper" knowledge, there is the risk that actions undertaken by employees would, at worst, reproduce inequalities or otherwise not lead to any real change.

Gender awareness is a constant process and not a one-time effort

Another discussion at the analysis seminar concerned the ideal expressed in the interviews and training sessions that staff should have acquired knowledge about gender and gender equality so that they could act at an "unconsciously conscious" level, that is that they could practice equality without even thinking about it. Questions, and doubts, were raised about how to reach that level of awareness and how to manage to stay there. Some research points to the creation of awareness as a long-term process, and not something acquired in a few training sessions (Andersson et al., 2009). "Unconscious consciousness" was seen by the participants as something that you had to actively work on to create and maintain.

On the other hand, simply focusing on a strategy based on external control, that is, the starting point of the dissonance theory, was also regarded as problematic, in that gender mainstreaming is very clearly about knowhow. Without knowledge about what is to be done, why it is important, and how it can be done, achieving the desired results in gender mainstreaming is difficult. Past research also shows that resistance often occurs when it is not explained why something is important or how it might be done (Halford, 1992).

Policy instruments must be chosen based on actual needs, not theoretical beliefs

In the discussions, there was no clear-cut preference among the participants for a strategy built on a gradual and self-generating development (incremental) or a tougher approach (fast track) in gender equality work, as discussed above. A conclusion from the seminar was that it was not simply a matter of choosing between a more radical or incremental approach when working with gender mainstreaming. Different organizations, situations, and people or positions may need their own special combination of "tools", such as training and behaviour-oriented control with regard to gender equality work. It might also be possible to apply the two perspectives at the same time, in a rotating or parallel process. An interesting question raised by a seminar participant was whether gender equality as a policy area is generally characterized by a culture that emphasizes softer policy instruments, such as training and reflection, in contrast to other policy areas where stricter controls are stressed.

Conclusions and discussion

It is time to turn back to the questions raised initially and to draw conclusions from the wider discussion in the chapter on gender training as a policy instrument for the outcomes of gender mainstreaming initiatives. The model for gender mainstreaming in Gothenburg shifted from being

more attuned to the classical learning perspective to reflecting the dissonance model towards the end of the research study. But was the change in
attitudes due to new knowledge gained through gender training, or was it
the shift in the objectives and steering introduced by the new manager that
brought about change?

One conclusion from the case study is that gender mainstreaming developed from being more oriented towards acquiring new knowledge and
awareness to being more about control and follow-up as a way of moving the work forward. This development took place as a parallel process
and included both learning among participants and the actions of the new
Director. The results can be seen as an indication that gender mainstreaming should steer towards specific results to be achieved in practical work,
rather than providing only the means to do so, that is gender training. Simply offering managers and staff new knowledge about gender, and skills in
how to work with gender mainstreaming, was not sufficient. Even so, such
knowledge was essential for *tackling* gender mainstreaming and creating
understanding about why gender equality issues are important, including for
managers. In the Management Training project, the strategy was to "transfer
ownership" from the gender equality experts to the managers. Without this
transfer, the training of the managers and the production of action plans
would probably not have been as effective.

Research has shown that, in general, policy areas often develop from softer
forms of control, such as capacity-building approaches, to stricter controls,
such as stricter rules and use of sanctions. In the context of the Education
Department, this meant that the departmental Head included the developments achieved in gender mainstreaming work in his follow-up talks with
school principals, which was also a foundation for their own career development and salaries. Correspondingly, research has shown that there is a
tendency for "newer" areas, largely characterized by uncertainties about
objectives and strategies, to use learning strategies for development. Later,
when uncertainty has abated and the area "ripens", stricter forms of control can be applied (Schneider and Ingram, 1990). This may explain the
changeover from softer to stricter controls. When the uncertainty about
what should be done was reduced, it became easier to demand results. The
Management Training project played an important role in this.

Another conclusion is that the content of gender training must be clearly
linked to the activities and work under focus. At first, gender theory and
national gender equality objectives were perceived by the participants as
abstract and out of place in their daily work. Only when theories and gender equality objectives were linked to core activities were they understood as
important. Significant work in the Management Training initiative involved
linking theory and objectives to everyday work. Aside from improved knowledge being important for the reasons outlined above, it is also important
to create conditions that generate new knowledge if this is lacking, which

seems to be particularly important in gender mainstreaming. This requires a knowledge-based, unreserved exploration, similar to the innovative learning discussed above. At the same time, adaptive learning is needed to adjust daily work in line with existing rules and objectives on gender equality. Here, a more top-down approach is warranted.

One question that emerged in the case study was whether it is possible to change power disparities through gender training in the first place, an issue which reflects the concerns of this book regarding the transformative potential of gender training. This can be linked to the discussion above about the incremental model and the *fast track* model, as well as the different assumptions underlying these approaches. According to the *fast track* model, gender inequality cannot simply be "informed away" because it rests upon power imbalances. Gender equality should mean a shift in the balance of power, for instance with regard to economic and decision-making positions. This perspective holds that change must be "forced" upon people. According to the incremental approach, on the other hand, the power perspective is not as striking. Instead, creating conditions that secure equal treatment is regarded as more important. What the actual end result will be is not quite as clear; it mainly depends on individual choice. According to the incremental approach, change is deterministic – it will happen gradually and be facilitated by new knowledge and altered insights.

The results of the case study indicate that neither of these two approaches can be adopted in isolation to the other: they must be balanced. Gender training might in itself be an insufficient instrument for gender mainstreaming, but it might still be necessary. However, it must be oriented towards both individual and organizational learning in order to be efficient and to allow for innovative learning, while being combined with a top-down approach that demands results of the actions undertaken. The case study shows that only focusing on creating prerequisites, that is merely providing gender training (even if made compulsory), was not enough. It was not until results were demanded from the gender mainstreaming work, monitored, and followed up, that managers stopped regarding the work as optional.

A final conclusion to be drawn is that it is impossible to evaluate the effects of gender training for gender mainstreaming separately from other policy instruments in use. For example, the prerequisites for training changed radically when the departmental Head started to demand results from gender mainstreaming. The fact that the initiative, by the end, emphasized a top-down approach in combination with a bottom-up approach is probably one of the more important contributing factors to the results.

Notes

1. According to the Swedish government, this means that decisions in all policy areas must have a clear gender perspective. The argument is that equality between

women and men is created where everyday decisions are taken, resources allocated, and norms established, and that the gender perspective must therefore be an integral part of daily work. This is similar to the description offered by the European Council in 1998.

2. In this context, gender scanning means making observations from a gender perspective and subsequently analysing the significance of these for one's own situation.

References

Abrahamsson, Lena (2000) *Att återställa ordningen. Könsmönster och förändring i arbetsorganisationer.* Umeå: Boréa Bokförlag

Andersson, Susanne, Eva Amundsdotter, Marita Svensson, and Ann-Sofie Däldehög (2009) *Middle managers as Change Agents.* Stockholm/Hudiksvall: Stockholms University/Fiber Optic Valley.

Bemelmans-Videc, Marie-Louise, Ray C. Rist, and Evert Vedung (eds.) (2003) *Carrots, Sticks & Sermons: Policy Instruments and Their Evaluation.* New Brunswick: Transaction.

Billig, Michael, Susan Condor, Derek Edwards, Mike Gane, David Middleton, and Alan Radley (1988) *Ideological Dilemmas: A Social Psychology of Everyday Thinking.* London: Sage Publications.

Borchorst, Anette (1999) "Den institusjonaliserte likestilling: Hvad er det vi studerer?", in Christina Bergqvist, Ann-Dorte Christensen, Anette Borchorst, Viveca Ramstedt-Silén, Nina Raaum, and A. Styrkársdottir (eds.) *Likestilte demokratier? Kjønn og politikk i Norden.* Oslo: Universitetsforlaget, pp. 151–156.

Callerstig, Anne-Charlott (2014) *Making Equality Work: Ambiguities, Conflicts and Change Agents in the Implementation of Equality Policies in Public Sector Organisations.* Doctoral Dissertation, Linköping University.

Callerstig, Anne-Charlott and Kristina Lindholm (2011) "The Contradictory Work with Gender Mainstreaming", *Tidskrift för genusvetenskap (TGV)*, 2–3, 79–96. English translation of article.

—— (2013) "Effects of Gender Mainstreaming", in L. Svensson, Lennart, Göran Brulin, Sven Jansson, and Karin Sjöberg (eds.) *Capturing Effects in Programmes and Projects.* Lund: Studentlitteratur.

Council of Europe (1998) *Recommendation No. R (98) 14 of the Committee of Ministers to Member States on Gender Mainstreaming.* Strasbourg: Council of Europe.

Dahlerup, Drude and Lenita Freidenvall (2005) "Quotas as a 'Fast track' to Equal Representation for Women", *International Feminist Journal of Politics*, 7(1), 26–48.

Daly, Mary (2005) "Gender Mainstreaming in Theory and Practice", *Social Politics*, 12(3), 433–450.

Dewey, John (1989) *Demokrati och utbildning.* Göteborg: Daidalos.

Elkjaer, Bente (2001) "The Learning Organisation: An Undelivered Promise", *Management Learning*, 32(4), 437–452.

Ellström, Eva, Bodil Ekholm, and Per-Erik Ellström (2008) "Two Types of Learning Environment: Enabling and Constraining A Study of Care Work", *Journal of Work place Learning*, 20(2), 84–97.

Ellström, Per-Erik (2010) "Organisational Learning", in Penelope Peterson, Eva Baker, and Barry McGaw (eds.) *International Encyclopedia of Education*, Vol. 1. Oxford: Elsevier, pp. 47–52.

Engeström, Yrjö (1996) "Development as Breaking Away and Opening Up. A Challenge to Vygotsky and Piaget", *Swiss Journal of Psychology*, 55, 126–132.

Government of Sweden (2007) *Gender Mainstreaming Manual Gender Equality in Public Services*. SOU 2007:15. Stockholm: Swedish Government Official Reports.

Hafner-Burton, Emile M. and Mark A. Pollack (2009) "Mainstreaming Gender in the European Union: Getting the Incentives Right", *Comparative European Politics*, 21(7), 114–138.

Halford, Susan (1992) "Feminist Change in a Patriarchal Organisation: The Experience of Women's Initiatives in Local Government and Implications for Feminist Perspectives on State Institutions", in Michael Savage and Anne Witz (eds.) *Gender and Bureaucracy*. Oxford: Blackwell Publishers, pp. 155–185.

Hearn, Jeff (2012) "Contextualising Gender Mainstreaming: Text, Context, Subtext", in Kristina Lindholm (ed.) *Gender Mainstreaming in Public Sector Organisations: Policy Implications and Practical Application*. Lund: Studentlitteratur, pp. 13–30.

Jahan, Rounaq (1995) *The Elusive Agenda: Mainstreaming Women in Development*. London: Zed Books.

Kemp, René and Rifka Weehuizen (2005) *Policy Learning: What Does It Mean and How Can We Study It? Innovation in the Public Sector*. Oslo: Nordisk Institutt for Studier av Innovasjon, forskning og utdanning – STEP.

Kvale, Steinar (1997) *Den kvalitativa forskningsintervjun*. Lund: Studentlitteratur.

Lascoumes, Pierre and Patrick Le Galès (2007) "Introduction: Understanding Public Policy through Its Instruments – From the Nature of Instruments to the Sociology of Public Policy Instrumentation", *Governance: An International Journal of Policy, Administration, and Institutions*, 20(1), 1–21.

Lombardo, Emanuela, Petra Meier, and Mieke Verloo (eds.) (2009) *The Discursive Politics of Gender Equality: Stretching, Bending and Policymaking*. London: Routledge.

Martin, Patricia Y. (2006) "Practicing Gender at Work", *Gender, Work & Organization*, 13(3), 254–275.

Nentwich, Julia (2006) "Changing Gender: The Discursive Construction of Equal Opportunities", *Gender, Work & Organization*, 13(6), 499–521.

Olofsdotter Stensöta, Helena (2009) *Jämställdhetsintegrering i statliga myndigheters verksamhet. Hur långt har myndigheterna nått? Vad beror det på? Hur kan arbetet utvecklas vidare? JÄMI 2/09 Rapport*. Göteborg: Swedish Secretariat for Gender Research, University of Gothenburg.

—— (2010) *Processer i arbetet med jämställdhetsintegrering. Ett samtal med 10 myndigheter*. Göteborg: Swedish Secretariat for Gender Research, University of Gothenburg.

Rubery, Jill, Hugo Figueiredo, Mark Smith, Damian Grimshaw, and Colette Fagan (2004) "The Ups and Downs of European Gender Equality Policy", *Industrial Relations Journal*, 35(6), 603–628.

Sabatier, Paul A. (1993) "Policy Change Over a Decade or More", in Paul A. Sabatier and Hank Jenkins-Smith (eds.) *Policy Change and Learning: An Advocacy Coalition Approach*. Boulder: Westview Press, pp. 13–39.

Sainsbury, Diane and Christina Bergqvist (2009) "The Promise and Pitfalls of Gender Mainstreaming: The Swedish Case", *International Feminist Journal of Politics*, 11(2), 216–234.

Sannerstedt, Anders (2001) "Implementering – hur politiska beslut genomförs i praktiken", in Bo Rothstein (ed.) *Politik som organisation – förvaltningspolitikens grundproblem*. Stockholm: SNS förlag, pp. 18–48.

Schneider, Anne and Helen Ingram (1990) "Behavioral Assumptions of Policy Tools", *The Journal of Politics*, 52(2), 510–529.

Svensson, Lennart, Per-Erik Ellström, and Göran Brulin (2007) "Introduction: On Interactive Research", *International Journal of Action Research*, 3(3), 233–249.

Timmers, Tanya M., Tineke M. Willemsen, and Kea G. Tijdens (2010) "Gender Diversity Policies in Universities: A Multi-perspective Framework of Policy Measures", *Higher Education*, 59, 719–735.

Van der Doelen, Frans C. J. (2005) "The 'Give-and-Take' Packaging of Policy Instruments: Optimizing Legitimacy and Effectiveness", in Marie-Louise Bemelmans-Videc, Ray C. Rist, and Evert Vedung (eds.) *Carrots, Sticks & Sermons: Policy Instruments and Their Evaluation*. New Brunswick: Transaction, pp. 129–148.

Vedung, Evert (1991) *Utvärdering i politik och förvaltning*. Lund: Studentlitteratur.

7
Between Knowledge and Power: Triggering Structural Change for Gender Equality from Inside in Higher Education Institutions

Viviane Albenga

Introduction

Tackling gender inequality in higher education institutions implies specific challenges for the politics of feminist knowledge transfer. Such institutions tend to reproduce gender inequalities in their own structures and functioning as well as in the process of knowledge production. For this reason, both aspects are addressed by gender mainstreaming, as has been the case as part of the EU-funded structural change projects undertaken under the FP7 and Horizon 2020 framework programmes. Higher education has been a key area of concern for the EU's gender mainstreaming strategy. Gender mainstreaming, moreover, has been promoted at the impetus of the European Union (EU) (see, e.g., the *Roadmap for Equality between women and men, 2006–2010*; and the *Strategy for Equality between women and men, 2010–2015*). Teresa Rees defines gender mainstreaming as "the promotion of gender equality through its systematic integration into all systems and structures, into all policies, processes, and procedures, into the organization and its culture, into ways if seeing and doing" (Rees, 2005). Its implementation requires the work of "gender mainstreaming advocates" (Hafner-Burton and Pollack, 2000, p. 440) struggling to ensure that their own institution leads on gender equality policies.

In terms of higher education, the "leaky pipeline" – through which many women "leak" from academic careers – has become an issue with regards to the EU's commitment to a knowledge-based society (Rees, 2007, p. 7). While expert groups, such as the Helsinki Group and the Expert Group on Women and Science, were established already by the late 1990s, a structural change approach has appeared far more recently. The relevance of gender for a knowledge-based society is thus promoted in the perspective of Europe 2020.

The French national context has also recently proved favourable to a mainstreaming approach. The actions of the Women's Rights Ministry between May 2012 and May 2014, which clearly stood up for mainstreaming equality in all policy fields, led the Ministry of Higher Education and Research to adopt its own actions and training plans in the area of gender equality.

Drawing on a survey carried out at Sciences Po Paris University, wherein the most significant stakeholders were interviewed, this chapter aims at highlighting the tensions and leverages for academics conducting a diagnosis to trigger structural changes within the institution, as gender mainstreaming implies this structural change. More broadly, it aims at questioning the conflicts of knowledges that occur when diagnosing gender inequalities in a knowledge production institution. As emphasized in the Introduction to this book, transferring feminist knowledge implies structural and institutional change as well as individual learning and transformation. Several notable studies have shown the resistances at play in institutions where a gender mainstreaming approach has been implemented by gender-sensitive professionals (Perrier, 2015). At first sight, it may appear that being a gender scholar diagnosing inequalities in one's own institution, as occurred in the case considered here, might limit the resistances and the tensions regarding that diagnosis. Nonetheless, I will demonstrate that conflicts of knowledges still do exist, highlighting the political nature of feminist knowledge transfer and unravelling the power relationships at stake. Power relationships can be read, for instance, in the denial of the scholarly capital retained by the gender expert. Indeed, drawing upon the theoretical framework of Bourdieu (1998), several works have already analysed the academic institution as a field with an unequal distribution of different kinds of capital that reproduce gender inequalities (Beaufaÿs and Krais, 2005; Vásquez-Cupeiro and Martín Fernández, 2007).

Specific attention must, therefore, be paid to the scholarly capital constituted by feminist knowledge and gender expertise. Possessing scholarly capital in gender studies – which can materialize in a specialized and recognized PhD, for instance – enables the use of feminist knowledge in gender expertise. However, the transfer of this knowledge into gender expertise implies taking into account different degrees of awareness regarding gender equality. In a higher education institution, many stakeholders are academics and recognize the scholarly capital of gender studies. Moreover, some are themselves gender-sensitive, which means that they might already have incorporated feminist knowledge, and/or are eager to increase their own knowledge on, and awareness of, gender equality. They can detail their own representation of what gender equality means and learn from expertise. Other stakeholders, moreover, can recognize the expertise held by gender scholars without themselves being academics. Still others can deny it, whether they themselves are academics or not. All of these configurations contribute to framing the conflicts of knowledges and power relationships that I will highlight in this chapter.

The first section of this chapter consists of setting up the institutional context to be placed under scrutiny and discussing the theoretical and methodological background of the study. In the second section, I will draw upon critical framework analysis to stress the conflicts of knowledges at play in the definition of gender equality, and the way this questions both the positioning of the gender expert carrying out the diagnosis and issues of individual and institutional resistances. In the third section, I will focus on gender-sensitive frames and the conflicts between structural and individual change that should be challenged by gender expertise.

Mainstreaming gender in a knowledge production institution

Stakeholder interviews were conducted as a part of the survey carried out at Sciences Po Paris under EGERA (Effective Gender Equality in Research and the Academia), a project funded by the Seventh Framework Programme (FP7) of the European Commission (2014–2017). This adopts a structural, multi-level approach to gender (in)equality in research and academia. EGERA brings together eight research and higher education institutions across the EU and Turkey, bound by a shared commitment to a dual objective: achieving gender equality in research and academia and strengthening the gender dimension in research. The project intends to cover the full scope of gender inequalities as well as challenge the governance and evaluation rules and practices (i.e. power structures) in which these are embedded.

Sciences Po Paris is a French university that dates back to 1872. At that time, it was a private higher education institution named the "Free School of Moral and Political Sciences" (Ecole libre des sciences morales et politiques), established shortly after the Paris Commune to make sense of major political events. In 1945, it was nationalized and divided into two different governing structures: the National Foundation of Political Science (Fondation nationale des sciences politiques – FNSP), a private foundation; and the Paris Institute of Political Studies (the Institut d'études politiques de Paris– IEP de Paris), a public establishment.[1] Sciences Po is neither a university in the true sense of the term nor a French "higher school" ("Grande école"): its status differs from both kinds of institutions. The dynamics of its evolution are also specific and follow neither the content nor the pace of French higher education reforms. It aims at training the future elite in a wide array of professions, from journalism to public affairs and diplomacy.

It has also internationalized its recruitment, in terms of both students and academics. The Sciences Po website emphasizes that, according to the QS World University Rankings, "Among the 200 [top] ranked universities, Sciences Po ranks among the best. In Political Science and International relations, as in Sociology, Sciences Po is ranked 1st among French universities."

International rankings matter for Sciences Po's governance. With the exception of researchers who are members of the National Center for Scientific Research (CNRS), and are therefore civil servants, the majority of Sciences Po employees are hired under private law through the foundation. In 2013, a total of 1,026 employees – 58.2% of whom are women – worked at Sciences Po. This figure excludes both CNRS researchers and associate professors contracted by other universities and teaching part time at Sciences Po as well as approximately 4,000 external associate lecturers from a wide variety of backgrounds involved with specific courses.[2]

To complete the picture of its background, it must also be noted that Sciences Po is characterized by its specific commitment to gender studies through the Gender Knowledge Teaching and Research Programme (Programme de Recherche et d'Enseignement des Savoirs sur le Genre – PRESAGE). PRESAGE was established in 2010, under the patronage of the former General Director of Sciences Po. Due to the central position of Sciences Po in the landscape of higher education and research in social sciences in France, this programme has drawn considerable attention from the media and the general public. Furthermore, the EU's EGERA project, as an innovative programme aiming at mainstreaming gender knowledge throughout research and academic curricula, constitutes a step further towards effective gender equality. It aims at fostering structural change through the implementation of transformative Gender Equality Action Plans. These plans articulate a structural understanding of gender inequalities and bias in research, alongside a set of measures and actions. These actions cover issues of recruitment, retention, appraisal, and empowerment of women in research as well as the mainstreaming of gender knowledge across disciplinary fields. The project is led and managed by Sciences Po, as both the leading institution of the consortium and an institution, among others, involved in the implementation of a gender equality plan.

EGERA primarily involves carrying out detailed diagnoses of the gender inequalities at play in implementing organizations. As such, from early 2014 onwards, a core team of two economists, a political scientist, and a sociologist began collecting data on a variety of indicators through econometric analysis and personal interviews with key stakeholders. Two main surveys were conducted in Sciences Po since the launch of EGERA in March, 2014. The first survey, which provides the data used for this chapter, consisted of semi-structured interviews with 15 stakeholders, including five individuals in management positions within the institution's Education Department; the Scientific Director; the Director for Communication; the Director for International Affairs and Cooperation; the Director of the On-the-job training Programme; the Fundraising Director of Strategy and Development; the Director of Human Resources; the Financial Director; a member of the Equality Committee attached to the Workplace Council; the Chief Administrative Officer; and the General Director of Sciences Po. In total, eight women and seven men were interviewed. This gender balance illustrates the parity that has been achieved in the Executive Board. Important positions, such as that of Scientific Director, Director of Education, and Chief Administrative Officer, are currently held by women.

Interview grids focused on the diagnosis of gender inequalities in the institution and the prognosis of what should be done in terms of each specific position. Moreover, each stakeholder was asked to express their personal definitions of gender equality and their diagnoses of key points regarding gender inequalities at Sciences Po. For instance, the members of the Department of Education acknowledged more freely the gender gap between students than the gender pay gap, although the issue of work–life balance is a matter of concern for them as members of Sciences Po's staff. Other sources were also used, such as the latest legally enforced annual Gender Equality Report (*Rapport de situation comparée*, 2013) by the Human Resources Department. Data collected through the interviews was complemented by a second survey, conducted through an econometric analysis. However, I have decided not to explore this second survey in this chapter, as my primary focus, in keeping with the scope of this book, is the politics of gender and feminist knowledge transfer within the specific context of a knowledge production institution.

Drawing upon the empirical material outlined above, my analysis is twofold. First, I focus on the interactions between the female gender scholar conducting the interviews and the stakeholders, each of whose academic capital differs from that of the other stakeholders and from that of the author. According to their institutional positions and knowledge of gender issues, I identify different discursive framings that oscillate between denial, underestimation, and the willingness to engage with gender inequalities. Drawing upon critical frame analysis, I then identify frameworks that emphasize potential leverages for change and those which are worth discussing from a feminist point of view. Critical frame analysis has been mobilized to make sense of the discursive aspect of gender equality policies in Europe. This approach emphasizes the open meaning of "gender equality". The concept of a "policy frame" is crucial here, employing the sense that Verloo (2005, p. 20) suggests when she defines it as "an organizing principle that transforms fragmentary or incidental information into a structured and meaningful policy problem, in which a solution is implicitly or explicitly included" (Lombardo et al., 2009, p. 11).

The open meaning of gender equality implies several assumptions. The most obvious is that the actors do not share the same meaning or definition of the term. In our case, the stakeholders interviewed at Sciences Po differed when diagnosing gender inequalities in the institution, and when defining what gender equality should encompass, and how it should be achieved. However, the open meaning of gender equality also highlights the inherent contradictions or fragmentary nature of a framework for any actor. The interactions between actors, embedded in power relationships, impact upon the meaning of gender equality, but do not fix it completely. Critical frame analysis also adds a normative dimension that highlights the construction of problems and policies. A "frame" in terms of gender equality "is a configuration of positions on dimensions of diagnosis and prognosis", which includes "normative assumptions" that "affect the interpretation of policy problems and the construction of policy measures formulated to solve them" (Verloo, 2005, in Lombardo et al., 2009, p. 11). It is important to emphasize that frames are conscious or unconscious, discursive, and practical. All these dimensions will be brought to light by the discourses of Sciences Po's stakeholders. In this sense, the competing frames unravel the conflicts of knowledge between the sociologist conducting the interviews and the stakeholders as well as between the stakeholders themselves.

In an institution of academic knowledge production, the moment of diagnosing the gender inequalities at play is crucial for negotiating the effective implementation of gender equality policies. It is at this stage that institutional stakeholders are likely to use their own intellectual and scholarly capital to frame the issue in accordance with competing views. How these competing frames are constructed is precisely the point I wish to underline. This provides a valid entry point for exploring the tensions between gender expertise, feminist knowledge, and the frameworks embedded in institutional practices. This is true even when an institution is firmly committed to a plan for structural change, as in our case study. All of these dimensions are illuminated by the discourses of Sciences Po's stakeholders, following the discursive-sociological approach developed by Lombardo and Forest (2012, 2015). While this method refers to studies focused on the larger-scale implementation of gender equality policies, adopted at the regional or national levels, or at the level of supranational institutions, it can also inform the analysis of policies adopted at the level of a single organization, such as a university.

The critical frame analysis I refer to can also be illustrated by the analysis of Malin Rönnblom (2009) concerning the issue of gender equality in a growth- and knowledge-based society. She characterizes the EU's discourses as contradictory:

> Even though the concept of discrimination is mostly applied to individuals and generally not in a collective manner [...] this articulation at least enables an understanding of gender equality in terms of relations and conflicts.
>
> (Rönnblom, 2009, p. 115)

This analysis stresses some points relevant for the analysis put forth in this chapter. Notably, the overarching goal of gender equality can imply targeting only women, or both men and women, as well as individuals or groups.

As such, in the second section, I will focus on the most gender-sensitive frames articulated by significant stakeholders. They emphasize that gender inequalities can be explained both by specific gender bias in higher education and by the way in which the masculine and feminine trajectories of career paths are embedded and interdependent. Consequently, the masculine standard of scientific excellence, coupled with the effects of masculine trajectories on feminine ones, is taken into account. This means that both women and men should be targeted by the measures implemented. It is this tension between structural change and individually based positive actions that reveals a challenge in play for feminist knowledge transfer.

Conflict between knowledges: Being an academic gender expert in a higher education institution

Feminist knowledge transfer implies linking a range of issues involved in gender mainstreaming: gender balance in decision-making and positions of power; issues of human resources, such as inequalities in career progression and wages; the gendering of research and curricula; and building a gender-friendly work environment through an effective work–life balance policy, and fighting both gender-based violence and sexual harassment. When these issues were discussed during the interviews, very different degrees of knowledge and awareness were revealed among stakeholders. For example, during one interview, I asked a stakeholder about the gender pay gap highlighted in Sciences Po's latest annual Gender Equality Report. As he was not even aware of the existence of this data, his denial of gender inequalities was sincere. This reveals that working as a gender expert entails more than simply transferring academic feminist knowledge. Rather, gender expertise should be an inclusive tool, taking into account the existence of a lack of awareness as well as of denial and resistances regarding gender equality.

In this sense, gender expertise can produce both inclusive and academic knowledge, but the assessment of the value of this knowledge remains a major issue. Indeed, the scholarly capital in gender studies can be underestimated – or even denied – by stakeholders who refute the very existence of gender inequality, or who underestimate certain key issues. In this section, I illustrate how, and to what extent, the interviewed stakeholders were aware of certain gender inequalities in higher education in general, as well as in the specific case of Sciences Po. Some stressed the processes that reproduce inequalities. However, in other interviews, certain aspects of gender knowledge were dismissed or marginalized. These resistances are not only a challenge to be tackled; they also reveal that expertise has to be undertaken in the form of an exchange of views, which is not merely a transfer of knowledge from academic to institutional stakeholders. Indeed, stakeholders may be placed in a much more powerful institutional position than academics conducting a diagnosis. This positioning regarding the relative power positions of stakeholders are reflected in the process of the interview itself.

With respect to these conflicts between the stakeholders' knowledge(s), on the one hand, and the structural approach to be provided by gender expertise, on the other, three main findings can be set out:

- Narrow meanings of equality may be in play, wherein equality means "parity" and gender inequality is replaced by "discrimination";
- Structural sexism, homophobia, and gender-based violence may be hidden by "discrimination"; and
- The denial of gender inequality, particularly relating the gender pay gap to seniority and sector-based gaps.

The first finding sheds light on the limited meanings afforded to gender (in)equality, as French public debates and policies place an emphasis upon issues of parity and discrimination. The first element that must be analysed is the willingness to embrace a deeper knowledge of gender inequality. Challenging gender inequality is a matter of awareness, but also one of knowledge and action, as argued by the General Director of Sciences Po, who frames gender equality as a political goal for both students and staff:

> As the director of Sciences Po, I feel accountable in two ways regarding gender equality. Firstly, as the Director of a higher education and research institution, I consider that gender equality is a fundamental concern for anyone in charge of training future stakeholders for many professions. [...] Secondly, and that is not of lesser importance, I am a kind of company manager and I am accountable for gender-based relationships within our institution which [have] reproduce[d] structural inequalities for a long time. I am accountable for being aware of these inequalities in order to eliminate them. This task is not the easiest one because we must not assume that assessing inequalities is enough. [...] It would not be appropriate to consider the issue [of gender equality] resolved within our institution merely because we are politically aware of it.
>
> (Interview with the General Director of Sciences Po, 2014)

All of the Directors interviewed stressed that parity has been achieved in the Executive Board. The female Chief Administrative Officer highlighted that "the most important management positions are currently held by women". The General Director assumed that parity in executive boards is even more important than parity in administrative boards. This emphasis upon gender balance in decision-making refers to a meaning of equality which is close to "parity".

Here, a gap may be discerned between this frame and the academic knowledge regarding the issue at hand. Indeed, the underrepresentation of women in positions at the top of the academic career ladder has drawn considerable scholarly attention, recalling the notion of the leaky pipeline (Alper, 1993), that is the gradual exit of women from academia along their way to top positions or the glass ceiling acting as an invisible barrier. The explanations for the existence of these phenomena rest upon gender norms. These norms refer to the implicit masculine standard regarding full commitment to professional careers (European Commission, 2008), or specific skills and specialization. Therefore, these norms underline opaque selection and promotion procedures (Alonso et al., 2011; European Commission, 2009; Forest and Mergaert, 2015). The issue of gender imbalance in positions of power within academia is therefore considered to be the result of the gendered inequalities in professional trajectories. As argued below, some gender-sensitive stakeholders highlighted these processes.

However, for the majority of the stakeholders interviewed, parity in terms of Sciences Po's Executive Board demonstrates that equality prevails in the institution. Two female stakeholders noticed that this gender balance in decision-making disappears when looking at positions of academic power. For instance, there is currently no female head of a research centre, where most of the knowledge within the institution is produced. Therefore, gender expertise opened up the meaning of equality in the interviews conducted, revealing that the research process itself, by being inclusive, can be considered a form of feminist knowledge transfer. This transfer is not always efficient as resistances can rely upon the de-politicizing nature of more general framing, such as diversity or anti-discrimination. Structural sexism, homophobia, and gender-based violence can thus be easily hidden behind "discrimination" or "diversity politics" (Sénac, 2015), which have developed much to the expense of gender (in)equality concerns in France since the mid-2000s.

As such, the second finding to be highlighted in this section relates to the interviews opening up about these issues. I systematically questioned stakeholders about sexism, homophobia, and gender-based violence. According to those interviewed, sexism is not a structural behaviour at Sciences Po, but a marginal one, concerning a minority of individuals. Gender inequality is mainly framed through the category of "discrimination". Sciences Po's Scientific Director stressed that indirect discrimination prevents female academics from advancing further along the career ladder, as the "right" candidate is implicitly represented as a man entirely devoted to science. Such gender-based representations, she argued, discriminate against women applying for academic positions. This widespread use of the term "discrimination" should be related here to "the French invention of discrimination", as Didier Fassin (2002) dubbed the common use of the term since the end of the 1990s, a category that can hide other public problems, such as gender-based violence. As shown by Sénac (2012, 2015), discrimination is even more loosely framed within the context of diversity politics, wherein diversity, merely used as a portmanteau word in France, tends to empty out the political meaning of all the forms of discrimination it claims to cover.

While gender-based violence has not been directly targeted by the institution so far, sexual harassment has been a matter of concern. It was one of the first issues identified for the Gender Equality Officer, hired in May 2014, who has since developed a Watch Unit and designed a booklet about sexual harassment and violence, for both staff and students. As part of our survey, a member of the Executive Board had already emphasized the gap between Sciences Po and its foreign partners regarding sexual harassment:

> We do not know how to manage these situations. We have no written rules while our foreign partners do have texts to refer to. Some female students complain when they come back to their University, they have lived difficult moments at Sciences Po, so we are asked about what our rules are and our definitions of harassment differ drastically.
>
> (Interview with a member of the Sciences Po Executive Board, 2014)

He consequently suggested that we investigate gender norms at Sciences Po according to the perceptions of foreign students, an investigation which is currently led by two female students via focus groups as part of the EGERA project. This highlights that interviews have caused leverages for change to arise, but this change implies deeper expertise. Moreover, this expertise involves students who are eager to be trained in gender studies as well as to take part in awareness-raising within the institution from the perspective of students. Yet, if the process of gender expertise can be reinforced by a certain lack of knowledge or certain resistances, certain aspects of gender knowledge can also, conversely, be denied or marginalized.

The third finding cited above illustrates this trend. The gender pay gap is denied as a manifestation of gender inequality and is instead related to the seniority of staff, and the sectors in which they work. It must be emphasized that, according to the Gender Equality Report (2013), the gender pay gap for administrative staff is not significant: 5% for 64% of staff. For another 24% of staff, a more significant gap appears but "is explained mainly by age and seniority distributions" (Sciences Po, 2013, p. 24). If the Report reveals a wider gender pay gap for academics, the interviews highlighted this as a sector-related and seniority-related impact. According to the General Director, the former highlights the need to target the students' choices in their early careers:

> The sector-related impacts really matter, as a graduate of the Communication School cannot achieve the same starting wage as a graduate of Finance and Strategy Studies working in a bank. This factor works also for our permanent academic staff. Some disciplines enable people to earn more money than other ones.
>
> (Interview with the General Director of Sciences Po, 2014)

A member of the Equality Committee of the Working Conditions Council, however, wondered if gender inequalities are completely related to indirect causes:

> We asked clear questions about wage equality between men and women and the only answer we got was that there wasn't any inequality. And if inequalities did exist, they are seniority-related.
>
> (Interview with a member of Sciences Po's Equality Committee
> of the Working Conditions Council, 2014)

The denial of our scholarly capital and gender knowledge emerged when we interviewed one stakeholder, who was convinced that gender inequality does not exist in career trajectories or in terms of wages at Sciences Po. First, he refused permission for his interview to be recorded, despite my appeal that this would help our work. The fact that I consequently had to take notes implied the existence of a more unequal position in this interview than in those with other stakeholders. The situation was all the more paradoxical given that this stakeholder was not an academic, unlike the other stakeholders, but it also helps to explain why the very situation of a sociological interview was misunderstood. His denial of gender inequality was brought to light when he remarked that:

> If two applicants are similar, we will prefer the female applicant. But we examine applicants at a given moment of their career. Gender equality is a nice idea in the absolute. But this issue makes no sense.
>
> (Interview with a non-academic stakeholder at Sciences Po, 2014)

As the denial was explicitly expressed, I attempted to encourage him to detail his opposition to the very issue of gender inequality. The institution's annual Gender Equality Report sets the objective of achieving gender balance in positions overwhelmingly occupied by women or men – including academic positions. Consequently, I asked him whether this indicator was relevant according in his view, to which he replied: "No, I do not think so, this issue is not relevant. I suppose that what I am saying is the opposite of everything you were taught!" (Interview with a non-academic stakeholder at Sciences Po, 2014). At this precise moment, our scholarly capital and expertise concerning gender were depreciated. However, I sought to take advantage of this situation to enquire as to his general point of view. He revealed his belief that gender discrimination could not exist in the institution because it would be "artificial", and would, therefore, be fought against.

This section closes with an example of clear denial both of gender inequality and of the capital of the gender expert. This aims to illustrate that gender expertise also has to negotiate with positions of power – when a stakeholder denies the very existence of gendered structural relationships when interviewed by a female sociologist in gender studies, she or he dismisses the very purpose of their analysis. This power relationship takes part in expertise itself, as it mirrors both institutional gender inequality and the lack of recognition of gender studies in the academic sphere. Resistances are part of expertise, and when they do not consist of denial, but rather of narrow meanings of gender equality, they can be used as a means of supporting the transfer of knowledge by a broadening of meaning and an exchange of views. This last situation appears specifically in the interviews with stakeholders who offer a sociological analysis of gender inequality in the institution, as well as leverage for change. The next section shows how the most gender-sensitive stakeholders provided a critical analysis and calls for action but also need critical gender expertise to trigger structural changes in gendered academic fields.

Gender-sensitive frames: Challenging masculine standards of excellence and enhancing women's careers

This third section demonstrates that resistances to structural change are not necessarily related to power relationships and conflicts of knowledge(s). They also rely on the difficult shift from targeting individuals, especially women, to a structural change approach. Schiebinger (2008) has emphasized the trend in higher education to "fix the women" rather than "to fix the institution" that produce gender inequalities. The challenge for gender expertise then consists of intertwining the structural analysis of gender inequality with actions targeting both women and men. Three main findings depict this tension between structural and individual change, as well as between feminist analysis and positive actions:

- Awareness regarding the masculine standard of excellence;
- Achieving gender equality through a modern and inclusive management of academic work; and
- Implementing positive actions, but targeting only women.

Regarding evaluation, two main biases can be identified, one "qualitative" and another "quantitative". The first bias is the implicit masculine standard of excellence. The second gender bias concerns the productivity-based definition of excellence, which pays attention to a number of publications and is related to the most recent evolutions of management in higher education (Forest and Mergaert, 2015). It discriminates against academics who take a break in their careers for several reasons, but especially against women because of maternity leave and because they take parental leave more often than men do.

The masculine standard of excellence may be the most difficult gender bias to challenge as it addresses the whole process of assessment and conferring value in the academic sphere. In other words, it is the very principle of academic capital which is threatened. Focusing on the recruitment and selection of full professors in The Netherlands, van den Brink and Benschop (2012) note that "excellence is not something one is born with but is the outcome of a stimulating work environment, infrastructure and social capital that has to be given meaning and valued in a certain context" (2012, p. 83). They highlight the processes of continuous and informal support between male academics, as "academic male elites nurture their male successors from the beginning of their career and teach them the informal rules of the field, so that they know how to survive in this highly political culture" (2012, p. 83).

Practices targeting gender equality thus differ from one academic discipline to another. However, according to van den Brink and Benschop, the difficulty remains in engaging with structural change, rather than just supporting some female individuals whose professional careers will be enhanced. Challenging the "masculine standard" in evaluation, as well as the gendered and unequal access to informal information, seem to be the major changes at stake. This specific gender bias is reinforced by an overarching blindness about the masculine standard that underlies academic excellence. Nonetheless, stakeholders who take part in processes of recruitment and promotion emphasize this bias without any specific questions being posed on the issue during our interview. Sciences Po's Scientific Director highlighted the fact that the main gender bias in evaluation resides in the criteria of selection and promotion:

> Things arose when they are asked [in selection committees] who is the best candidate for them. They won't say a man or a woman, they are not such fools, but the way they describe who is the best candidate is gendered. And I don't know really how we could fight against this. They have the sense that their criteria are objective: if I count the number of papers, the opportunities of being visiting professor, and if men have more, it will mean that they are objectively better. It is very difficult to make them understand that men are more inserted in appropriate networks and that they have more opportunities of being visiting professors, all things that have already been shown regarding the gendered processes in academic careers.
>
> (Interview with the Scientific Director of Sciences Po, 2014)

In the same way, another member of the Executive Board brings into light the gendered biases behind the criteria of excellence:

> I have very precise memories regarding the choice of candidates to get "honoris causa" and the few women who were proposed were "swept" away because if they were not the first one in their discipline, they did not represent a matter of interest. What matters are papers, which means we

can go on reproducing inequalities for a long time. I think that displaying a chart, on every website, concerning each element of recruitment, this idea of transparency and equal access, would be important.

(Interview with a member of the Executive Board of Sciences Po, 2014)

Despite this awareness regarding the gendered biases of "objective" excellence, these are left mostly unchallenged in practice. As highlighted by the aforementioned quotations, the criteria of publications remain core to evaluation. This brings us to the second finding related to an inclusive management of academic careers.

Challenging the criteria of academic excellence cannot be confronted directly as it is an overarching issue of the higher education system. The issue of evaluation and governance in higher education questions the implementation of the New Public Management, and the role of the stakeholders, when institutions of higher education and research become more autonomous from state institutions. Consequently, taking into account parental leave in the evaluation process is the only measure currently considered by Sciences Po's stakeholders.

The General Director addressed the issue of the wage inequalities as a consequence of the gendered bias in publication-based evaluation:

We benefit luckily from a kind of flexibility in matter of evaluation rules. The evaluation of the quality per se of an academic relies upon objective criteria related to publications. But we can decide that the absence of production of a significant paper for two years, related to the birth of a child, cannot discriminate [against] someone for their wage increase.

(Interview with the General Director of Sciences Po, 2014)

Nevertheless, productivity is a matter of scientific legitimacy, even more so for women. The Scientific Director evoked a current debate at Sciences Po about the evaluation of the tenure-track for those women who have had a child during the tenure-track process:

I know that here, in this department, women who have had a child are given a seventh year to get tenured. This means that they enter their careers later, since they expect one year more to get tenured because they have had a child. As we were discussing this procedure, female academics said that they preferred to be evaluated one year more, instead of being evaluated with less demanding criteria. Indeed, they feared that they might be perceived as being less legitimate if they obtained tenure based on lower academic criteria due to maternity leave. As far as I am concerned, this measure does not mean getting tenured with lower standards. Because they were on tenure track for six years, they had a child and were given a year for that, so they should be evaluated on their work

for five years. [...] We finally decided that it will be a free choice, to get one more year or ... we'll see what the women in this situation will choose.
(Interview with the Scientific Director of Sciences Po, 2014)

Resistances here are expressed by female academics who fear being misjudged and losing scientific legitimacy. This suggests that limited discussion has been engaged in so far at Sciences Po regarding the implementation of positive actions in any field related to Human Resources Management. Nonetheless, these positive actions are forecasted.

The third finding to be discussed in this section stresses the tension between positive actions to enhance women's careers and the lack of a structural approach inherent in targeting only women. Here, gender expertise leads to highlighting the fact that actions implemented do not fit within a structural change approach. For instance, the Scientific Director of Sciences Po observed that gendered inequalities continue to deepen all along academic career paths. According to her own research, it is not before entering their careers, but rather once they enter them that women take on less highly valued tasks. She highlights the fact that "in the French case, all [the gendered career] is played [out] during the first five years after being recruited", because this is the moment when "careers are being adjusted inside [within] the couple" or when "couples get separated and they [the female academics] become alone in charge of the children" (Interview with the Scientific Director of Sciences Po, 2014). Thus, when academics are in their 30s, the beginnings of their careers draw gendered and unequal trajectories in academia. Masculine and feminine trajectories are embedded and dependent on each other. In other words, women's careers cannot be the only target when fighting against gendered inequalities. The intertwining between the careers of their spouses, for example, also matters for understanding the key moments at which to enhance women's careers.

This outlook stresses both masculine and feminine trajectories in the achievement of gender equality, which is a feminist and structural analysis. Moreover, women are not always put in charge of the most highly valued tasks, which highlights the overarching issue of a lack of career management in French higher education. Nevertheless, the Scientific Director emphasized the fact that young female academics tend not to project themselves in a career of their own. She suggests supporting women's careers by encouraging them to apply and by preparing those who are eager to take charge of scientific direction as the heads of research centres. She herself explained having already guaranteed more gender-balanced selection committees to this end:

We compel the selection committees to have at least one woman among their members, and actually, often there is more than just one. I have never believed that this would change the world, but it limits the direct discrimination: when a woman is there, men cannot say certain things, when there are several women indeed because only one is not enough, that's what we have shown in researches to which I have participated. It limits open or direct discrimination, but not indirect discrimination.

(Interview with the Scientific Director of Sciences Po, 2014)

This issue of "indirect discrimination" addresses a challenge for gender experts: how can we trigger structural change in which stakeholders are aware of the structural nature of gender equality, but are required to challenge processes instead of targeting individuals? A return to a critical feminist perspective is therefore needed to better inform the actions to be implemented in this regard.

Conclusion

To summarize the context of the gender expertise, I provided at Sciences Po as part of the EGERA project, I have shown that the scholarly capital of the gender expert can be underestimated, denied, or remain un-acknowledged. Moreover, this appears paradoxical in an institution where a teaching and research programme for mainstreaming gender knowledge was implemented several years ago. Gender mainstreaming in higher education has to face conflicts of knowledge(s) and power relationships regarding scholarly capital and institutional positions. In this context, the expert conducting a survey on gender inequality must remain comprehensive during the interview itself, while at the same time opening up gender issues to make the frames involved very explicit. Considering that gender equality implies different definitions helps experts to pose questions to stakeholders without increasing conflicts of knowledge(s). The meaning of gender (in)equality has to be opened up when the existing frames tend to narrow it. In addition, the structural nature of gender inequality has to be shown or highlighted by experts.

First, we have seen that narrow meanings of gender equality (such as parity) have to be broadened. Moreover, definitions of inequality which equate it with discrimination or diversity can hide several crucial issues such as structural sexism, homophobia, and gender-based violence. Feminist knowledge can be dismissed when the gender pay gap is not considered to reflect a gender-based inequality, but is instead related to issues of seniority or the specificities of a particular sector. Gender expertise has to shift from the analysis of these conflicts of knowledge(s) in terms of resistances to a structural and shared definition of equality in an institution. This could be achieved by the dissemination of the diagnosis undertaken by the expert(s) and the exchange of views in participatory seminars. This addresses the issue of the step from gender expertise to gender training within a single institution.

Van den Brink and Benschop (2012) suggest that gender inequality in academia is like a "seven-headed dragon". Even if gender equality is not completely problematized as a structural issue, the range of issues stressed by the stakeholders interviewed validates this metaphor of a "seven-headed dragon" to be fought against. Understanding the frames involves enables the inclusion of stakeholders in future negotiations for structural change. That is why interviewing the most important stakeholders in an institution and determining the widest possible range of points of view matter immensely. Some questions remain open, however, such as the involvement of men in the design and implementation of gender equality policies. For example, work–life balance can trigger resistances when it appears to seek to manage private life. Nonetheless, the most gender-sensitive stakeholders are conscious that masculine and feminine trajectories impact one another other, but men are not yet considered a target for change. Therefore, a tension does exist between the recognition of the structural nature of gender inequality and the positive actions that only target women. This tension has to be challenged by gender expertise.

Finally, gender expertise should be an inclusive tool in a knowledge production institution, opening up the range of gender-related issues and linking them in a structural approach. It should be an instrument that includes a community of actors to produce knowledge, even if this production must face power relationships. Yet, gender expertise should also remain a critical tool, embedded in feminist knowledge, and contributing to transferring and further developing this knowledge within each institution.

Notes

1. For further information on the governing structures of Sciences Po, please see http://www.sciencespo.fr/en/content/5/governance-sciences-po
2. Further information pertaining to the staff of Sciences Po may be accessed here: http://blogs.sciences-po.fr/recherche-news/2013/07/17/sciences-po-ranked-as-frances-top-university-in-political-science-international-relations-sociology-and-history/

References

Alonso, Alba, Marta Lois, and Isabelle Diaz (2011) "Is Gender Mainstreaming Helping Women Scientists? Evidence from Research Policies in Spain." Paper Presented at the *ECPG Conference*, Budapest.

Alper, Joe (1993) "The Pipeline Is Leaking Women All the Way Along", *Science*, 260(5106), 409–411.

Beaufaÿs, Sandra and Beate Krais (2005) "Femmes dans les carrières scientifiques en Allemagne: les mécanismes cachés du pouvoir", *Travail, genre et sociétés*, 14, 49–68.

Bourdieu, Pierre (1998) *Practical Reason*. Stanford: Stanford University Press.

European Commission (2008) *Mapping the Maze: Getting More Women to the Top in Research.* Luxembourg: Office for Official Publications of the European Communities.

———— (2009) *Monitoring Progress Towards Gender Equality in the 6th Framework Programme – Synthesis Report.* Luxembourg: Publications Office of the European Union.

Fassin, Didier (2002) "L'invention française de la discrimination", *Revue française de science politique*, 52, 403–423.

Forest, Maxime and Lut Mergaert (2015) "Incorporating Gender and Diversity", in R Dingwall and L. MacDonnell (eds.) *The Handbook of Research Management.* London: Sage.

Hafner-Burton, Emile M. and Mark A. Pollack (2000) "Mainstreaming Gender in the European Union", *Journal of European Public Policy*, 7(3), 432–456.

Lombardo, Emanuela and Maxime Forest (eds.) (2012) *The Europeanization of Gender Equality Policies: A Discursive-Sociological Approach.* Basingstoke and New York: Palgrave Macmillan.

Lombardo, Emanuela and Maxime Forest (2015) "The Europeanization of Gender Equality Policies: A Discursive-Sociological Approach", *Comparative European Politics*, 13(2), 222–239.

Lombardo, Emanuela, Petra Meier, and Mieke Verloo (eds.) (2009) *The Discursive Politics of Gender Equality: Stretching, Bending and Policy-Making.* Abingdon and New York: Routledge.

Perrier, Gwenaëlle (2015) "L'objectif d'égalité des sexes dans la mise en oeuvre des politiques d'emploi à Berlin: de la diffusion professionnelle aux difficiles réappropriations profanes", *Politix*, 109.

Rees, Teresa (2005) "Reflections on the Uneven Development of Gender Mainstreaming in Europe", *International Journal of Feminist Politics*, 7(4), pp. 555–574.

———— (2007) "Pushing the Gender Equality Agenda Forward in the European Union", in Mary Ann Danowitz Sagaria (ed.) *Women, Universities and Change: Gender Equality in the European Union and the United States.* New York: Palgrave Macmillan, pp. 7–21.

Rönnblom, Malin (2009) "Bending Towards Growth: Discursive Constructions of Gender Equality in an Era of Governance and Neoliberalism", in Emanuela Lombardo, Petra Meier, and Mieke Verloo (eds.) *The Discursive Politics of Gender Equality: Stretching, Bending and Policy-Making.* Abingdon and New York: Routledge, pp. 105–120.

Schiebinger, Londa (2008) "Introduction: Getting More Women into Science and Engineering – Knowledge Issues", in Londa Schiebinger (ed.) *Gendered Innovations in Science and Engineering.* Stanford: Stanford University Press, pp. 1–21.

Sciences Po (2013) *Rapport de situation comparée entre les femmes et les hommes.* Paris: Sciences Po.

Sénac, Réjane (2012) *L'Invention de la diversité.* Paris: Presses Universitaires de France.

———— (2015) *L'Egalité sous conditions. Genre, parité, diversité.* Paris: Presses de Sciences Po.

van den Brink, Marieke and Yvonne Benschop (2012) "Slaying the Seven-Headed Dragon: The Quest for Gender Change in Academia", *Gender, Work & Organization*, 19, 71–92.

Vásquez-Cupeiro, Susana and Juan Martin Fernández (2007) "Insiders Kingdoms – Mechanisms of Career Advancement in Spanish University", in Renata Siemienska and Annette Zimmer (eds.) *Gendered Career Trajectories in Academia in Cross-National Perspective.* Warsaw: Scholar, pp. 97–128.

Verloo, M. (2005) "Mainstreaming Gender Equality in Europe. A Critical Frame Analysis". *Greek Review of Social Research*, 117 (B'2005), 11–35.

Conclusions

María Bustelo, Lucy Ferguson, and Maxime Forest

Introduction

As set out in the introductory chapter, this book is an attempt to offer a critical reflection on the politics of feminist knowledge transfer, bringing together analytical and theoretical work on gender expertise and gender training. Grounded in both the theory of feminist knowledge transfer and experiences of gender training and gender expertise, the chapters elaborate on emerging bodies of literature to advance further what have, to date, been primarily practice-oriented debates. This book articulates an understanding of processes of feminist knowledge transfer as pursuing a transformative agenda, rooted in a structural approach to gender inequality. Feminist knowledge is framed as situated, depending on the standpoints of different knowers. These standpoints do not only result from different disciplinary backgrounds and status. They also reflect different knowledge transfer scenarios – for example, EU member states and countries of the Global South. This book also articulates an explicit acknowledgement of the political nature of the contexts (cultural, institutional, or organizational) in which this knowledge is being transferred and of the potential for contestation. All chapters embrace a reflexive approach, adopting varying degrees of critique towards the biases and limitations this transfer process can reveal. Indeed, the very notion of transfer has been placed under scrutiny, in order to challenge hierarchies of knowledges and place increased emphasis on the dynamic and participatory nature of such a process. For this reason, this book also addresses resistances and contestation as inherent to transferring knowledge from a feminist perspective.

The contributors to this book have engaged with the idea of feminism as a vehicle for gender knowledge, exploring to different extents how the current political and economic climate is shaping new constraints for a transformative feminist agenda. To this end, our main concern was the "instruments" and sub-set of tools and methods used to actively transfer feminist knowledge. By shedding light on how these instruments are being used in different knowledge transfer scenarios, the chapters contribute significantly to further refining notions of gender expertise and gender training. Both are analysed in the light of their relation to gender mainstreaming as a broader transformative strategy. More specifically, they are analysed as devises for governmentality, through which social relationships and representations, that is ways of doing things and embedded power structures, can be challenged.

In this concluding chapter, we will first identify the differences and complementarities that have emerged between the respective contributions. We explore how different authors engage with the broader questions and research agenda set out in the Introduction. With respect to similarities, authors largely converge in terms of challenging gender mainstreaming processes; reclaiming the feminist nature of gender knowledge transfer; and underlining the importance of contexts in which such knowledge is transferred. At the same time, differences are evident in terms of the level of analysis; the knowledge transfer scenarios on which they focus; and their level of optimism with respect to the potential of gender expertise and gender training to transform gendered power relations. Second, the Conclusion develops a set of key reflections from this comparative analysis of the contributions, elaborating upon the contested notion of knowledge transfer; the different standpoints and scenarios reflected on by the authors; and the attention paid to intersectionality. Finally, we develop an overarching proposal based on the findings and analysis of the book. Namely, to reclaim the "feminist" nature of knowledge transfer processes. Calling attention to attempts at de-politicizing gender knowledge, and the risk of co-optation by a neoliberal framing, we insist on the development of professional ethics for feminist knowledge transfer. In this vein, we follow Elisabeth Prügl's insights, drawn from Jürgen Habermas' deliberative ethics, on the need for gender experts and trainers. The approach we call for must create conditions for deliberation and contestation, thus reclaiming the political content of gender knowledge transfer. These broad reflections are complemented by a series of recommendations for moving forward, coupled with a tentative future research agenda.

Convergences and differences

As set out in the Introduction, this book presents a diverse range of approaches to feminist knowledge transfer. In order to tease out some of the richness of this diversity, we first explore the similarities between the chapters, before addressing what makes them both different and complementary. In terms of similarities and convergences, first, the chapters are all located in a particular political-economic context in which gender mainstreaming processes are being increasingly questioned, by both feminist and non-feminist actors. Beyond early feminist critiques, emphasizing the risks of diluting gender equality policies via mainstreaming, and of de-politicizing feminist claims by incorporating them to governance structures, new critical voices also arise. These denounce the unachieved institutionalization of gender mainstreaming two decades after it was established as a new global policy paradigm in this field. Whereas "dilution" was also triggered by the merging of gender into broader diversity mainstreaming (Sénac, 2012), the financial and economic crisis that began in 2008 also brought about changes in policy agendas, with gender equality moving down the ladder of political priorities (Bettio et al., 2012; Bustelo, 2014).

This book demonstrates a need to reflect not only on the broader processes of gender mainstreaming but also to engage with the conceptual and practical issues involved in its implementation. By providing different perspectives on the knowledge transfer mechanisms offered by gender mainstreaming in a variety of contexts, the authors collectively contribute to this broader reflection and offer a range of case studies to better understand the power dynamics involved in such an implementation process. Their contributions are especially welcome as gender expertise and gender training have been cited as the two main supporting instruments – if not the actual pre-conditions – for effective gender mainstreaming strategies. By exploring the practice of feminist knowledge transfer, and its accompanying challenges and tensions, these chapters challenge the potential of gender expertise and gender training as resources for gender mainstreaming strategies. The authors' standpoints matter immensely here. For instance, one critique that has grown in the field of international development and post-conflict management points at gender expertise and training as instruments of power which need to be mitigated by other types of "knowledges" on gender. This critique resonates far differently in the European context, where gender mainstreaming has clearly lost its momentum after having materialized to some extent in institutional and policy design over the late 1990s and 2000s.

Moreover, while the political and methodological standpoints of authors may vary, all express a concern for knowledge transfer to be "more feminist" in some way. This concern varies in scope and scale. For example, both Kunz and Davids and van Eerdewijk question the fundamental premise of a "transfer" of knowledge and the political implications of this for feminist transformation. Other chapters, such as that by Prügl in this book, argue that:

> [...] principles for the ethical conduct of gender experts can be derived from theories of deliberative democracy and from feminist methodology. [... The former] suggest that wielding feminist power should be approached as engaging in debate and struggle [...] that respond to principles of rational and un-coerced deliberation among equals and should produce institutional spaces where such deliberation is possible.

Principles of feminist methodology and ethics complement these because they provide additional attention to hierarchies and difference, and append to the democratic demand of inclusiveness a demand for reflexivity with regard to power relations" (p. 34).

Together, these principles offer a set of ethical guidelines for ensuring that knowledge transfer processes are committed to the feminist principles of deliberation and participation. Still other authors identify and address resistances to the term "feminist" itself, namely Lombardo and Mergaert, and Ferguson and Moreno. They propose ways to navigate such resistance while maintaining a commitment to feminist transformative politics.

As set out in the Introduction, there are strong debates at play over the difference between "gender" knowledge transfer and "feminist" knowledge transfer. Some authors, for example, distinguish between feminist and non-feminist gender experts in order to delineate more clearly the political commitments of practitioners. Davids and van Eerdewijk are among the most critical with regard to the "smothering" of feminist knowledge in gender knowledge transfer, emphasizing that:

> [... the] governmentalities that seek to govern gender relations are not only informed by feminist knowledges. In a neoliberal context, gender mainstreaming and with it gender knowledge intersect and articulate with neoliberal governmentalities and knowledge (p. 113).

This interruption of the relationship between feminism and gender, they argue:

> [...] occurs at certain points, places and phases of the organization. Instead of a mentality of gender difference as unequal power relations and institutional bias, as gender mainstreaming governmentalities set out for (see also Prügl, 2011), an unproblematic version of gender difference is installed; that mentality contributes to reproducing rather than challenging gender inequalities (p. 122).

In terms of the transformative potential of gender training and expertise, authors vary on the extent to which they consider this to be embedded in feminist knowledge and practice. For Kunz, as well as for Davids and van Eerdewijk – who are concerned with the circulation of gender knowledges in the Global South and with working from a postcolonial perspective – feminist knowledge should not be considered immune to reproducing unequal power relations. By contrast, those contributors who focus on interactions with international organizations, the EU or domestic policy bodies, and private organizations, highlight how the feminist content of transferred knowledge is subject to a continuous process of negotiation. This process is directed both towards commissioning organizations, to preserve the transformative potential of gender expertise and training from co-optation and de-politicization, and towards experts and trainers themselves, to ensure their collective ethics within the framework of a deliberative space.

Despite these differences in focus, all chapters in this book reaffirm the importance of context for exploring the potential for feminist knowledge transfer processes to contribute to transformation. In the EU case studies presented here, for example, the authors are concerned with navigating bureaucratic and individual resistances to gender training, within a context of a relatively institutionalized gender mainstreaming framework (see the chapters by Lombardo and Mergaert (Chapter 2); Callerstig (Chapter 6); and Albenga (Chapter 7). Other chapters, however, discuss the kinds of challenges presented for practitioners in contexts in which gender knowledge is neither institutionalized nor widely respected. This is the case in Ferguson and Moreno's study of the private sector, and in Kunz's research on Liberia, wherein conflicting perspectives on the meaning of gender equality rendered feminist engagement with such norms highly challenging. As such, as the chapters demonstrate, any analysis of feminist knowledge transfer needs to reflect explicitly on the institutional and policy dynamics in which it is embedded. So too must it explicitly reflect on the channels through which such transfer takes place, whether at the national or EU level, in development agencies, UN bodies, or the private sector. In terms of similarities, the chapters are united by the following premises: a desire to actively reflect on the practice of feminist knowledge transfer; a concern for the feminist content and politics of gender expertise; and a recognition of the importance of the context in which knowledge transfer takes place. We now go on to explore these in turn and pull out some key points for overall reflection. In terms of differences, three key dimensions can be identified: geography/scale; background/standpoint; and level of optimism for the possibilities of feminist knowledge transfer.

The first key difference between authors is the geographic region and scale on which they focus their analysis. Three chapters – those by Prügl, Ferguson and Moreno, and Davids and van Eerdewijk (Chapters 1, 3, and 4, respectively) – approach the concept of feminist knowledge transfer at the global level. Indeed, Prügl's chapter is concerned with overarching questions regarding the process of feminist knowledge transfer, without reference to a specific geographical or regional context. Ferguson and Moreno adopt a political economy approach to address concerns surrounding feminist knowledge transfer in the private sector from a global perspective, focusing on a range of case studies with private sector organizations in a number of countries. While Davids and van Eerdewijk are concerned with development institutions specifically, they do not limit their analysis to a specific geographical context. As such, they adopt a global approach to exploring feminist knowledge transfer. These broad-level analyses allow for a more conceptual and abstract discussion of some of the key issues involved in feminist knowledge transfer and contribute to the more analytical aspects of the debate.

By contrast, the chapters by Lombardo and Mergaert, Callerstig, and Albenga (Chapters 2, 6, and 7, respectively), are very much concerned with the relationship between feminist knowledge transfer and gender mainstreaming processes in the EU. All three chapters begin with a discussion of gender mainstreaming in the EU context, before going on to explore how this has played out in terms of gender training and expertise in different country contexts, specifically in Belgium, Sweden, and France, respectively. These chapters focus primarily on analysing the ways in which processes of feminist knowledge transfer represent the tensions inherent in the implementation of gender mainstreaming strategies. Whereas Lombardo and Mergaert adopt a broader perspective on these processes, by comparing data collected through different EU-funded projects, both Callerstig and Albenga focus their analyses on the level of specific organizations and policy areas. These different focuses are also to be characterized by the emphasis placed on training (Lombardo and Mergaert, and Callerstig) and expertise (Albenga). More limited to a specific geographical area is the chapter by Rahel Kunz (Chapter 5), which is concerned with post-conflict interventions in Liberia. Here, there is an explicit recognition of the complexities and tensions at play in the process of feminist knowledge transfer and the ways in which this interacts with different agendas concerning gender in the context of a society in transition. This combination of a global perspective with case studies in very different settings offers an interesting contrast for understanding the opportunities and limitations of feminist knowledge transfer in diverse contexts.

A second important feature that distinguishes the chapters concerns whether the authors are writing from a primarily insider or outsider perspective. It is important to acknowledge here that this is not a straightforward or absolute distinction. As set out in the Introduction, and as evidenced by the authors' biographies, most contributors work in various different capacities at once. Therefore, they have multiple identities related to feminist knowledge transfer – for example, gender trainer and academic, UN gender expert and researcher. These standpoints are not only related to the roles played with regards to feminist knowledge transfer, nor are they limited to the sole issue of status. Instead, they also potentially entail different sorts of resources, as well as a wide range of rationales behind each role or capacity, from knowledge production-oriented to market-driven activities. The fact that these authors shoulder different capacities is a feature typical of gender training and gender expertise activities. In fact, it is rare to find gender trainers or experts who do not engage, in one way or the other, in some type of research or academic activity. Conversely, almost every feminist academic in this sphere also engages in some form of gender training or consultancy work as a gender expert. These multiple hats worn by the authors offer a very interesting perspective for approaching and understanding feminist knowledge transfer.

Nevertheless, it is possible in each chapter to identify whether the author has approached the analysis primarily as an insider or an outsider. For example, insider perspectives are offered by Lombardo and Mergaert, Ferguson and Moreno, and Albenga, all of whom chart their experiences in the field of gender training and/or expertise to draw out the tensions and frustrations involved in such work. These authors use their own reflections as practitioners to reach broader conclusions on many of the pragmatic and political challenges involved in the process of feminist knowledge transfer. In contrast, this book features chapters which adopt a primarily outsider standpoint in their analysis. Prügl, for example, calls for professional ethics for gender experts and trainers. However, these are developed from the perspective of an outside observer, rather than a practitioner seeking to develop her own practice or that of her colleagues. Likewise, Callerstig adopts an external analytical focus on the impact of gender mainstreaming through gender training at the local level in Sweden. Approaching the analysis from a sociological-institutionalist perspective, she explores the capacity of gender training to act as a driver for change, and as an effective supporting instrument of gender mainstreaming. Gender experts and trainers in these chapters are the *object* of research, thus the perspective adopted is not that of a more embedded approach to reflecting on practice from an insider perspective. Again, these standpoints need not be mutually exclusive, as shown in the chapters by Davids and van Eerdewijk (Chapter 4) and Kunz (Chapter 5). Both these chapters are concerned with research on gender expertise in their respective contexts, but in a way which also aims to trigger reflection on practice.

The background and standpoints of authors, moreover, matter a great deal as they contribute to conditioning the kinds of questions asked, and the kinds of conclusions drawn. At a more implicit and prospective level, they also feed into differences between the chapters' approaches in terms of their level of optimism for the possibilities of feminist knowledge transfer. Among the chapters most optimistic, or least critical, of the potential which feminist knowledge transfer has for bringing about actual change are those by Lombardo and Mergaert, Callerstig, and Albenga. These maintain a positive outlook overall as to the possibilities of gender mainstreaming as an overarching approach to achieving gender equality, as well as the role of feminist knowledge transfer in such an endeavour. All three chapters consider that the implementation of gender mainstreaming may be achieved under certain conditions. These encompass political and organizational commitments; strong and continued diagnoses; reviews, and monitoring systems which act as a "watch-dog" for commitments; and improved use of tools

and methods. Such conditions are seen to increase the possibilities of suc-
cessfully implementing gender mainstreaming, whether through addressing
general resistances to gender training (as argued by Lombardo and Mergaert)
or through specific policy sectors, such as secondary and higher education
institutions (as discussed by Callerstig, and Albenga).

A second set of chapters, specifically, those by Prügl, and Ferguson and
Moreno, adopt a broadly critical approach to feminist knowledge transfer, highlighting some of the key tensions and contradictions involved in
such a process. However, in spite of this overarching critical stance, these
authors attempt to engage with such challenges in pragmatic ways. They
do so either by challenging practitioners to develop professional ethics and
bring forward the principles of rational deliberation (as in the case of Prügl)
or by engaging in feminist ways with private sector organizations (as discussed by Ferguson and Moreno). Finally, the chapters by Davids and van
Eerdewijk, and Kunz demonstrate the most critical stance towards the possibilities for feminist knowledge transfer. Grounded in postcolonial theory,
these authors are primarily concerned with the power dynamics involved in
knowledge transfer processes, and how gender training and gender expertise
are embedded in broader global power relations and dynamics of inequality, particularly those between the Global North and the Global South. This
eventually leads these authors to frame gender training, gender expertise,
and feminist knowledge transfer, as asymmetrical dynamics through which
knowledge from the North is being mainstreamed in a variety of situated
contexts wherein local knowledges on gender are marginalized and silenced.

This more critical stance on feminist knowledge transfer is reflected in references to Foucault's "governmentality" approach defined by Prügl in this
book as "the art of governing through the application of knowledge". Particularly present in the chapters by Prügl, and Davids and van Eerdewijk's,
this notion suggests that feminist knowledge, when co-opted by the discourse of institutions and organizations and/or mobilized for the purpose
of gender mainstreaming, can convert itself into an instrument of power.
This instrument can either contribute to de-politicizing feminist claims, as
Prügl suggests, or it may be turned against other types of situated experiences and knowledge(s) on gender, as posited by Kunz. This governmentality
approach must be discussed, however, as the powerful critique it offers
could potentially provide arguments *against* feminist knowledge transfer,
whether through gender training or gender expertise. Indeed, while borrow-
ing Foucault's notion helps reveal the ambiguity of processes at play, we
suggest that it may take the critique too far. In its original sense, *gouverne-
mentalité* refers to governing people's minds and means of action through
knowledge, processes, and incorporated power devices. As such, we would
ask whether gender training and expertise actually belong to that category,
or are these intrinsic ambiguities better grasped when framed as "social
engineering"? As Jacquot (2010) puts it, gender mainstreaming is derived

from "public willingness to modify social relationships and representations" through policy instruments. One could argue that it is this instrumental character and pursuant transformation, rather than the exertion of power through "soft" modes, which better account for the processes entailed in gender expertise and training, as explored in this book. Here, insights derived from Habermas' version of a deliberative space are especially useful. These underline the possibility for gender experts and trainers to remain legitimate by exercising reflexivity, demonstrating inclusiveness and contributing to generating "spaces of deliberation to democratize international governance", as Prügl underlines in this book.

Key reflections

Having set out the contours of the debates presented by the chapters in this book, we now go on to draw out some key themes for further reflection. Following the analysis of the differences and similarities between chapters, a number of issues can be highlighted for consideration. Four areas of interest in particular stand out: whether to focus on the "transfer" or "circulation" of knowledge; the different scenarios in which feminist and gender knowledge are being transferred, with different sources of legitimacy; the influence of the backgrounds and standpoints of experts and trainers on their experiences with feminist knowledge transfer processes; and the challenges of intersectional approaches to gender expertise and gender training.

  The first question addresses the terminology and concepts used throughout the book. In the title and Introduction, we discuss the notion of "feminist knowledge transfer". However, other authors – in particular Kunz – prefer the term "circulation of feminist knowledge" or, in the plural, "feminist knowledges". This issue is of particular concern to those authors working on the Global South, who highlight a plurality of knowledges on gender in a range of contexts that may differ from those of international and development institutions. This draws on standpoint approaches to feminism which acknowledge the validity of different ways of knowing and the politics of situated knowledge (Haraway, 2004; Harding, 2004). However, while we agree with the idea of circulation of knowledges, and are keen to avoid assumptions of top-down knowledge transfer processes, we suggest the need for a very specific classification. That is, we would insist on classifying such knowledges as feminist, as opposed to merely knowledge on gender, devoid of feminist analysis and/or politics. This kind of classification makes it necessary to make judgements on whether knowledge can be deemed feminist, which of course raises further questions about hierarchies of knowledges that need to be taken seriously. Nevertheless, we maintain that in order to develop a concept of "circulation", we would need to be clearly discussing a "circulation of feminist knowledges", rather than merely "circulation of knowledge on gender". Of course, knowledge on gender is a vital tool for gender expertise and training scenarios and must be used by trainers to engage participants in discussions about equality and transformation. Moreover, the situated knowledge of such participants on gender and other areas – such as specialism and local contexts – is also vital for any such situation. Unless such knowledges are explicitly or implicitly "feminist", however, we continue to defend the concept of knowledge "transfer", maintaining an emphasis on the feminist nature of such a transfer. This necessarily involves participation and the acknowledgement of a plurality of knowledges on gender.

The second key point on which we wish to reflect is the existence of different scenarios in which feminist knowledge is circulated or transferred. By scenarios, we do not refer here to the differentiated contexts posed by organizational cultures and patterns, specific contexts of interaction, mandates granted by commissioning organizations, or cultural environments. As the chapters have illustrated, this diversity is intrinsic to the very notion of feminist knowledge transfer, and dealing with it is part of the process itself. Instead, here we refer to the different sources of legitimacy and justification for feminist knowledge transfer or circulation. In the chapters by Albenga, Callerstig, and Lombardo and Mergaert, this transfer is to be read in light of the implementation of both "hard" and "soft" institutional mechanisms in favour of gender equality. The fact that these mechanisms were often transferred from the EU to national or regional levels does not affect the legal type of legitimacy that underlines their implementation. Implementing a transformative agenda in specific organizational settings thus partly consists in implementing this policy agenda and/or aligning it with the rationale of the organization. This, in turn, precipitates negotiation regarding the feminist content of the knowledge which will be transferred. This scenario sharply contrasts with that of international development politics, wherein international norms and conventions only remotely legitimate the agenda of gender equality. In such a scenario, the transfer of feminist and gender knowledges is incorporated into more imbalanced power relations, as highlighted in chapters by Kunz, Prügl, and Davids and van Eerdewijk. Exploring these different scenarios, it appears that those chapters dealing with EU contexts adopt a less critical stance, overall, towards feminist knowledge transfer. The authors dealing with cases in the Global South, however, are far more critical. The latter must grapple with issues such as postcolonial and post-conflict politics and further focus on how these processes interact with gender expertise and gender training in problematic ways.

The background and standpoint of experts and trainers with respect to their experiences with feminist knowledge transfer processes is also relevant here. As argued above, in this book, authors can be categorized as primarily insiders or outsiders in the approach they have taken to the analysis of feminist knowledge transfer. Some reflect as practitioners and others as researchers, although it is important to acknowledge that most contributors play both roles at different times and in different ways. These differences raise key questions, such as the extent to which policy areas and academic disciplines impact the ways in which authors explore feminist knowledge transfer. It also prompts questions of whether a more critical position is required in international settings wherein the unequal power relations of global political economy are embedded, such as development cooperation agencies. Knowledge transfer in contexts where both gender trainers and experts, as well as the knowledge transfer itself, is mediated – and paid for – by development donors may require a more critical stance. As such, can we sketch a rough conclusion that the more unequal the power dynamics of the training/expertise scenario, the more we are forced to question the politics of feminist knowledge transfer? This does not mean, however, that the dialogue between these two broad scenarios is not fruitful. On the contrary, postcolonial feminism and the experiences of feminist and gender knowledge transfer in the Global South can help us to adopt a more critical point of view regarding global political economy. This affects not only North–South international relations but also "domestic" settings, whether in the North or the South.

Finally, we return to one of the key issues posed in the Introduction – *intersectionality*. Despite attempts to focus on this issue, the subject matter of the chapters did not give rise to substantive discussions of intersectionality. Indeed, in the studies presented here, intersectionality is not discussed as a systematic feature of either gender training or gender expertise. Rather, it is discussed in the context of a broader trend towards "diversity" mainstreaming, particularly in the private sector, as demonstrated by Ferguson and Moreno. The rise of diversity management and training has often proved detrimental to more feminist approaches to knowledge transfer, with a tendency to focus more on multiple discriminations rather than on inequality and structural power relations (see, for instance, Sénac, 2015, and Prügl, 2011). While we initially asked authors to reflect on the role of intersectionality in their chapters, the majority of the experiences on which they draw concentrated on *gender* training. This suggests that there is still much work to be done, as intersectionality is not fully integrated in regular gender training experiences in any explicit way.

This finding in itself is interesting and worth some reflection here. Does the fact that we are not currently able to integrate intersectionality systematically simply imply that we are at an early stage in the development of feminist knowledge transfer? Or does this reveal resistance to intersectional approaches by gender experts and trainers, due to its association with "diversity" and the dangers of diluting feminist approaches and feminist politics? While the latter arguments certainly prevent practitioners from systematically embracing an intersectional approach, the first – normative – assumption could be easily turned the other way: can intersectionality effectively inform a transformative approach to gender and other inequalities in an already complex intervention context? Whereas there is no doubt that, whatever the context, gender intersects with a number of other inequality or discrimination strands, how far can knowledge about these intersections be circulated and bring about actual change? As demonstrated in the collection by Kriszan, Squires, and Skjeie (2012), there have been few signs that intersectionality can become a policy paradigm and be institutionalized. From this more critical perspective, do gender expertise and training constitute a specific case? Or do they illustrate the fact that we are at an extremely early stage in the development of intersectionality as a policy paradigm?

It is important, however, to note that while intersectionality may not be a key part of a specific training or expert interventions, most authors do reflect on the ways in which intersectionality influences how power dynamics play out in knowledge transfer scenarios. That is, while this may not be explicitly integrated into the "content" of a training course, for example, practitioners and researchers nevertheless reflect on the intersectional power dynamics of a training scenario and how this produces hierarchies of knowledge in different contexts. As such, this suggests that intersectionality is always present in any knowledge transfer scenario, just as gender is always necessarily one hierarchy among many in any context. Moreover, the situated knowledges on gender drawn upon in such scenarios are embedded in intersectional power dynamics. Therefore, we suggest that the different authors find feminist ways of bringing intersectionality on board in training and expertise scenarios, whether this is done in an explicit or implicit manner. We argue that any feminist knowledge transfer process will necessarily be *gender+*, since any expert or trainer committed to feminist politics will always pay attention to the specific power dynamics at work in any knowledge transfer scenario. Indeed, we propose that attention to intersectionality is a key aspect of what makes such a process feminist. As such, while there may not always be a focus on intersectionality in terms of the content of gender training or expertise, the "process" itself should explore intersectional power relations and dynamics in order to be embedded within a feminist approach to knowledge transfer. In sum, we argue that an intersectional perspective is embedded in any truly feminist knowledge transfer processes and should be claimed as an explicit component of gender training and gender expertise.

Reclaiming feminist knowledge transfer

Drawing on the findings and reflections presented in this book, we now propose some ways forward for feminist knowledge transfer. Two main questions are considered here. First, should we continue to pursue feminist knowledge transfer agendas? And, if so, what role could professional ethics play in the future of feminist knowledge transfer? In considering the first question, we take into account the range of analyses of feminist knowledge transfer addressed in the chapters, as outlined in detail above. In spite of the substantive critiques of the conceptual foundations and practical implementation of feminist knowledge transfer – or circulation – we nevertheless uphold the value of such an endeavour as a key component of feminist transformative politics in action. Moreover, in a climate of political and economic crisis in which feminist progress is being challenged and rolled back in many areas, we suggest that renewed feminist engagement with key national and international institutions is vital. As argued above, in many areas, the space for feminist transformation may be considered to be contracting, for instance in EU policies. In the EU context, however, it could also be argued that gender mainstreaming has been sufficiently institutionalized so as to make it difficult to reverse feminist progress, although vigilance is needed to avoid the technocratization and de-politicization of feminist knowledge transfer. In these scenarios, feminist experts and trainers can draw on this legacy of institutionalization to continue to seek space for transformation, adopting the approach set out above. In other spaces, it can be considered that gender training and expertise are continuing to grow. Recent changes in the UN, for example, point to this. The UN-SWAP process makes gender training mandatory for all staff in UN agencies and has led to the development of the compulsory "I Know Gender" online course, run by the UN Women Training Centre in Santo Domingo. Such opportunities should be seized as potential openings for feminist transformation, despite the inherent tensions and restrictions involved.

The process of feminist knowledge transfer draws on several decades of debate and research on gender inequalities, which continues to grow and engage new areas and issues. There are few comparable bodies of knowledge and analytical frameworks which propose pragmatic ways of tackling inequalities in global society. Knowledge on gender is extensive and covers, for example, all 12 critical areas of concern of the Beijing Platform for Action. Moreover, each subfield – for example armed conflict, macroeconomic policy, political power, and decision-making – contains a cadre of gender trainers and gender experts. More recently, gender knowledge has further expanded to address the areas covered by the Sustainable Development Goals and to engage with core challenges such as climate change from gender and feminist perspectives. The proliferation of experts on gender and other issues demonstrates the ways in which feminist knowledge transfer is driven by conviction and commitment to an overarching transformative project. This ever-growing body of feminist knowledge can and should be deployed through feminist, *gender+* knowledge transfer processes in order to address the multiple crises in which we find ourselves at the time of writing. However, we suggest that in order to be considered part of this transformative project, feminist knowledge transfer processes need to meet certain conditions and criteria. At the heart of this is a commitment to feminist politics and transformative outcomes and a focus on "feminist knowledges" as opposed to merely "knowledge on gender", as discussed in more detail below.

In order to address some of the issues raised in this book, we follow Prügl's call for "professional ethics" in feminist knowledge transfer, in particular the claim that "wielding feminist power requires ethical guidelines". Prügl proposes that the purpose of gender expertise and gender training should be to make "truths" on gender the subject of deliberation. In turn, this shifts the focus of feminist knowledge transfer from a primary concern with the "quality of outcomes" to one which pays more attention to the "quality of processes" in which gender experts engage. In addition, such an approach requires that experts and trainers acknowledge more explicitly the political character of expertise, and in so doing, they make the exercise of such power more conscious.

A key part of operationalizing the approach suggested by Prügl involves an explicit engagement with the very status of resistances in the process of feminist knowledge transfer. In this book, Lombardo and Mergaert engage with resistances in detail, drawing up conclusions which primarily apply to the macro policy level. They suggest that "recognizing and typifying resistances can help to more exhaustively diagnose the problem and thus design more adequate implementation strategies" for gender mainstreaming. However, a focus on process also highlights resistances as necessary for a deliberative approach to knowledge transfer. As such, resistances should be viewed as a vital part of any feminist knowledge transfer scenario, also on the micro, individual level, as pointed out by Albenga in this book. Indeed, we would suggest that resistance and contestation must be present in order for such a scenario to be considered "feminist" and "transformative". The risk of de-politicization inherent in many knowledge transfer scenarios, as extensively referred to in this book, often leads to experts and trainers engaging in trying to limit areas of contestation, which includes resistance from participants. However, as demonstrated in this book and elsewhere, when feminist knowledge is de-politicized in order to meet purely strategic ends – be they market-driven or geared towards conforming to the broader process of change in which an organization is involved – its transformative potential is lost. This is seen, for example, when the term "feminism" is dropped from training courses or policy work. In an attempt to "get feminism in through the back door", the reality is often a transfer scenario in which the political dimensions of feminist knowledge have been marginalized, returning to our key point about the relative weakness of "knowledge on gender" as opposed to the more politicized notion of "feminist knowledges".

We suggest that, as part of a field of professionalization in the making, gender experts and trainers need to engage more explicitly with resistances and develop tools and strategies for dealing with this. Otherwise, there is a danger that they – we – will become agents of the reproduction of unequal power relations, rather than the agents of feminist transformation we wish to be. Nevertheless, from a pragmatic perspective – as raised in the chapters by Albenga, Ferguson and Moreno, and Davids and van Eerdewijk – many knowledge transfer scenarios require compromise and negotiation in a variety of forms. In many areas, funding for gender expertise is being cut, leaving experts in a potentially weaker position to negotiate than in the past. Moreover, it is important to point out the precarious conditions in which many gender experts and trainers currently operate, notably as freelancers working on a contract-to-contract basis without financial stability. As such, a middle ground is needed between embracing resistances and deliberation and delivering feminist expertise and training in less than ideal circumstances.

In this book, Prügl suggests that we should be more explicit about "recognizing complexities in practice", an approach which allows for an understanding of negotiation and compromise. In practical terms, experts and trainers have to work within the specific confines of each knowledge transfer scenario. This entails taking into account the political economy considerations of the expert, the various standpoint knowledges on gender with which to engage, and the climate of the institution with which one is engaging – for example, having to make a "business case" or to "drop the feminism". While this climate can be described as "political", since it will impact the conditions in which the intervention or training will be performed, it often depends, in the first place, on the purpose and field-specific features of the organization. For this reason, it is vital for experts and trainers to fully grasp the contexts in which they operate and to determine whether or not these are compatible with minimum standards as regards the content, scope, format, and transformative potential of gender expertise and training. Here, once again, we appeal to the professional ethics Prügl proposes. We suggest that there is work to be done here, a path to be carved which, on the one hand, takes into account the politics of feminist knowledge transfer scenarios, while on the other, pays maximum attention to process and deliberation. The overall aim is to seek out the space for transformation in each knowledge transfer scenario. In order to close the book, we now go on to propose some practical and strategic ways forward with this agenda.

Ways forward and future research

Taking into account the analytical and normative objectives of this book, as set out in the Introduction, how can we take the lessons learned and move forward with feminist knowledge transfer? In particular, having identified a number of critical areas for reflection, what practical and pragmatic steps could be collectively taken to advance this agenda? In the concluding section of this chapter, we propose four preliminary recommendations for further debate among gender experts, trainers, and those concerned with feminist knowledge transfer. These are to promote further exchange between "insiders" and "outsiders" in feminist knowledge transfer; to re-politicize feminist knowledge transfer; to ensure that feminist knowledge transfer processes pay specific attention to intersectionality; and to drive a bottom-up process of professional ethics for gender experts and gender trainers. We now address these recommendations in turn, before setting out some remaining gaps in knowledge.

First, we propose that is important to promote further exchange between "insiders" and "outsiders" in feminist knowledge transfer. We consider this book to be an important step in such an endeavour. In reflecting on more critical and pragmatic approaches to knowledge transfer, both practitioners and researchers are able to reformulate their ideas and practices in response to a broader range of experiences and perspectives, with better prospects for transformative processes and outcomes. This exchange not only entails individual standpoints but also encompasses the different knowledge transfer scenarios in which we operate. Taking into consideration the experience of feminist and gender knowledge transfer in the framework of postcolonial debates, particularly as they play out in the Global South, can help us adopt a more critical point of view with respect to dynamics elsewhere. Overall, moreover, greater reflection is needed both at the individual and at the collective levels. Should we, as practitioners and researchers in this area, strive to be more open about the sources of our own training and education in gender; the policy and other networks in which we are embedded; and how this conditions the ways in which we view knowledge transfer processes? How does our own training affect what we can and cannot see about gender expertise and gender training? And, should we, as a community of practitioners, adopt a more critical epistemological point of view, questioning the origins of gender training?

Second, we argue for a "re-politicization" of feminist knowledge transfer. The current context of feminist knowledge transfer is marked by the growing professionalization of gender experts and trainers; a political economy of knowledge transfer entrenched in a neoliberal framework; and severe limitations on the financial and policy resources available. With this in mind, we argue that it is time to recast gender knowledge transfer not only as feminist but also as "political". By political, we mean an endeavour which is not merely one of social engineering, that is, of transforming social relationships and representations to achieve some form of common good. Rather, it is an endeavour which also challenges embedded power structures, unravels hidden hegemonies, empowers, and creates a space for collective deliberation.

Third, it is from this point of view that we collectively need to ensure that feminist knowledge transfer processes pay specific attention to intersectionality. As argued above, intersectionality is not always an explicit aspect of the content of feminist knowledge transfer. However, as argued throughout this chapter, an increased emphasis on process and deliberation in feminist knowledge transfer scenarios allows for a more feminist engagement with participants and institutions. In such an approach, intersectionality can be addressed through engagements with hierarchies and stratified knowledges, which can be brought out in training and expertise contexts.

Finally, we propose a "bottom-up process of professional ethics" for gender experts and gender trainers. Building on work already done on this sphere, such as the Madrid Declaration (see Appendix for full text) and the proposals developed in this chapter, there is a need for further development. We consider it timely to reopen a debate on the professionalization of gender expertise, and the standards and criteria to which such a profession should be held. We believe that further developing Communities of Practice (CoPs) for feminist knowledge transfer is an appropriate way to address these key areas of collective enhancement. Such communities, which can be of different scopes and natures, are not only a way for practitioners to increase the exchange of experiences with the overarching aim of more feminist knowledge transfer. They can also act as an effective support network for professionalization and the collective development of common standards. So too do they stand to contribute greatly to the collective development of feminist knowledge transfer more widely, while increasing the capacity of gender experts and trainers to engage with intersectionality and to harness resistances for achieving feminist transformation.

The chapters in this book offer a complement to existing research on feminist knowledge transfer, gender training, and gender expertise. Here we have aimed to combine researcher and practitioner perspectives to develop broad reflections on the current state of the field of feminist knowledge transfer. However, gaps in our knowledge remain. We are lacking, for example, basic information on the extent and nature of gender training and gender expertise worldwide. Moreover, we do not have consistent information on the kinds of contracts, conditions, and rates of pay in the field. A baseline study on such issues could be used to complement and reinforce the arguments presented in this chapter. In addition, the development of professional ethics for feminist knowledge transfer could be supported by more in-depth research on the kinds of tools and methods used in knowledge transfer scenarios, and the collective development of criteria for assessing methodologies and approaches. In sum, with this book, we aim to make a contribution to the growing field of research on feminist knowledge transfer. It is hoped that the case studies, reflections, and arguments put forward will lead to enhanced debate around the politics of feminist knowledge transfer and collective solutions for promoting the transformative potential of such an endeavour.

References

Bettio, Francesca, Marcella Corsi, Carlo D'Ippoliti, Antigone Lyberaki, Manuela Samek Lodovici, and Alina Verashchagina (2012) *The Impact of the Economic Crisis on the Situation of Women and Men and on Gender Equality Policies*. Brussels: European Commission.

Bustelo, María (2014) "Three Decades of State Feminism and Gender Equality Policies in Multi-Governed Spain', *Sex Roles*, DOI 10.1007/s11199-014-0381-9.

Haraway, Donna (2004) "Situated Knowledges: The Science Question in Feminism and the Privilege of Partial Perspective', in Sandra G. Harding (ed.) *The Feminist Standpoint Theory Reader: Intellectual and Political Controversies*. 1st Edition. New York: Routledge, pp. 81–102.

Harding, Sandra G. (ed.) (2004) *The Feminist Standpoint Theory Reader: Intellectual and Political Controversies*. 1st Edition. New York: Routledge.

Jacquot, Sophie (2010) "The Paradox of Gender Mainstreaming: The Unanticipated Effects of New Modes of Governance in the Gender Equality Domain", *West European Politics*, 33(1), 118–135.

Kriszan, Andrea, Hege Skjeie, and Judith Squires (2012) "European Equality Regimes: Institutional Change and Political Intersectionality', in Andrea Kriszan, Hege Skjeie, and Judith Squires (eds.) *Institutionalizing Intersectionality: The Changing Nature of European Equality Regimes*. Basingstoke: Palgrave Macmillan, pp. 209–239.

Prügl, Elisabeth (2011) "Diversity Management and Gender Mainstreaming as Technologies of Government", *Politics and Gender*, 7, 71–89.

Sénac, Réjane (2012) *L'Invention de la diversité*. Paris: Presses Universitaires de France.

—— (2015) *L'égalité sous conditions: genre, parité, diversité*. Paris: Presses de Sciences Po.

Appendix: Madrid Declaration on Advancing Gender+ Training in Theory and Practice

Complutense University, Madrid, February 3–4, 2011

Important note: This Declaration is meant to engage all gender+ trainers, gender+ training commissioners, and gender+ training experts who express a commitment to further development and improvement of gender+ training as an emerging professional field. In this Declaration, many concepts are inherently contested. We have put those in *italics*, signalling our intention to use them in as inclusive a way as possible and to have intensive productive dialogue at a later stage in order to avoid lack of clarity or exclusion due to these concepts.

Preamble

As *gender+* trainers, *gender+* training commissioners, and *gender+* training experts, we understand ourselves as part of a broader movement for change towards more *gender equal democratic* societies. We are committed to delivering, commissioning, and further developing the highest quality training. With the use of the concept of *gender+*, we signal that we work with gender as intersected with other structural inequalities. Gender+ training should work towards engaging both men and women.

In order to provide the highest quality training, we acknowledge and commit to the following:

Concerning the positioning of Gender+ training

- Gender+ training should ideally be carried out as part of a broader explicit gender mainstreaming strategy.
- Gender+ training ultimately is a means towards making policies work better for people through improving the quality of policy making.
- Gender+ training is linked to the broader community of gender+ scholars, researchers, and students and learns from and contributes to this community.

Concerning the content and methods of Gender+ training

- The content of gender+ training should include the structural character of inequalities, the power mechanisms reproducing these inequalities, and the privileges and power enjoyed by some groups, so that gender+ biases and gender+ blindness are understood as a result of the inequalities that are to be overcome.

- Intersectionality should be integrated into gender+ trainings.
- Transformative learning methodologies such as participatory and experiential methods should be used whenever possible in order to maximize the learning experience for participants.
- Resistances to gender+ training should be embraced and dealt with as part of a necessary process of organizational/institutional, societal, and personal change.
- Gender+ training is based on *feminist and gender theories* translated to practitioners. Trainers should actively search for ways to communicate up to date *feminist and gender theories* in the training.
- Gender+ training should combine knowledge transfer with *competence and capacity building* while also confronting attitudes that could hinder the application of knowledge and competences.

Concerning the further development of high-quality Gender+ training: Sharing, reflecting, and professionalizing

- Innovations in theory and methodology should be developed, shared, and applied in order to remain on the cutting edge of expertise in both training and gender+.
- Experiences should be shared by engaging in (sub)national, European, and transnational networks and Communities of Practice based on transparency, inclusiveness, an appetite for "practices with potential", and recognition of others' work.
- Reflexivity enhancing practices should be an integral part of any gender+ training and mainstreaming proposal and activity, using methods such as questioning, peer review, and intervision.
- Gender+ trainers, commissioners, gender+ training experts, and representatives of equality institutions should work together in an open dialogue to develop professional quality standards on theory, methodology, format, and ethics, including sufficient time for training and sensitivity to context.
- Gender+ trainers, commissioners, and gender+ training experts should be realistic in their expectations and in the design and implementation of gender+ training, specifying the level of training and the time and resources allocated to the training.

Index